The 8 Steps to Strategic Success

Unleashing
the power of
engagement

The 8 Steps to Strategic Success

Unleashing the power of engagement

Gerben van den Berg
and Paul Pietersma

With the participation of:
Wieke Ambrosius, Simone Heemskerk,
Roel van Lanen and Lindy van der Veen

KoganPage

LONDON PHILADELPHIA NEW DELHI

First published in Great Britain and the United States in 2014 by Kogan Page Limited

2nd Floor, 45 Gee Street	1518 Walnut Street, Suite 1100	4737/23 Ansari Road
London EC1V 3RS	Philadelphia PA 19102	Daryaganj
United Kingdom	USA	New Delhi 110002
www.koganpage.com		India

© Berenschot BV (Gerben van den Berg and Paul Pietersma), 2014

The right of Gerben van den Berg and Paul Pietersma to be identified as the authors and of Berenschot as proprietor of this work has been asserted by them in accordance with the Copyright, Designs and Patents Act 1988.

ISBN   978 0 7494 6919 1
E-ISBN   978 0 7494 6920 7

British Library Cataloguing-in-Publication Data

A CIP record for this book is available from the British Library.

Library of Congress Cataloging-in-Publication Data

van den Berg, Gerben.
  The 8 steps to strategic success : unleashing the power of engagement / Gerben van den Berg, Paul Pietersma.
    pages cm
  Includes index.
  ISBN 978-0-7494-6919-1 – ISBN (invalid) 978-0-7494-6920-7 (e-ISBN)   1. Strategic planning.
2. Success in business.   I. Pietersma, Paul.   II. Title.
  HD30.28.B45495 2014
  658.4'012--dc23

                                                                    2013037262

Typeset by Graphicraft Limited, Hong Kong
Print production managed by Jellyfish
Printed and bound in Great Britain by CPI Group (UK) Ltd, Croydon CR0 4YY

CONTENTS

LIST OF FIGURES

FOREWORD

Strategic success is much sought after, but far from commonplace. In most industries, only a handful of organizations manage to outperform the great majority of contenders. Their shining results make them stand out – whether in terms of customer appeal, bottom-line numbers, growth prospects or otherwise. Yet even they are subject to decline, for sustaining success in a turbulent world is far from a sinecure.

So, why is it that strategic success is so elusive, and what does it take to sustain success?

To a large degree, the answer lies in how firms approach strategy. Without a sound strategy, organizations tend to underperform. Without a master plan that guides pivotal decisions and commitments, it is exceedingly hard to give shape to an organization's future, especially in a changing setting. In a fast-paced world with relentlessly mounting customer demands, there is an acute need to scrutinize one's bearings and direction, and thus to rethink strategy. Yet, all too often firms shy away from mapping out a path ahead. Some organizations are reined in by the status quo. Others assume that being flexible and reactive is the preferred way to cope with strategic uncertainties and day-to-day pressures. In my view, that is a tricky assumption – it can easily lead to directional drift and misallocation of scarce resources.

In contrast, we know that strategic success and directional clarity go hand in hand. This was already evident some 20 years ago in the research that led to my co-authored and best-selling book, *The Discipline of Market Leaders*. The companies featured in that work, as well as the many outperformers I have come across since, did not succeed by being all things to all people. Instead they chose to excel on particular dimensions deemed most pertinent to certain customers. In other words, they made hard choices and commitments. In these and other outperforming firms, strategy acts as a pervasive framework and guiding force. Management teams align around their firms' strategy along with its multitude of implications. Deeper down in these organizations, a clear sense of direction, commitment and purpose prevails, which reassures customers, suppliers and shareholders as well as other stakeholders. Results ensue.

While strategy's importance is beyond question, the process of creating an effective strategy and putting it solidly in place takes diligence and perspective. It is far from easy – which is why strategic success is not commonplace. But that is also why this book, *The 8 Steps to Strategic Success*, is in my view so valuable. The authors' deep experience (and plenty of hard-learned lessons, I imagine) make this a rich resource.

What resonated in particular with me is the book's strong advocacy of a dialogue-driven approach to strategy. I wholeheartedly agree with that approach: it is eye-opening to engage managers in dialogues involving strategic choices and models. As an example, consider the strategic framework laid out in *The Discipline of Market Leaders* which in essence asks management to contemplate three choices for their firm: offer the best price (aka operational excellence), the best product (aka product leadership) or the best total solution (aka customer intimacy). Each of these choices has considerably different – and often conflicting – operational, financial and organizational implications. Simple as it appears, this framework has for decades stimulated deep and passionate discussions among managers as to what they believe their firms should be best known and recognized for.

The *Discipline* framework is but one of a multitude of models and tools covered in the book. Clearly, there is no shortage of pertinent and sound insights. The great contribution that the authors make is to show how to apply these at the appropriate time (in each of the *8 steps to strategic success*), thus fuelling powerful dialogue and constructive engagement.

Let's get ready for strategic success.

Dr Fred Wiersema
Customer Strategist, Chair, B2B Leadership Board,
Institute for the Study of Business Markets at Penn State,
and co-author of the top-selling
The Discipline of Market Leaders

ABOUT THE AUTHORS

Gerben van den Berg (b 1979) is a consultant at Berenschot in the Netherlands. He has advised clients in a range of industries across Europe and the Caribbean. In his consulting practice his core area of work is in strategy development, competitive positioning, corporate governance and (complex) organizational transformation. Gerben has a special interest in professional service firms. He is the author of numerous books and articles on strategy and management, including the best-selling title *Key Management Models* (2nd edition) and *The Great Book on Strategy*, a leading title in Dutch, both co-authored with Paul.

Paul Pietersma (b 1965) is a strategy consultant and Managing Director of Strategy Funding and Innovation at Berenschot in the Netherlands. He has more than 15 years of experience in the consulting business in which he has advised many CEOs and boards of directors on various strategic issues. He has won the Dutch Professionals Award for Management Consultancy. He has published several articles on strategy and, with Gerben, is the co-author of the internationally best-selling title *Key Management Models* (2nd edition) and *The Great Book on Strategy*.

Paul and Gerben would like to thank their colleagues at Berenschot for their contributions to this book. Their views, the group discussions and their enthusiastic support made our editorial work for this book, for which (a translation of) *The Great Book on Strategy* was the foundation, much more rewarding. We would especially like to thank Wieke Ambrosius, Sascha Bruggink, Simone Buijs, Klaas de Gier, Hendrik Jan Kaal, Martijn Laar, Roel van Lanen, Titia Tamminga and Vera van Vilsteren. Also, many thanks and appreciation for Fred Wiersema, our fellow strategist, for writing the foreword.

We would also like to thank our editor, Liz Gooster, for her enthusiastic support and professional guidance. Thanks to her patience and resilience, and – amazingly – her belief in us when we told her that a manuscript written in Dutch would be worth bringing to market internationally, we were able to complete this book.

Berenschot is a leading Dutch consultancy firm with offices in the Netherlands, Belgium, the Caribbean, Brazil and South Africa.

Introduction
Time to rethink strategy

How the world in the 21st century will look after the '2009–2013' crisis, no one knows for sure. Opinions vary considerably. Some are already concerned about staff shortages, while others think the worst is yet to come. Certainly it seems likely that after this crisis the world will not be the same as before. Phrases such as 'system crisis' and 'this time it's different and definitely not like it was before' are frequently heard.

The external context of organizations will remain uncertain and un-predictable. This requires a different way of determining strategy: not a static planning event once a year, but a strategy process in which the organization is in constant dialogue with its environment and itself on the strategic direction. A process which can be directly adjusted when and where necessary, and one which engages all the relevant stakeholders in an open and constructive dialogue. To continue to create opportunities in an increasingly transparent and unpredictable world, organizations need a strategy that makes them more authentic, interactive and decisive, especially as organizations are becoming increasingly interrelated, with relationships reaching across industry, country, public-sector and private-sector borders.

In the world of today, the economy and society require that organiza-tions can quickly change course. In an unpredictable environment, decisiveness and speed are of the utmost importance, because the changes are by definition temporary. Future winners are thus able to pick up signals faster and combine them more quickly into new services and products than others. This can only succeed if the ideas are decisively implemented. Only then can an organization quickly and efficiently adjust to a supply chain, alliance or branch network in which new initiatives unfold, each time in different combinations. And the only way an organization can respond in a timely manner to changes in demand and the increasing availability of alternative products and market entrants is when organizations master greater decisiveness.

As organizations today are increasingly involved in interrelationships, information about new products, new activities and prices is also increasingly transparent and often widely shared. Organizations are judged publicly on who they are and what they do. Reputations can quickly be destroyed. From the perspective of corporate social responsibility and sustainable reputation, business will increasingly be done not on what a company offers, but on who and what a company is. This means that the reputation and values of a company should precisely reflect its actual performance. Authenticity and accountability are increasingly important requirements for partners and not least for customers. Also, the core values and principles of the company play an increasing role in attracting and retaining employees. It is therefore important that organizations stay true to themselves: acting according to their DNA and willing to be assessed on this. On a strategic level, this means that given the need for decisiveness, organizations hardly have the time or space for playing different roles in each of their relationships. Organizations should foster their corporate identity and promote their authenticity, especially as interaction and interdependency between organizations are expected to become even stronger in the coming years. Organizations will have to find a place in the relevant networks and alliances to innovate jointly, to get finance or to develop and market new products or services. This demands an organization that connects continuously with its relevant physical and virtual networks. Organizations must be interactive and interact with all of their stakeholders: customers, suppliers, employees, partners, shareholders, competitors and government institutions.

To do so, organizations' strategic foundation has to be enriched with a new approach to strategy: an approach that contributes to making them more authentic, interactive and decisive. The strategy processes of today should allow for decisiveness in a world full of uncertainties: it should enable the organization to keep all its options open on the one hand and to make clear choices on the other. At the same time these processes should foster the organization's authenticity to make consistent choices that are recognized and trusted inside and outside the organization. And they should be about making the right choices while obtaining a priori support for them, so that choices can be immediately transformed into action. So both strategy formulation and strategy implementation processes should enable the organization to involve its network and to interact with all relevant stakeholders on a timely basis. This requires a process of strategy formulation and implementation that allows for involving the right people on the right topic at the right moment in the process. However, although all organizations and managers recognize the importance of strategy formulation and implementation, too often the process of strategy formulation is more difficult than they initially expected, and following the logical steps of the process of strategy implementation often seems more difficult in practice and slower than they would have wished.

But one of the critical determinants of strategic success is to see strategy not just as expert planning, but also as a process that involves dialogues with multiple stakeholders, both within and outside the company. In our strategy consulting practice, we learned that these dialogues are key to strategic success, and that strategy processes with high levels of engagement deliver results more quickly and more permanently. This practical experience prompted us to describe a new approach to strategy, an approach in which engagement is key. This generic approach we named the 'strategic dialogue': a proven 'route' to strategic success. This is the approach we present in this book: an easy-to-grasp and empirically proven model/method for formulating and implementing strategy.

In our approach we combine the process of strategy formulation with the process of strategy implementation. For us, these two processes are interlinked and interrelated and thus part of an integrated model. We identified 8 steps in this model, with distinct elements of the strategy to be addressed per step, using state-of-the-art models and instruments and with the facilitation of modern-day methods and techniques. This book presents our strategic dialogue model and will enable you to discover how you can organize the strategy process for your own organization effectively and how strategy should be formulated, developed and executed in the 21st century: through unleashing the power of engagement.

Unleashing the power of engagement

In a strategy process there are three critical success factors:

- A good understanding of the *context* of strategy definition: without shared understanding of cause, necessity and ambition, a company trying to formulate its strategy will drift. And without knowing where you stand, there is no way to set a course.

- An adequate use of *content* in terms of quality, completeness and depth: thorough analysis with appropriate models and instruments is needed to really understand what is and is not possible for the organization and the environment in which it is active. Thorough analysis is the basis for finding the right strategic options.

- An effective and inspiring *process*: who are involved at what time, what are the roles, how is participation organized? In other words: applying the correct methods of engagement. These help to increase the intrinsic level of understanding, stimulate creativity and develop ideas. Three things are essential in engagement:
  - the quality of the participants' contribution;
  - the numbers, both in analysis and in vision and in willingness to think fundamentally about the future;
  - simultaneously initiating and pacing the implementation process.

For strategic success, organizations will have to understand the essence of context, the essence of content and the essence of the process.

The essence of context

The context or situation in which a new strategy is to be formulated affects both the content of the strategy and the process of how the strategy is formulated. This starts with the question of why a new strategy is needed and why a strategy process should be initiated. It is important to formulate why the organization's ambition, its reason for existing and its distinctiveness are valid at the point where the management wants to formulate a new strategy. Where does the urgency come from? Why should the new strategy be different or why should the current strategy at least be confirmed?

Also, it is important to understand the point of departure: what are the questions that management wants answered? What is the time horizon? What is meant by strategy and therefore what is and is not in scope?

Finally, it is helpful to get common agreement regarding what prompts the start of the strategy process and what this means for the nature of the process and the quantity of resources and processing time that can be made available. If a growth strategy is sought, the process will be different from when a new perspective is sought in an economic downturn.

We have observed that the process of strategy is often confined to a small circle of people. Because of the danger of leakage of strategic information, doors are kept closed. At the end of the process the result will be a big surprise for the stakeholders. In a one-hour presentation, the strategy is explained to the organization, first to the board, then to supervisors, then to employees and finally, with luck, to customers and suppliers. After the presentation everybody is expected to understand the meaning of the new strategy and to start acting accordingly. All too often it turns out that most people have not understood the real meaning of the new strategy, even when it has been thoroughly explained. Or stakeholders had other directions in mind, so they start asking questions, making comments or, worse, completely undermining the strategy by producing new facts and figures based on everyday experience. Making the context clear to all stakeholders at the very beginning of the process will help their understanding of its outcome: the new strategy. Corporate communication is often used to broadcast the strategy to all concerned, incorporating the message repeatedly in speeches and written communications. But it should also be used to explain the underlying reasons for the final strategic choices. Such early communication about the context of, and necessity for, a new strategy will help in getting the right people involved and contributing to a better strategy.

The essence of content

The current circumstances demand clear and realistic strategies, strategies that express the distinctiveness and added value of the organization, and that make the organization authentic, interactive and decisive. A clear strategy will lead to the correct valuation of the company and increase the chance that venture capitalists or other investors will be willing to invest in it because they are convinced that the strategy will lead to a good return on their investment. Companies with a need for investment will find that having a clear strategy in place is the best way to get financing from private equity. Again, attack is the best means of defence. A realistic strategy will explore the opportunities offered both by new business models and by new products and markets, while keeping operational excellence and a competitive cost level in mind as a licence to compete.

Thinking about strategy in an organization is thus extremely valuable. The point is to capture the essence of the company and get an answer to the existential questions: what added value does the company provide and how will it distinguish itself from its competitors? The company states in which markets it will operate and what position it wants to gain or maintain. In other words, what is its playground? What game does it play and how can it play the game successfully? These questions should be captured in the strategy of the organization and they will determine its future.

The future is uncertain by definition, however stable some business environments seem to be. The past few years have proved that even relatively stable companies and industries can drift in turbulent environments. The financial services industry is perhaps the biggest example. Real choices mean that some old habits must be abandoned. Sometimes this means literally saying goodbye to products or services that have been successful for a long time, saying farewell to some loyal customers or processes that the company has developed and perfected over a long period, and also, and perhaps this is the hardest part, saying goodbye to employees who have been loyal to the company over the years – and all this based on the belief of a small number of people who are convinced (or hopeful) that their strategic choices will bring the company greater prosperity in the future. No wonder many enthusiastically deployed processes of strategy ultimately result in only marginal adjustments of the strategy and policy of recent years. Sometimes the radical consequences of radical choices have been rejected and old certainties reinstated. As the saying goes: 'Managers often choose certain misery over uncertain happiness.' This does not mean that a company always has to change course. Minor adjustments may be sufficient and perpetuation of certain choices is sometimes equally valuable. A company is not served by an erratic course. Such a course is difficult to explain to employees and often punished by shareholders. What is needed is a thorough review of the current strategy, of developments in the market and in the organization, and of the financial situation. On this basis, you can opt for a limited adjustment of the strategy or choose a radical change of course. A well-organized strategy process is thus needed.

The essence of the process – an integrated approach based on engagement

It is often the case that defining a strategy is a laborious process and its subsequent implementation turns out to be even more difficult and slower than anticipated. Almost all firms struggle with this. In general, it is difficult to reach a joint decision on the future direction of the organization, let alone understand the full meaning and implications of it. Everyone translates the strategy in their own way; 'internalize' is the correct term. So how can better orchestration of the strategy process overcome this?

Strategy processes require effort: it is perspiration and inspiration, thinking and doing, committing and very confrontational. The illusion is that these processes are best carried out by experts in solitude and through a top-down approach. Although it may seem to be a paradox, as it requires some additional effort in organizing the strategy process, involving more people during the process will help to increase both the quality of the strategy and the acceptance and understanding of it. Asking for the knowledge, insights and opinions of the right people will lead to a better and more realistic strategy. The stakeholders and employees thus engaged will feel involved, which is key to getting them mobilized for successful implementation. Jointly building the future gives rise to joint confidence in that future. So the way the strategy process is organized will have a positive effect on both the content of the strategy and its successful realization.

Introducing strategy through dialogue

Executives take some six months to think of a new strategy.

They then take some six weeks to put it on paper.

In six days they convince their team.

In six hours the 'troops' are informed.

They have six minutes to understand the strategy.

And a mere six seconds to pose questions.

Ever wondered why they don't follow the strategy?

Organizing both strategy formulation and strategy implementation processes as a dialogue will lead to strategic advantages and strategic success. Our consulting practice has proved that the success of a strategy can be displayed in a formula:

Strategic success = Formulation × Mobilization × Realization

That is to say: strategic success comes from successful strategy formulation multiplied by mobilization (or engagement) of the right people times successful strategy realization (or implementation).

Formulation

Many companies devote most of their attention to the F of Formulation. They formulate a strategy which, if correct, shows them the way through the uncertainties of current and future markets. It could lead to the perfect plan. And then it is 'only' a matter of perfect execution. All too often, however, strategic plans aren't flawless. It is difficult to make the right choices upfront for unforeseen future developments. The choices made – if they are really made in the first place – do not always reflect a combination of thorough analysis and sound entrepreneurship. And often the strategy states what the company will do, but not what the company will stop doing (which is often inherent in making choices). Emphasis on formulation is no guarantee of a consistent story or of execution of the strategy.

Realization

Next to formulation, typically the R of Realization receives the most attention in strategy processes. Sometimes there are elaborate and detailed implementation plans, as comprehensive as an encyclopaedia. And sometimes they are only fragmentary. Most of the time there is something of an implementation plan and attention will be given to communication and progress. Milestones and required breakthroughs in the implementation plan are monitored and periodically scheduled on the management agenda (however, often not really addressed, as operational fires must be extinguished first). But even if there is a brilliant strategy with elaborate implementation plans and well-managed change projects, all too often everyone is still surprised that the strategy is not working and does not deliver what they had expected.

Mobilization

The demands of the world in the 21st century are structurally different, and that is reflected in the strategy process, which has to become more agile and decisive. Strategy is inherently about the long term, but today there is great pressure from banks and shareholders to achieve results in the short term. Tolerance of mistakes and risks is low. Adjustments must be made instantly. You must therefore focus more than ever on the third variable: the M of Mobilization. This is about organizing involvement in and engagement with the processes of both strategy formulation and strategy implementation. In short: Who will be involved and how? Who has which responsibilities in the process and what powers? Who is allowed to perform the analyses? Who appoints whom to lead the implementation? How does decision making take place, not just on the strategy but throughout the entire process? The following guidelines will help:

- Interact and take your time. Enter into dialogue with employees, but also with the working environment: customers, suppliers and other stakeholders. A strong vision with tightly controlled execution seems attractive, but it is not. The temptation to extend 'exclusive invitations' is great, but the apparent benefits of timesaving and clarity will be lost.

- Convince not only the board and shareholders, but focus particularly on involving managers and heads of departments, as their teams have a decisive role in executing the strategy. If they experience the strategy as clear, inspiring and feasible, the chances of success are increased.

- Do not hesitate to engage external stakeholders. Sending them an invitation to contribute is a signal that they are of strategic importance to your organization. Posing questions or asking for opinions is not a sign of weakness or ignorance, but a sincere invitation to think alongside you and to co-create. An open exchange of ideas can benefit everyone. It can even strengthen the authentic position of your organization in its relationships with its stakeholders.

- Facilitate an effective dialogue. A dialogue on strategy is not a group session where everyone can put forward their opinion. Participation is not free. Nor does it imply a democracy. If you participate, you have to stick to facts, contribute ideas, be constructive and energetic. And you have to conform to the procedures. This demands good process control and professional guidance.

If as much attention were to be paid to the M of Mobilization as there is to the F of Formulation and the R of Realization, many companies would gain a real strategic advantage. Mobilization is perhaps the trickiest but also most valuable, hence our emphasis on it.

Formulating strategy through the engagement of multiple stakeholders, both within and outside the company (customers, suppliers, knowledge institutions, researchers, academics, employers' associations, industry organizations etc), is essential to benefit from all relevant insights and is key to mobilizing for successful and speedy execution. In our strategy consulting practice, we learned that high levels of engagement lead to effective mobilization, delivering more lasting results faster. This practical experience prompted us to describe a new approach to strategy, in which this concept of engagement is central.

Unleashing the power of engagement makes strategy come to fruition. Dialogue with external and internal stakeholders additionally emphasizes the importance and role of their relationship with your organization. Engaging key external and internal stakeholders brings quality input to your strategy. And this in turn leads to more effective and more efficient implementation. Jointly building the future creates confidence in the shared ambitions for that future.

Next to organizing an engaging and effective process, one of the complicating factors in the process of strategy remains the multitude of possible models, methodologies and methods. In the management literature, an enormous variety of insights, instruments, models and methods can be found. Each can provide valuable insights, but with so much available, it is difficult for managers to make a pragmatic choice. In other words, which model, methodology or method should be used for which analysis or question?

This question is not easy to answer. In our opinion, neither the model nor the method used is decisive, but the insight that the manager wants to obtain from it. A model helps to arrange information and can give new insights by looking at information in a different, coherent way. However, you will always have to draw your own conclusions and verify them by discussing them with the others involved in the strategy process. You should beware the risk of taking a model or the outcome of an analysis obtained with the help of a model for an absolute truth.

This also holds for our own strategic dialogue model. We see it as a recipe: a combination of the right ingredients and a clear procedure. As we all know that any delicious dish is the result of the improvisations of the chef reflecting his or her own taste, we foresaw that our strategic dialogue model should be flexible enough to let organizations tailor it to their own strategy process. Our approach is therefore presented in this book as a generic recipe with several suggestions on how to flavour it to make it your own. Let the strategic dialogue model be your guide on the bumpy road of strategy.

Structure of the book

In this book, the reader is guided through the strategy process of the strategic dialogue, with an introduction to all models and methods in a practical manner that will allow the reader to shape his or her own strategy. The book consists of four parts.

In Part 1, we present our strategic dialogue model. We emphasize the importance of the strategy process and show how all requirements for strategic success are covered in our strategic dialogue approach. We introduce the 8 steps for strategic success and a case study that will be used throughout the book to show what a strategy process following the strategic dialogue model looks like. Based on real-life experiences, it will also highlight some of the social and political elements in each stage of a strategy process.

Part 2 describes each of the 8 steps in depth, explaining their purpose and scope, introducing applicable activities, identifying focal points, providing warnings of pitfalls and bottlenecks in the process and giving hints on how to take this step for your own organization. At the end of each step there is the case study, not only to give insight on how to perform the particular step, but also to let readers experience the power of engagement in performing the thought process and focusing on the way that analyses are performed and the vision and strategy are developed. Also, it shows how stakeholders are involved and their support obtained, and how it is implemented and monitored. Part 2 is the backbone of this book.

In Part 3, we introduce a selection of key strategy models that can be applied in each of the 8 steps. For each of the strategy models we provide a brief introduction and a recommendation on how to use it. These models are linked systematically to each of the 8 steps. With Part 2 being the core of the book, Part 3 is intended to be used as a guide to, and reference for, relevant strategy models that can be used in each step. This is the set-up stage of the book. The selection of key strategy models introduced in Part 3 is based on our practical experience. It is certainly not our claim to be exhaustive or exclusive, or that all of these models have to be used. There are many more models and methods available than those described in this book; you can find them on numerous websites or in books on key management models or on key strategy models. In the end it should be you who picks the models that appeal most to your situation, as each model should help to organize and interpret the information you regard as relevant and help you to understand what choices you have to make based on that information. We have tried to illustrate the flexibility and usefulness of the selected models in the structure of the book, with Part 2 as the core and Part 3 as an additional reference and guide.

Part 4 consists of a selection of methods of engagement that may be used throughout the strategy process. These methods are linked to the characteristics of the strategic dialogue introduced in Part 1. As already mentioned, we see strategy as an integral process of formulation, implementation and mobilization. To us, it is a process that involves (or should involve) elements of participation, creativity, decision making, analysis and commitment. Part 1 of this book elaborates on this. In Part 4 we introduce a selection of methods of engagement for each of these characteristics. Together with a brief introduction and recommendation on how to use them for each of the methods, we will also provide suggestions on how to use them in the 8 steps of the strategic dialogue. Thus, Part 4 also serves as an additional guide and reference.

Part 5 shows you how to embark on a strategy process using the strategic dialogue model. It presents some hints and tips on how to get started, and some points that you should keep in mind when using the strategic dialogue model in different contexts. In our opinion, seasoning your recipe depends on the specific situation; as this final part will show, some aspects of, and steps in, the strategy process will differ depending on the situation at hand.

This book is a useful guide for managers, academics, consultants, students and all who are interested in the art of strategy. It is not a scientific work, but makes existing theory and the latest practical experience accessible and translates them into guidelines that are useful in practice when defining and implementing your own strategy. We invite you to experience what unleashing the power of engagement can mean for your organization and to walk the 8 steps towards strategic success with us.

PART 1
Engagement on a strategic level

Introducing the strategic dialogue model:
8 steps to strategic success

01

Our strategic dialogue approach treats strategy as an integral process of formulation, implementation and mobilization. It focuses on content and process: doing the right things and doing things right. It is an iterative process that leads to choices while leaving room to keep options open. And it is an approach – the name 'strategic dialogue' says it all – that is based on engagement with key stakeholders: what the organization can and will do is not invented in an ivory tower, but in dialogue with key external partners and stakeholders, and is explored and discussed with internal stakeholders. However, a dialogue doesn't imply a democracy: those responsible will still have the final say and have to make the strategic choices.

The strategic dialogue model is an integrated methodology of strategy formulation and implementation which has been developed on the basis of practical experience. It is not a one-size-fits-all standard prescription on how to do strategy, but it's a generic approach that you can customize to your organization and circumstances. Every company and every environment is different and requires a customized approach. The strategic dialogue model offers an iterative process which is applicable to a multitude of situations and strategic issues. In the model we identified eight distinct steps, each with distinctive purposes, scope and activities:

- *Searchlight*: setting up the process of strategy formulation and implementation and finding a shared ambition and business scope.

- *Outside-in: scenarios*: mapping potential strategic positions from plausible future business environments.

- *Inside-out: analysis*: exploration of strategic options based on the abilities and limitations of the company.

- *Options*: translating analytical information to insights and then generating strategic options.

- *Choice*: estimating the risks and feasibility of the various options, leading to the choice of strategy.

- *Operationalization*: making an implementation plan, deciding the implementation process in detail and cashing in on 'quick wins'.

- *Execution*: the actual implementation of plans, policies and actions for change.

- *Monitoring*: the assessment of ongoing developments in the environment and organizational performance in relation to the strategy and strategic goals.

The schematic diagram of the strategic dialogue model looks like two circles linked together: the processes of formulation and implementation. These two circles also form a lemniscate – the symbol for infinity – representing the integrated and iterative character of our approach to strategy (see Figure 1.1). It depicts how everything is connected with everything else in logical connections.

Ideally, the strategy process will go through all 8 steps of the model (an entire cycle run) from left to right in Figure 1.1. The process of developing a mission statement, vision and strategy is described in the left-hand cycle. This process is fluid, interactive and creative. In the middle, the actual process of selection of strategic options takes place. This is where different options are weighed and choices are made. In the right-hand cycle, the emphasis is on the realization and implementation of the choices made. This process is more rigid and action oriented.

FIGURE 1.1 Strategic dialogue model

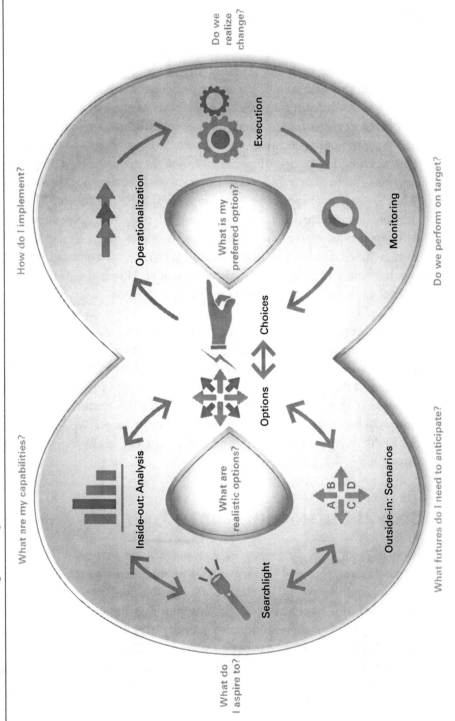

What are my capabilities?

How do I implement?

Do we realize change?

What do I aspire to?

What futures do I need to anticipate?

Do we perform on target?

Operationalization

Execution

Monitoring

What is my preferred option?

Choices

Options

Inside-out: Analysis

Outside-in: Scenarios

What are realistic options?

Searchlight

Step 1: Searchlight

In Step 1, the playing field for the strategic dialogue is determined. This requires defining both the scope of the content and the scope of the process. In this first step of the strategic dialogue model, the content is scoped by formulating a working hypothesis of the mission statement and vision of the company based on dialogue with internal and external parties, commonly executives and non-executive members of the board. This working hypothesis aims to determine the scope of the company's activities and to match the level of ambition of the different stakeholders: What is (or is not) in scope? What do we want for our future? What is the time horizon we are looking at? Next, the process is scoped through defining the degrees of freedom for the process: What is the overall approach, what is the overall planning of activities, who will be involved in what role and how will decisions be made? This helps to make the level of expectations for all participants clear.

The determination of the playing field can be seen as a design of the 'window' through which the company will look at the outside world and at itself to determine the future. It sets a first framework for the strategic direction of the organization. This direction also helps to focus the scope of the next steps in the strategy process, hence the name 'searchlight': where the beam shines determines what will be in scope. And by holding the flashlight in this first step, you can adjust the beam to your own situation.

Step 2: Outside-in: scenarios

In Step 2, all relevant external developments are mapped. The focus is towards the future. This step can be characterized as straying from conventional paths and exploring all possible and plausible futures (scenarios) in a structured way. In this step it is important to keep in mind all relevant stakeholders, to identify trends and uncertainties, and to help construct scenarios of the future. The objective is to detect opportunities and their consequences. The main question is: what do we have to take into account in the coming years and how do we deal with it? Discuss this with all relevant stakeholders – the usual ones (customers, suppliers, scientists, politicians, etc) but also the more unusual ones, for instance from other industries or an artist, to freshen your insights and perhaps to identify cross-over possibilities from other industries. Usually Step 2 generates a lot of questions that need to be answered. What do stakeholders expect of our organization? Which developments should we consider or deal with? What is the future purchasing power and behaviour of customers? What expertise and technologies will become available? Which networks and partnerships are interesting? Which positions in the supply chain will give the best value? What is our relative position in comparison with our competitors? With what products do we control which markets and are there opportunities in new markets? What are the unknown but inevitable surprises?

Patterns from past and present times offer guidance for the estimation of possibilities and opportunities. Therefore, in this step, there is an analysis of the total market in which the company wishes to operate and of the forces that influence those markets. Not only should the current market segments and customer groups of the company be analysed, but also adjacent segments and potential customer groups. This broad approach forces us to think outside the traditional patterns. It explores new opportunities and leads us towards a nuanced understanding of the market position that the company actually has.

Step 3: Inside-out: analysis

In Step 3, we map all relevant internal developments that determine the possibilities and impossibilities for the company. This step includes all relevant aspects linked to the existing working processes, procedures, structure and governance of the company. Discuss this with all relevant internal stakeholders and get them engaged: board members, employees, councils, former customers, customers, former competitors.

In this step we answer questions such as: Do we fully utilize our capacities? Can we do more with our current assets? Where do we make a profit and where not? Should we be doing different things? Should we be doing things differently? What can we learn and develop? What should we change and what can we change? What are our core competences? What are our core values and what is our organization's identity? How is the organization structured and governed? What is our current financial situation and our room for investment? How much risk can and should we take?

Focusing on the capabilities of the organization, which are assessed by performing a financial, operational, structural and risk analysis, and on the (potential) capacity for change in the organization, Step 3 gives insights into the possibilities and impossibilities facing the organization.

Step 4: Options

Step 4 serves three goals:

- To integrate the outcomes of Steps 2 and 3: interpreting the analyses enables you to identify the options the organization has.
- To finalize the working hypothesis of the vision and mission statement drafted in Step 1 by confronting (or combining) the beliefs of the management of the organization with the actual data from the analyses. If necessary, the vision and the mission statement should be adjusted.
- To generate a number of strategic options in line with the formulated vision, mission statement and ambition.

The questions to be answered in this step are: Which business concepts are appropriate? What are the advantages, risks, limitations and (financial) implications of each option? How do we take our own abilities and conditions into account? How do the options relate to each other? Do we have all the information needed to make a choice?

The strategic options are determined using data and insights from the outside-in and inside-out steps and are then sharpened and further developed creatively. From the multitude of options, the most promising options must be selected based on their contribution to the strategic objectives as expressed in Step 1. This often entails making a shortlist of the options. These shortlisted options are then broken down further into business cases, target groups and competences to give more insights into the pros and cons of each of the options and to facilitate decision making.

Step 5: Choice

In Step 5, the various options are put side by side. First, they are scored on three criteria: usability, feasibility and applicability. This results in a choice of an initial strategy or strategic direction. The challenge lies in making choices and at the same time keeping options open. This sounds ambivalent and indeed it is: a choice must be made, but at the same time there has to be sufficient flexibility to allow quick adaptation to changing circumstances and to make a quick exchange of options possible. After an initial choice, it is therefore common to look again at the options not chosen and to identify which elements are very strong and should ideally – somehow – be combined with the chosen overall strategic direction. This combination can lead to a new, adapted option. It can also lead to a combination that is sequential in time: go for one strategic option but keep things flexible enough in the implementation of the chosen strategy to be able to switch to the other option. This sequential combination is often chosen in situations with high levels of uncertainty about future developments. You might call it having a Plan B for the case of a specific change of circumstances.

The questions in this step include: What are our preferred options and what is their ranking? What criteria and weighting factors do we apply and how do we apply them? Who chooses (process)? How do we choose (procedure)? Do we still need more information? What will we choose given our risk profile? How many resources do we put in? Which stakeholders must approve our choice or will have to be advised? When (under what circumstances) would another option be preferable? Do we choose one option or a combination of options? What elements from other options do we want to combine with our preferred option?

The choice of strategy can then be made based on all available information and options. This step is concluded with the production of a brief document which outlines the vision, mission statement and chosen strategy.

Step 6: Operationalization

In Step 6, the main consequences of the chosen strategy are identified and the implications for the organization detailed. This step usually takes quite a long time as, depending on how radically different the new strategy is, many aspects of the current organization need to be looked into: the necessity for change needs to be identified, aspired-to future situations drafted and change plans written. In this step the participation of management and key employees in earlier steps will thus pay off. As they already understand why the new strategy has been chosen, what the underlying rationale and intent are, they can more easily and quickly make plans for what needs to be changed in their part of the organization. The questions in this step include: What business model do we need for this strategy? What is our organizational model? What are our business unit strategies? What are our functional (HR, Finance, IT, etc.) strategies? What are our policy frameworks? What is our approach to making all necessary changes? What is our implementation plan and roadmap?

Often the attention of the participants involved in the strategy process wanes from the point at which choices have been made. Pressure ebbs from the process. It is likely that management's attention will be focused on the operational day-to-day business. So, top management and strategic staff must constantly encourage and maintain strategic thinking. At this point in the strategy process it is essential to communicate, first with people inside the organization, later also with people outside. You are about to make real changes and will need understanding and support from employees. The anchoring of the strategy in the consciousness of the employees takes time and the message must be repeated through various communication channels (speeches, internal communication magazines, social media, intranet, fixed agenda topic in department meetings etc).

Step 7: Execution

In Step 7, the emphasis is on directing and executing the plans and guiding the actual change throughout the organization in systems and in contacts with clients. Good project management and sometimes interim management are very important in this step. Questions to be answered are: How do we change our organization and can we implement the strategy effectively and efficiently? Are we realizing the desired change? Are we still on schedule according to our strategic script or is intervention needed? When is the implementation completed?

Several actions have to be taken and measures can be incorporated in business and department plans. Most efficient is to have the line managers perform this deployment as part of their regular management task.

Step 8: Monitoring

In Step 8, the performance of the organization is assessed in relation to the strategic goals. Also, an assessment is made of ongoing developments in the environment in relation to the strategy. This step focuses on exercising control over performance and keeping it aligned with the strategy. The strategy has been devised, communicated and executed. Now, it is important to keep an eye on the realization of the strategy and to stay on the course set out.

In this step the following questions have to be addressed: Are we reaching our desired strategic position? Are we realizing our strategic objectives? Are we still on track or do we need to intervene? How can we actively monitor trends and developments in the environment of the organization? Do we know what (early-warning) signals to look for? Can we continue on our strategic course or is a strategic review needed?

The activities of this step are to monitor the performance, trends and uncertainties, and if necessary to evaluate, report and adjust. Reports on progress should be produced periodically with clear, transparent and SMART (specific, measurable, acceptable, realistic, and time-based) performance indicators. These indicators should be defined at different levels. Deviations from desired scores on these indicators should be reviewed and discussed. This can lead to two types of adjustment. When the periodic review, for example, shows that a business unit is not pulling its weight, appropriate measures to bring its performance into line with the strategic goals can be discussed and carried out by (line) management. This is the first type of adjustment, which will be common in any organization and part of regular general management. Another type of adjustment is applicable when, for example, multiple periodic reviews over a longer period show the same deviation occurring again and again. Then it might be appropriate to discuss the need to review the strategic goals themselves. These adjustments imply starting the strategy process all over again, beginning at Step 1.

An important remark needs to be made about the numbering of the steps. In the strategic dialogue model (see Figure 1.1), the steps have no number. The reason for this is that in reality strategy processes do not start at Step 1, but are often triggered by a finding in one of the other steps. We will go into this in more detail in Part 5 of the book. Throughout this book, however, we will refer to steps by the number introduced in this chapter (ie from Step 1: Searchlight to Step 8: Monitoring). The numbering of the steps serves the purposes of increasing recognition and facilitating cross-referencing.

Each of the steps in a strategy process using the strategic dialogue model involves elements of participation, creativity, decision making, analysis and commitment. Together, these are the five most important characteristics of a strategy process. We elaborate on them in the next chapter.

The five characteristics of the strategy process with the strategic dialogue model

02

The approach to strategy with the strategic dialogue model has five characteristics: the process is participatory, creative, analytical, decisive and committing. All at the same time: they can be found in each of the 8 steps of the strategy process, albeit differently in each step. They require ongoing attention in every step of the strategy process, but the intensity of that attention necessarily varies by step. In Part 2 of this book, where we go into more detail on each of the 8 steps, we will also cover the characteristics of each step. The five characteristics of the strategy process contribute to the success of the approach. The right emphasis on these characteristics in each step ensures that the quality of the outcome will be high(er) and that the feasibility of the strategy and the appropriate engagement of stakeholders are assured. The characteristics are as follows:

 Participatory. This is about getting people involved, and about getting large and comprehensive groups of key internal and external stakeholders contributing enthusiastically on the right topic at the right moment and in the right role. This could be in conducting analyses, developing ideas and discussing consequences. Or perhaps even in making choices.

Creative. This is about getting people in creative mode and collecting creative input. Searching for new playing fields and new challenges requires thinking 'out of the box' and going where you have not gone before. Be encouraged to look for the new, rather than automatically doing the same as you always have. Design a new game if necessary.

 Analytical. This is about getting the facts on the table and guaranteeing objectivity, about getting a clear, factual and thoroughly supported picture of all current and future playing fields. Substantiate discussions with good business cases and a clear assessment of the implications.

 Decisive. This is about coming to realistic and supported choices. Choices should be based on external and internal comments. The real choice lies in determining the playing field, the game that you want to play and the way you want to play and win the game. But choices are also made on smaller issues during the process.

 Committing. This is about getting support for conclusions and outcomes, and about getting people started on the outcomes. Ensure that people understand the logic and consistency of the choices made and that they acknowledge the underlying factors and movements. It must be clear what the consequences are: so communicate and interact!

These five characteristics can be seen in all of the 8 steps of the strategy process, but with different needs for attention and variation in intensity per step. We will elaborate on this in the next part of the book, Part 2, with the detailed introduction of each of the 8 steps. The five characteristics also allow effective steering of the process. With the right method it is possible to put the correct emphasis on, and give appropriate attention to, all of the characteristics. In Part 4 of the book we present a selection of methods of engagement which give practical advice on how to influence a characteristic and steer the strategy process.

The amount of attention a characteristic needs is also determined by the context of the strategy process. In a 'normal' context the strategy process is highly participatory and committing in most steps, engaging employees and external parties to gather and exploit all available knowledge and to mobilize the right people for the strategy. There is also a good balance between steps that are more analytical, steps that are more decisive and steps that are more creative. But often the context is different. For example, with a merger at hand, a differently organized process is required. Or, if the strategy is intended to help convince a bank to prevent the organization from defaulting, the process will be organized differently. These differences in how to organize the process and how to alternate emphasis from one process characteristic to another will be elaborated in Part 5.

03 Introducing the DuSoleil case study

In Part 2 we will describe each of the 8 steps of the strategic dialogue model's strategy process in detail. Each step is also illustrated by a case study which sums up the essence of the step. The case study illustrates both how the process will typically unfold and what substantive challenges the participants have to deal with. It describes how a company states its vision, makes its analyses, comes to conclusions and makes its choices. And it describes the highs and lows that occur in every strategy process. The case studies will emphasize that strategy is an iterative rather than a linear process.

This case study is based on real-life experiences in our consulting practice. Of course, names are fictitious, but the issues, questions, challenges and emotions are very realistic. In this chapter we will introduce DuSoleil, a company that produces sunbeds. At the end of each chapter in Part 2 introducing a step in the strategy process, the case study illustrates that step. In this way, the strategy process at DuSoleil is presented step by step. With one episode per step, you can follow how the strategy process using the strategic dialogue model unfolds. By the end of Part 2, all 8 steps of the strategic dialogue model and all the characteristics of the strategy process will have been comprehensively introduced.

CASE STUDY DuSoleil

About DuSoleil: its origin and first steps to growth

Many years later, standing in the boardroom overlooking the city from the 26th floor, Will DuSoleil Jr was reminded of that long-ago afternoon when his father took him and his elder brother Henri to see the first tanning studio in Boston. DuSoleil senior had proudly shown him the space in which the first sunbeds produced and installed by DuSoleil were standing. DuSoleil senior, a former researcher and inventor at GE, had started a year earlier with nothing more than a pile of retrieved patents and a generous portion of entrepreneurship. The family business became a leading player in North America. The market for sunbeds exploded from the moment the first pre-tanned tourists were seen on the beaches of Miami in the 1970s. Many tanning studios were rapidly established in all big cities. The major resellers of electronic products jumped into this new segment and expanded their product range with this new high-margin product: the sunbed. When Phylight, a company from the Netherlands which was originally only a manufacturer of light bulbs, started producing sunbeds under its own brand, it caused a further growth spurt in the market.

In the mid-1980s Henri succeeded his father and DuSoleil became the market leader in North America in both the retail and the tanning studio markets. Henri entered Europe and established DuSoleil's own sales offices in the United Kingdom, the Netherlands, France and Germany, and created agents throughout what are now called the EU member states. Its own factories in Boston were greatly expanded and new facilities were opened in Antwerp (Belgium).

After completing his studies at MIT, Will DuSoleil Jr joined DuSoleil at the end of the 1980s. He immediately established a large R&D department and started to create an excellent external knowledge network that made DuSoleil supreme in tanning technology. Henri and Will Jr worked closely together as chief executive officer (CEO) and chief operating officer (COO), respectively.

Everything must change

In the 1990s came a major disruption. The first blow came when market volume decreased by 50 per cent, caused by a wave of negative publicity about the risks of skin cancer. DuSoleil had to reorganize, but the company soon recovered thanks to the entrepreneurship and sales power of Henri and the innovations of Will Jr. There was growth again, now in the top segment of the market and in the emerging markets of Brazil and Russia. With sales of all kinds of additional products and accessories, which were purchased in China, further growth was realized. The service levels provided to tanning studios by DuSoleil became legendary and major cost savings were achieved thanks to the purchase of non-critical parts in China. In 2007, an all-time-high profit figure was reached.

By the end of 2009, DuSoleil had suffered greatly from the worldwide economic crisis. Henri and Will Jr were desperate. The crisis had inflicted a hard blow on the sales of all the more expensive durable consumer goods and of sunbeds in particular. Although the worldwide tanning studio market was still a multi-billion market, sales of sunbeds were 40 per cent down. The sunbed market had diverged into a market with very cheap imports and a market for very exclusive and expensive sunbeds. Retailers had largely abandoned the DuSoleil mid-category of high-quality sunbeds for a reasonable (but not the lowest) price. At the low end, sunbeds were even downgraded to a seasonal product. Tanning studios consolidated everywhere: national chains evolved with reduced overhead costs and increased bargaining powers. Prices of mid-category sunbeds fell sharply. Also, quite a few studios worldwide had to close their doors owing to the competition they faced from large wellness centres (eg sauna plus gym plus tanning studio). Moreover, the inward-looking R&D department at DuSoleil was not able to follow the innovations of the competition who were moving towards wellness, electronics, software and sustainability (energy-efficient beds). Will Jr, however, refused to accept that DuSoleil was falling to a position of market follower instead of market leader. The factories struggled with understaffing and quality problems. Henri always managed finance and control in the evening, assisted by an old financial accountant who had worked for DuSoleil senior since the beginning. They had never invested in an enterprise resource planning (ERP) system or in financial IT systems. The financial data were consequently so opaque that Will Jr didn't have a clue as to where to start or how to make sense out of them.

In their quest for a brighter future, Will Jr and Henri had made a strategic plan and subsequent investment plans to turn DuSoleil around. For the required capital they were introduced by their bank to a private investor from Saudi Arabia. This investor had already acquired companies specializing in fitness and wellness equipment in the United States, but was looking for a producer of sunbeds. This was motivated by his ambition to become the world leader and total supplier to fitness and wellness centres.

To the displeasure of DuSoleil senior and under great pressure from their bank, Will Jr and Henri DuSoleil not only arranged a capital investment by the Saudi investor, but sold DuSoleil to the investor's company Al-Flous at an undervalued price. In return they received a capital injection to get back in business and to adapt to the changed markets. In the first year, however, this capital injection was increased to more than twice the original amount and still not enough change had been realized. The investor's money vanished in financing the working capital of

DuSoleil. More investments were about to be needed, but banks had diminished their lending and funding to DuSoleil owing to new financial rules.

This time it is different

By mid-2011, the Saudi investor was insisting that DuSoleil should undergo a total turnaround to become a profitable company again. The DuSoleil brothers were given an ultimatum by their new Saudi parent company Al-Flous: Will Jr and Henri had better come up with a sound and realistic strategic plan with a sustainable long-term perspective or the final closure of DuSoleil loomed and their father's life work would be destroyed.

The need for a drastic change in strategic direction was evident, but how could the brothers deal with this? What playing field would and could they enter and what options did they still have? They were very busy with day-to-day operation of the business and were already suffering heavy pressure. How could they combine that with an intensive, strategic discussion and a change operation? How would they be able to translate strategic choices to results and perspectives in which the employees, the investor and the banks would believe? Henri DuSoleil and Will DuSoleil Jr stared at the members of the board of their Saudi parent company and promised to come back with a strategy within six months. Then they called Berenschot, a leading Dutch consultancy firm and started the strategy process using the strategic dialogue.

To be continued...

PART 2
The 8 steps to strategic success revealed

The 8 steps to strategic success what do we aspire to?

 Step 1: Searchlight

Objective and results

Step 1: Searchlight is about setting the scope of the strategy process: both content-wise and process-wise. The first objective of the step is to explore and define the company's business playing field, shared ambition, and business scope. It leads to an overview of strategic opportunities and uncertainties, both subject to further exploration, without the inclusion of too many irreversible choices. The second objective of the searchlight step is to ensure that the strategy process is well organized, with the right people available in the right roles and tasks and with realistic planning. Obtaining a team with the right spirit is a particularly crucial part of this step in the strategy process.

> **THE RESULTS OF STEP 1: SEARCHLIGHT ARE:**
> - a working hypothesis of the mission statement, vision and business scope;
> - clarity on the degrees of freedom and level of ambition for the strategy;
> - a formulation of the organization's shared ambition;
> - clarity on the strategic process;
> - a team with high commitment and involvement;
> - increased inspiration, energy and feeling of urgency.

Scope and content

In this step, key questions to be answered are:

- *What is our mission statement? What is our identity?* The searchlight step answers questions concerning the organization's 'being'. What is the organization's right to exist? What role does the organization want to play in the social and economic environment? What are the core standards and values from which it operates?

  These questions are of crucial importance as clients and employees both search for companies with whom they can identify. A company's ability to differentiate itself through its identity and authenticity is a unique strength which many companies aim for. It is also the leading principle when making the final choice: do we stick to our current identity or is it subject to renewal?

  Strategies that lack authenticity that is as locked in as the company's DNA will be experienced as having low internal and external credibility. So it's important not to misjudge these principles of the organization's existence by identifying them as being irrational or vague. Instead, act on them in order to create a robust strategic foundation that stimulates the creation of new strategic insights.

- *What is our shared dream? What do we wish to achieve in the next few years?* A company's vision and level of ambition are more than a complicated sentence accompanied by some target figures. It is rather a matter of formulating the grand inspiring objective for the organization. This so-called 'Big Hairy Audacious Goal' ('BHAG' – introduced by James Collins and Jerry Porras in their 1994 book *Built to Last*, Harper Business, New York) represents the shared dream that inspires employees to wake up and go to work every morning in order to make this dream become reality. A strong BHAG expresses the company's vision and level of ambition. It is therefore a platform that gives employees direction and inspiration, and stimulates individual and group energy levels. In order to be able eventually to translate the BHAG into specific activities, it must first be defined as having specific, measurable, acceptable, realistic, and time-based (SMART) objectives. For each of these formulated quantitative and qualitative objectives, specific activities can be undertaken.

- *What will be our business scope?* The business scope determines the organization's current and possible future activities. It sets the playing field on which the organization wants to play. The business scope can be formulated using Derek Abell's business definition model (see Part 3), which expresses a business scope in three dimensions: who (a company wants to serve in terms of markets, customers etc), what (a company wants to offer them in terms of value-adding activities, products, services etc), and how (a company wants to realize their aims in these contexts by the use of technology, competences, capacity etc). Additionally, an overview of the core, supporting and exit activities is produced. These dimensions are examined to see whether they have potential to increase the organization's outcomes: might the organization be more successful by extending or limiting certain types of activity? Finally, new business models are explored. These new ideas might also identify necessary 'upgrades' in existing activities.

  The most important objective of determining the business scope is not to choose a specific strategic demarcation, but rather to identify and set a first framework for the strategic direction for the organization.

- *With whom will we formulate the strategy?* The starting point of a good strategy is a team that is willing and able to create an inspiring vision by combining their knowledge, time and mindset. This is not necessarily the management team. On the contrary, forming a team specifically to come up with the new strategy serves two purposes. A mixed team consisting of senior managers with an open mindset, staff with high potential and/or trusted outsiders (key stakeholders) can create the feeling that something is about to happen – something that awakens the interest and involvement of the rest of the organization. This, in turn, stimulates commitment, inspiration, energy and a feeling of urgency in the overall strategic process and can mobilize all stakeholders to take on the strategy and help execute it. Such a mixed team also allows management to take on a distinct role, most likely that of decision maker to whom the 'strategy team' has to report. And it keeps management available for the daily demands of the business.

- *How do we shape the strategy process?* Finally, the process needs to take on a distinctive form. Schedules that determine milestones, deadlines and responsibilities must be drawn up. Agendas for workshops and meetings must be drafted. And a communication plan must be put in place: who is informed when, on what and by whom?

Recommended models

Several strategy models can be used in the searchlight step. Models that help express ambitions or a vision and mission statement are particularly useful. We recommend using (see Part 3):

- Strategy 3.0;
- 'BHAG';
- Abell's business definition model;
- key market characteristics.

The process

Figure 4.1 gives a schematic representation of the sequence of topics and activities in the searchlight step:

- the dream and the identity;
- content demarcation;
- the team and the mindset;
- process demarcation;
- inspiration, ambition, vision and mission statement, objectives, business scope, core process.

In the searchlight step, initially both the content and the mindset should be free to roam without constraints: to break free from the ordinary and the usual and have a fresh look at opportunities and possibilities. In Figure 4.1 this is depicted as the beam of a flashlight: it first diverges and then travels in parallel. Subsequently, the content and process are framed by the organization's vision, ambition and goals, in order to provide and maintain focus. As depicted in Figure 4.1, scope and team go together simultaneously. It is, however, important to concentrate first on creating the right team with the right team spirit and then move on

FIGURE 4.1 Schematic representation of the searchlight step process

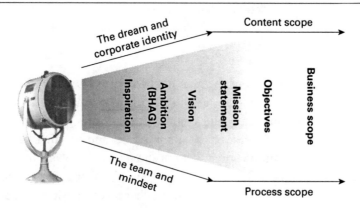

to determining the content. Once the content is on the agenda, most people dive into it and have little interest in thinking about teams. Besides, it is much more difficult to get a team together and fired up when the scope is already set.

Characteristics

The searchlight step provides direction to the strategy process. It involves top-level decision making. In this step, most emphasis is on the 'decisive' characteristic. Although all the characteristics of the strategy process within the strategic dialogue are relatively strongly visible in this step, it is foremost about initial decision making – about the scope of both the strategy and the strategy process.

A certain degree of creativity is truly necessary in this process, especially when it comes to considering new playing fields and new perspectives on the organization. It is also necessary to balance a very open and free approach, on the one hand, with enough constraints to overcome the potential hazard of an exercise so extensive that making a decision becomes impossible. Therefore creativity is needed alongside decision making, to define the scope and depth of what is expected and what is to be considered.

The analytical character of this step is mainly focused on substantiating the chosen course and ambition. Even though the next two steps will provide much more detailed data that will help in the eventual decision making, it is also crucial to emphasize the importance of the choices made during the searchlight step.

The participative nature of the searchlight step, as shown in Figure 4.2, has equally strong emphasis, as this step is very much about putting together an inspiring team and communicating information about the strategic project to the rest of the organization and to other key stakeholders. People within the organization should feel involved and excited about what is going to happen. It is thus important that many opinions are gathered when formulating the strategic process, business scope and level of ambition. However, compared to the other levels of the strategic dialogue, the group involved will still be limited to the management team and/or a core strategy team.

FIGURE 4.2   Characteristics of the searchlight step

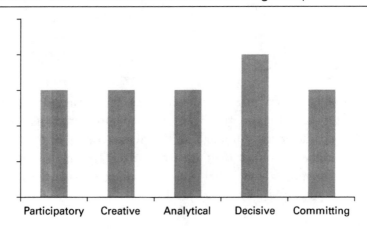

Participatory   Creative   Analytical   Decisive   Committing

The people involved

In the searchlight step there is plenty of room to shape the process and frame the content by using the organization's know-how and ideas. Some organizations organize (online) discussion forums that allow employees, supply chain partners and other key stakeholders to participate in this step. This stimulates the creation of positive and creative energy for the process and reduces the likelihood of narrow-minded views taking hold. Broad participation benefits not only support for, but also the quality of, the content. The strategy process has to be something special in itself. If it is perceived as nothing more than an annual ritual, nobody will feel truly involved. Involving a wide-ranging group of people is fully in line with the strategic dialogue approach. An alternative approach is to let the core team develop a framework, but only if it is then extensively tested within the organization and with some key external stakeholders.

The searchlight step in the strategic dialogue sequence

The searchlight step can be the beginning of the strategy process, but it does not have to be. As described in Part 1, a strategy process using the strategic dialogue is an iterative process which, depending on the circumstances, can be started at any of the 8 steps (see Figure 1.1 on page 19). It is entirely possible that the strategy process starts out as a tightening up of the strategy implementation in Step 7 or 8 but eventually causes revision of strategic principles resulting in the need to 'go back to' or continue with the searchlight step. Often companies end up stranded in the implementation stage of their strategy or fiddling around for a long time while knowing that their strategic course isn't leading them to where they want to go. In these cases it is perfectly normal to start at another step, but then make a conscious decision to go to the searchlight step, to widen their perspective and scope and open a discussion as to whether their current strategy is up for revision. The searchlight step is the one that stimulates new insights and forces a reconsideration of everyday thinking and acting. So Step 1 can be, but does not always have to be, the first step in a strategy process. In any process, however, it is usually the step that marks the beginning of new strategy formulation.

Another motive for going to the searchlight step from another step is when there's a need in one of the other steps to reconsider the company's ambitions and/or business scope. In these cases there will be an iteration between the searchlight step and the other step, often Step 4 or 5.

Dos and don'ts

✔ Prevent narrow-mindedness. Have the courage to dream and use the (physical and mental) space to consider divergent ideas before starting to converge into frameworks.

✔ Make sure you talk about the opportunities and solutions.

✔ Lay a basis for all the other steps in the strategy process by setting a frame of reference based on the formulated ambition, identity, BHAG and business scope. If the basic principles are compromised too much at a specific moment in the process, the chosen course of action ('how') or principles ('what') can then be changed.

✔ Organize an 'unfreezing event' to start off. During an unfreezing event an activity is organized outside the organizational setting. It's an inspiring event that brings team members closer together. This has an inspirational effect that stimulates people to take action.

✔ Involve external stakeholders.

✔ Assign a 'WOMMBA ratio': limit the number of White Old Males with MBAs in the strategy team to a maximum of half the team.

✔ Emphasize the focus on mindsets, instead of definite choices, when communicating results.

✘ Do not misjudge the value of discussions concerning the company's 'being', in which questions about the company's right to exist, identity and role in society are considered. Do not see them as irrational or vague. Instead, these considerations are of crucial importance to your clients and employees as they form an important source of inspiration and help create the right mindset.

CASE STUDY   DuSoleil

Previously...

At DuSoleil, Will Jr and Henri DuSoleil were in need of a drastic change in the strategic direction of the company. Their Saudi-Arabian parent company Al-Flous, backed by their Saudi investor, had demanded a sound and realistic strategic plan with a sustainable long-term perspective that would give rationale to additional investments. If they failed, final closure of DuSoleil loomed. The DuSoleil brothers had promised to come up with a strategy within six months. Then they called the consultancy firm Berenschot and are now about to start their strategy process with the strategic dialogue.

Getting started

When the decision to start a strategy process was made, a strategy team was formed, consisting of senior managers ('the realists') and creative newcomers ('the idealists'). Will Jr would lead the team. A steering committee, appointed to make monthly evaluations of progress and to make final decisions, consisted of Henri DuSoleil (as CEO), the financial director (the former accountant) and the chairman of the board of their parent company. In cooperation with the consultant, the team started by drafting a project and communication plan that described the entire strategy process: the steps to be taken, the amount of time expected to be needed to complete them, the desired result of each step, and what was to be communicated to whom. Henri DuSoleil, never very open to outside interference, was supportive of limited interference and a short-term project. After discussing the matter with Will Jr and the chairman of the board of the parent company, it was decided that the process would have high degrees of participation and interaction in accordance with the ideas of the strategic dialogue. In particular, customers, employees and suppliers were to be engaged, in order to create a good and complete picture of the dramatically changed environment and customer needs and to create support for the changes that would have to be realized. Given the financial situation and in accordance with Henri's wishes, it was decided that several broad and generic analyses would be undertaken, but nothing too detailed or fancy.

Speeding things up and creating a sense of urgency

The strategy team started out with some interviews and talks within the organization to get a better understanding of how things stood regarding the needed change in strategic direction. This first round made it very clear that without emphasizing the urgency and without inspiration, no new strategy would ever work at DuSoleil. Henri and Will Jr had to admit that they usually communicated an over-optimistic perspective and that the acquisition of the company by the Saudi Arabians had come as a surprise to the employees. Therefore, half the organization had not yet realized how serious the situation was, while the other half showed a pessimistic attitude to the change: why could this change of strategic direction be so urgent all of a sudden? There was much criticism of the management, but at the same time employees did have great passion for and loyalty to DuSoleil and a great sense of belonging. Although many feared losing their jobs, overall, people felt that the business had been stagnant for too long. So, in general, there was great support for starting the strategy process, and thanks to voluntary suggestions and input from many employees, the strategy team was able to produce a highly supported and qualitative project plan in a very short time. This plan also made it clear that even though a strategy process with the strategic dialogue would frequently ask for employee support and input, it was not a democratic process: ideas were welcome but decisions were agreed by the strategy team and finally presented to the management team after it had the assent of the steering committee.

In order to make the strategy process more inspiring and to increase the feeling of urgency, the strategy team next organized an 'unfreezing event' with participants from all departments, business units and geographic regions of the organization. Teams of senior and mid-level managers were sent out with cameras to visit customers in their region with one single assignment, which was to listen: What are the issues customers face? How is DuSoleil perceived? What is the competition doing? The next day the insights were shared via a web-conference: it turned out that overall and in all regions, DuSoleil had to be cheaper and more sustainable at the same time. The quality level was not what it should be, users wanted to see quicker tanning results, and the cosmetics industry obtained a greater market share than had been presumed.

The consultancy firm also shared their findings on the current financial and organizational situation of DuSoleil, a 'quick scan' analysis they had performed in parallel to the 'unfreezing event'. The insights and feedback of customers and consultants gained much recognition, but also much discussion. The senior employees in particular saw 'a picture taken at the wrong moment', that is, a market slump that would recover. However, there were also several managers who shared the opinion that DuSoleil had fooled itself long enough. What had begun as a nice company trip ended in a workshop in which departments and generations came into confrontation. Henri concluded that the family culture on which the business had been running for a long time was gone. Will Jr, on the other side, was happy to see that the underlying truths, emotions, contradictions and opinions were finally explicitly expressed.

Reinventing ourselves

The strategy team then organized its first workshop. Its agenda was to define the mission statement, vision, scope and ambition of DuSoleil. The session paid in-depth attention to the company's identity, passions and its right to exist: What is driving us? What are the core values and how valuable are they in today's market? With the use of the BHAG model, the team formulated a vision and mission statement that supported the true identity of DuSoleil. A new mission statement was formulated: 'DuSoleil is the innovative market leader of products, services, and knowledge in the area of body and facial tanning for the global professional and consumer market.'

The new mission statement builds on the core expertise of DuSoleil and extends the market perspective of exclusively producing sunbeds. It opened discussions for exploration of new opportunities, such as marketing the organization's knowledge on skincare, and offering all-inclusive packages of products and services to new markets. It even led to exploration of whole new business models for DuSoleil. The strategy team now got excited, but before it started to work out these new-found strategic alternatives, it was recalled: the searchlight step determines the playing field and formulates the hypotheses, but it does not yet go into any detail. Instead, the team was guided to first set the scope of the possible product and geographical business scope. There was much talk about the market activities of various countries, channels and segments. Can we operate in higher segments without operating in the lower ones? Were wellness and fitness centres a more attractive market than retail and studios? The overall conclusion was that there was simply too little information on the market and financials to say anything about this. This scope discussion, however, clarified what information was needed and should be sought in the outside-in and inside-out steps.

In accordance with the communication plan, the results of this workshop were first presented to the steering committee but not yet distributed further in the organization. The steering committee was not very specific in its feedback but did give its approval to the project and communication plan and allowed the strategy team to continue with the new mission statement as a working hypo- thesis. Afterwards, Henri argued that it had all been tried before, but the financial director and chairman encouraged the team and perceived the strategic frame- work as a good first step towards actually making decisions and transforming DuSoleil into a profitable company once again.

Don't wait for good things to come

As no strategy process is a linear process, and as the customer visits had brought to light some 'quick wins' and operational points of improvement that could be realized in a short time frame, a 'quick intervention team' was formed, consisting of some of the participants of the unfreezing event with the authority to implement improvements immediately, irrespective of the direction and step of the strategy process. The intervention team set up a 'war room' and started taking some improvement measures right away, including improving two of the quality checks in production. As these initial measures showed an immediate increase in customer satisfaction, it became clear to the entire organization: we do not yet know where we are heading, but, starting today, the customer is our main priority and we will interact more professionally, and more as a team.

To be continued...

The 8 steps to strategic success

what futures do we need to anticipate?

 Step 2: Outside-in: scenarios

Objective and results

Step 2: Outside-in: scenarios provides a comprehensive picture of the company's environment and the parties involved. To achieve this successfully, knowledge of who the most important external stakeholders are, now and in the future, and insights into what developments are most likely to determine the future are essential.

Organizations are increasingly dependent on the actions of other organizations. In business chains, task specialization and division of roles are increasingly applied. This is represented, for example, in the outsourcing of support and primary activities, and even the outsourcing of product development. Today, companies cannot exist without their network of knowledge institutions, suppliers and alliance partners. In addition, the market and customers are naturally a source of revenue and the desired financial results. Also, other parties can positively or negatively influence the company and its success, for example regulators, supervisors, trade organizations and educational institutions. In order to realize a successful strategy, a company needs a clear idea of what these organizations and institutions are doing, what drives them and what their ambitions are. Step 2 is therefore aimed at getting a clear view on the position, interests, development and mutual dynamics of all these stakeholders. Future winners will be the companies that are the first to capture and translate these external signals into new services and products and competitive position.

The viewpoint in the outside-in step is looking towards the future. And the future is uncertain by definition. Nevertheless, companies can perform a trend analysis in their strategic process to gain some insights and future guidance. In addition, uncertainties can be taken into account: these are merely external developments that can lead to various future situations, for each of which a strategic option could be defined. Hence the name of this step: from an outside-in perspective you will see how external developments will have implications for your (future) activities and through creating scenarios you can even see how uncertain external developments will affect you. Strategy is the managing of uncertainties and preparing the company for the future. It is not just the mechanical formulation of options and making decisions, but it is also about keeping the right options open for the future. The latter can also offer solutions when a decision appears not to have been the right one. So you will need a good understanding of all external developments that can influence your organization's future.

THE RESULTS OF STEP 2: OUTSIDE-IN: SCENARIOS ARE:

- an overview of all relevant stakeholders;
- insights into the development and value of the customer base, the market position and the company's competitiveness;
- insight into current and expected future external developments and their character: uncertainties or trends;
- insight into the potential impact on, and implications of external developments for, the company's performance and activities;
- plausible scenarios for the future business environment in which the company has to operate;

- identification of stakeholders' interests and behaviour in each of the scenarios for every stakeholder;
- identification of possible course(s) of action for the company in each scenario with an assessment of the potential consequences on the company's performance;
- indicators which act as early-warning signals for expected future external developments.

Scope and content

The outside-in step translates developments in the external environment into something that has meaning to the company. The width of the analysis of the external environment depends on the scope chosen in the searchlight step. In any case, parochialism should be avoided. This means that you shouldn't look solely at the parties currently involved in your network and value chain, but also take into account parties that might play a role in a future scenario and those that might drop out.

This step provides answers to many questions, including these most relevant ones:

- What will we have to deal with in the years ahead and how will we prepare for it?
- Where do our future opportunities lie?
- What is the perspective of our current product groups?
- What is expected of us by our stakeholders?
- Which markets and businesses are attractive to our company?
- What will be the future purchasing power of our customers?
- How will the prices of raw materials, semi-finished products and services develop?
- What expertise and technologies will become available?
- Which networks and partners are interesting?
- Which new business models can be successful?
- Which rules and regulation can be expected?

- How will the labour market develop?
- Which position(s) in the supply chain will allow us to capture the most value?
- What is our competitiveness?
- With what products do we serve which markets? And are there any other, possibly completely new markets with good opportunities (adjacent or 'out-of-the-box' product–market combinations)?
- What surprises might we face (or should we expect)?

The scope of the external exploration must not be too narrow. It might already be possible to identify limitations in, for example, geographical scope, customer groups or technologies used, based on the ambitions formulated in the searchlight step. This will set the width of the analysis. The depth of analysis required must be decided for each element, as sometimes it is sufficient to know the main issues and sometimes you want to know every detail of a development.

Another important aspect in setting the scope of external exploration is the time horizon. A good time horizon is approximately five years ahead. Obviously, this depends on the nature of the industries in which the company operates. The time horizon should be chosen so that it spans enough time for new developments to develop and so that you can really enrich your perspective, but also should not be so far away that it becomes more like science fiction. But be aware that strategy truly is a long-term matter.

Recommended models

Several strategy models can be used in the outside-in step. Models that help analyse developments in the market, with customers, suppliers, competitors, in society and all other relevant developments in the external environment are particularly useful in this step. We recommend (see Part 3):

- PEST (or PESTLE) analysis model;
- stakeholder analysis;
- competitive analysis: Porter's five forces model;

- customer analysis: Curry's pyramid;
- scenario planning.

The process

The topics and activities in Step 2 include the following:

- mapping the external environment (stakeholders, supply chains, competition, markets, etc);
- creating an overview of available expertise, visions, statements, and data about, for example, market developments, cost developments, customer satisfaction and competitors;
- organizing external involvement in discussions on external developments, their probability and potential impact;
- analysing all relevant external developments and assessing their impact and possible implications for the organization;
- building multiple scenarios of what the future could look like, based on the most relevant external developments (including uncertainties and trends spotted);
- determining the consequences and possible course(s) of action for the company in each scenario.

The business scope and ambition defined in the searchlight step indicate which customers, customer segments, suppliers, knowledge institutions, trade organizations, regulators and supervisors are relevant. In addition, in the outside-in step other relevant stakeholders that could influence the organization's activities are identified. There are many useful strategy models that help identify the most relevant players and influencing parties. It is important to consider their possible actions and interests, and how they will try to realize their ambitions in the years ahead, in order to consider how your own company can react. Once the stakeholders, chain partners and other relevant parties are identified and mapped, it is important to gather information about them. This can be done through research or by actually contacting them, for example by planning interviews or organizing theme-based expert meetings. Direct contact is the best way to gain a view on their driving forces and planned actions. Experience tells us that even though expectations at the start of these initiatives are low, they always produce new insights into the future. During these meetings, it is important to maintain a future perspective. Be conscious of the fact that looking forward is difficult. If you ask someone to look 10 years ahead, you will always receive an answer based on something that will happen 5 years from now. Also, employees within the company should be asked for their views on the stakeholders. Accountants and company representatives can tell a lot about customers, for example. Considering the variety and the number of parties involved, it is important to plan this step carefully and to pay close attention to the lead-time.

As well as the stakeholders' statements, visions and ambitions, you also need to gather information on markets, competitors, countries, product lines, returns, market shares etc. Some of this information can be obtained directly from external parties, but for the greater part it is research that needs to be executed by the company itself. If there is only a limited amount of information available, you might decide to hire an external party to do customer and/or market research. In the outside-in step, strategy models can be very useful as they help arrange and interpret vast amounts of market data and information on external developments. They are also useful to make sure that you have information on all relevant topics and that no one is overlooked.

When all the information is available, it can be analysed and scenarios constructed. In Part 3, scenario planning is described in more detail as a strategy model that can be used in this step. From our experience we have learned that using scenario planning techniques should not just be a suggestion. The activities in the outside-in step therefore follow the thinking process used for scenario planning (see Part 3). Figure 5.1 is a schematic representation of the activities.

First, you formulate a central question regarding what you would like to know about the future (for instance, 'how can we keep up our lead over our competition in our core markets?') and identify the time horizon (eg 5 or 10 years).

Next, a systematic inventory of external developments on both the micro and the macro level is made. The micro level covers developments in the organization's working environment (ie its customers, suppliers, labour unions etc), while the macro level considers the major global issues (which are at first sight thus less directly related to the organization),

FIGURE 5.1 Schematic representation of the activities in the outside-in step

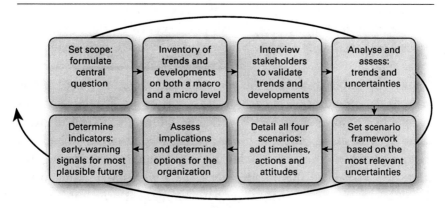

such as scarcity of food or the availability of energy sources. Based on the inventory, an analysis is made of the probability of these developments and their likely impact on the organization. Here a distinction is made between trends and uncertainties. Trends are highly probable external factors leading to a specific outcome that is largely predictable, for example the ageing of a country's population. Uncertainties are factors of great importance but whose development is not fully obvious and which could develop in different directions; that is, they are developments with outcomes that have an unpredictable chance of becoming reality, for example a government's ambition to turn the country into a knowledge-based economy. How certain is it that this will be realized five years from now? And to what extent will measures be taken to realize this to what level? In order to gain insight into the dynamics behind the uncertainties that have the highest impact on the company's future, the driving forces that stimulate the developments and their plausible outcomes are examined. Based on the two most relevant uncertain factors, a scenario framework (system of coordinates) that reproduces four scenarios in its four quadrants is developed. Each one of these scenarios is then further developed. Using the identified trends and the information gathered about the attitude and the possible or expected actions of stakeholders in each of the scenarios, the scenarios can then be further detailed. By using creative tools and techniques (see Part 4), a scenario can be brought to life. For instance, a clear picture will emerge of the possible alternative futures that lie ahead. By using a timeline per scenario that represents events, or by writing a story or a conversation between two or three important stakeholders, the degree of realism of the scenario will be increased. Additionally, the scenario will support communication of future perspectives to others involved in the strategy process and eventually to all key stakeholders.

Finally, the implications for the company and the course(s) of action open to the organization in each of the scenarios are investigated. This is done in a number of intensive workshops, during which participants come up with ideas, raise questions, provide suggestions and challenge them themselves, thus being able to contribute to determining the strategic direction of the organization. These workshops result in the definition of one or more strategic options; these are the outcomes of Step 2 that will become the input to Steps 4 (Options) and 5 (Choice). There, the options will be considered and reflected upon, using knowledge from other steps, particularly from Step 3 (Inside-out). A particular future positioning (as a strategic option) might seem to have potential from an external point of view, but that does not necessarily mean the company is able to achieve it. It is important to be clear about the focus on external developments in the outside-in step and to be clear about the step as providing only half the input that is required for a well-informed choice of strategy. Also, it is important to know that Step 2 can be organized as an iterative process; for example, when it appears that other developments are of more crucial importance than those initially assumed and considered in the scenarios, you can start again at that point in Step 2 and continue the strategy process from there.

Ultimately, in Step 2 the most relevant indicators are derived to monitor the probability of the scenarios: which one is to become reality. These indicators will eventually also be of use in Step 8 (Monitoring).

Characteristics

Step 2 is first and foremost analytical. What information do we need? What information can we find? Whom should we contact and who is willing to cooperate? How should we interpret the information? It is of great importance to know how you want to perform the activities in this step, preferably right at the start, in order to prevent excessive lead-times, especially when you want to consult and involve both internal and external stakeholders. The actual analysis mainly takes place at the start of this step. You should not simply accept that there are no available data: interviews with external stakeholders, sessions with experts on new trends and developments, documentation research, and the uncovering of tacit knowledge held by long-time employees of the organization can all lead to solid analyses. Tailoring the depth and width of the analyses is also important. Too few analyses will lead to a lack of factual substantiation of the scenarios, and too many analyses can lead to a false sense of security.

The knowledge of employees from many different disciplines can be very valuable in this step. They are likely to have substantive insights into developments in customer needs, technologies, supplier opportunities, labour market conditions and other factors that can be of relevance for your organization's future. Additionally, they have insight into identifying the relevant players in the environment. They can thus help create an equal degree of participation by third parties in the process. In the external analysis, customers, competitors, suppliers, regulators, trade organizations, politicians, policymakers and scientists are often involved or consulted. The outside-in step thus has high levels of participation from within and outside the organization, as shown in Figure 5.2.

FIGURE 5.2   Characteristics of the outside-in step

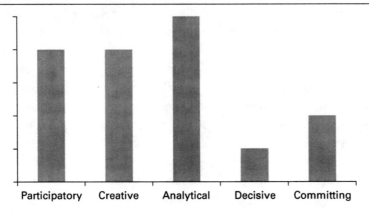

Participatory   Creative   Analytical   Decisive   Committing

Creativity is the third important characteristic of this step. Scenarios are images of the future which naturally does not exist yet and therefore should be shaped or sketched. In this process, it is required that participants imagine the ambitions, future roles and interests of stakeholders in order to identify their own possible future course of action. This requires a lot of creativity, which also indicates that this step can produce a lot of energy.

Actual decision making in this step is limited. Decisions will mostly be about assessing developments as uncertainties or trends, or the assessment of imagined courses of action in which some possibilities are inevitably eliminated. In terms of commitment, this step has some emphasis on this characteristic. The extensive involvement of stakeholders automatically ensures that the analyses made and the scenarios created will be wide-ranging and that acceptance of the organization's future perspective will be gained. As the stakeholders themselves were involved in shaping this future perspective (to a certain extent), they will feel committed to it (to a certain extent).

The people involved

Given the high degree of participation, it is not surprising that the number and diversity of the people involved (representatives of multiple stakeholders, experts and other invitees) are significant and much greater than in some of the other steps, including the searchlight step. You could even say of the outside-in step: the more, the merrier. It particularly concerns 'more' from outside the company. This includes consulting and interviewing external stakeholders and experts on expected future developments (trends and uncertainties) by suppliers, partner organizations, (current, potential and lost) customers, consumer organizations and, if possible, competitors, policymakers, political parties, academics, regulators, trade unions, works councils, industry organizations, knowledge institutes, international organizations (eg EU Commission), environmental organizations, and all other relevant stakeholders or sources of information.

The involvement within the organization is ideally shaped in line with the searchlight step: a core team which is involved throughout the strategy process. In this step they will be the ones doing (or directing) the analyses and building (or facilitating the creation of) the scenarios. But alongside this core team, employees from different backgrounds and from different departments can be involved. They can help in collecting information about the environment from both inside and outside the company, performing analyses, discussing trends and uncertainties, assessing the impact and implications of developments and building the scenarios. Different employees can be involved in different activities or a group of employees can be involved in all activities. Their involvement should be determined by reference to the knowledge of external developments they can bring and/or the contacts they have with external stakeholders.

In addition, expert meetings can be organized around a central theme (eg the application of a new technology). Both external and internal participants can be invited, although these meetings should have a smaller number of participants able to discuss the main theme in greater depth.

The outside-in step in the strategic dialogue sequence

The outside-in step often follows the searchlight step, which demarcates the external environment to be explored (see Figure 1.1 on page 19). You should thus always check, before starting Step 2, that the searchlight step has indicated a clear scope for the strategy process (and thus also for the external analysis). If not, you should first finalize the searchlight step.

The outside-in step can be performed simultaneously with the inside-out step. Strategic options are developed from both steps. The outside-in step provides market-driven options derived from, for example, customer questions, technical opportunities, new knowledge, expected actions of competitions, and regulation. The inside-out step provides opportunities based on the organization's own competences. Both steps are used as input for the option step (Step 4).

Apart from coming after the searchlight step, there are also situations where it makes sense to start with Step 2. There can be a particular situation where the current ambition is still valid but developments in the market have caused previous choices to become outdated and therefore new strategic options are required. In that case, a new external exploration is needed in order to create new options with a higher potential to succeed given the new external developments.

Also, the outcomes of Step 2 are input for Step 8 (Monitoring). In Step 8 the most relevant indicators of the probability of the scenarios becoming reality are monitored, so that the organization can change course in a timely fashion if necessary. Continuous monitoring of external developments is also carried out in Step 8 and the analyses and tools from Step 2 are very useful for that purpose.

Dos and don'ts

✔ When exploring the environment, choose a level of participation that is as broad as possible. Organize expert interviews and meetings.

✔ Go from thinking 'outside the box' to thinking 'beyond boxes': prevent any parochialism.

✔ Actively search for yet unknown developments that might influence the company in the future.

✔ Ask for input from cross-thinkers and obstinate thinkers within the company.

✔ Interview customers, including potential customers and lost ones.

✔ Prevent lead-times being too short for this step: in particular, take your time when building and discussing scenarios.

✔ During the analysis, continuously consider the following questions: is the answer to this question known, and if so, how relevant is that answer for identifying strategic options? Eventually it is all about insights. Facts are mere intermediate results, used during the creation of insights.

✘ Be careful not to pay too much attention to obvious trends. And don't look only at what is predictable 'as that's the only thing you can actually do something about'. Do not forget uncertainties, as otherwise they will inevitably surprise you.

✘ Do not hold on to particular insights: 'We know the market, we deal with it every day.' Even when you have frequent contact with clients or partners, don't act on their behalf but consult and involve them. You will be surprised to learn some new insights from them, which you hadn't discussed with them before.

✖ Do not search for the most likely scenario. Each scenario is equally plausible and relevant, even the less attractive ones, as you will want to be prepared for those too!

CASE STUDY DuSoleil

Previously...

In their quest to turn DuSoleil into a profitable company once again, Henri and Will Jr had started the strategy process by forming a strategy team and a steering committee and by setting up a framework for the strategy process and drafting a communication plan. The activities in the searchlight step – talks within the organization, the unfreezing event where customers were interviewed and the workshop to discuss the company's ambition – had already led to a promising start. A new mission statement was formulated and some quick wins were identified to 'cash in on' right away. But it also appeared that DuSoleil might have been lagging in knowing what its customers wanted and how the markets were developing. This they had to look into more closely.

Of course we know our business, we've been in it for ages!

As already concluded in the first workshop of the strategy team in the searchlight step, DuSoleil lacked market insight. Also, little was known about the competition and, except for the annual research into customer satisfaction, no market research was performed. However, insights about market sizes, growth and profitability were essential if the company was to be able to act on a substantiated market view. DuSoleil's strategy team therefore decided to map out the external environment. First, the PESTLE analysis that had been performed three years earlier was updated. Even though the members of the strategy team who had a commercial background thought the political and social trends were very abstract and general, and although the R&D members thought the technology trends lacked detail, their jointly putting together and prioritizing all the information still led to surprising insights into various markets. Almost half the trends appeared to be uncertain factors that had multiple directions in which they could develop. For instance, the availability of raw material was identified as very important for the future success of DuSoleil, though its future availability was very uncertain. The same applied to oil prices and to consumer behaviour.

As before, the team immediately felt the need to translate the PESTLE analysis into action plans for each market, and again, as in the searchlight step, the team was pulled back from this. The view on the external environment first needed to be further complemented. In doing so, it quickly became clear that the team members thought they understood the interests, wishes and demands of customers, users, suppliers and other stakeholders; however, from extensive interviews with, and site visits and calls to, the Saudi-Arabian parent company Al-Flous, important customers, suppliers and university researchers, it became clear that this was not always the case. They also learned that the opinions of DuSoleil's sales managers and country managers on market trends, supply chain developments and technological developments often differed from those of the stakeholders. It became clear that the market had gone through some significant changes and that, besides the traditional sunbeds, a whole new range of products was being offered in the areas of body and facial tanning, including spray studios, self-tanning creams and pads. The newest sunbeds offered high-pressure facial bronzers, breeze systems and special compositions of ultraviolet radiation. Users were increasingly looking for ease of use: quick, accessible and safe tanning.

Are we ready for the future?

In order to specify the trends and uncertainties, a three-day scenario planning workshop was held, attended by DuSoleil's sales and country managers, their largest customer, their largest supplier and two specialists from the parent company Al-Flous. The workshop was held at a mansion in Saudi Arabia. During the workshop, various future worlds were developed and analysed, incorporating the position of DuSoleil in each one. Although the team was nervous at the start ('Aren't we going to exhibit all the things we don't know and are unable to do?'), the scenario workshop led to great insights into, and better understanding of, the rapidly changing markets. Based on their shared knowledge and experience, the team could now make better predictions about what tomorrow's world might look like. It appeared that the growth opportunities in one scenario were entirely different from those in another scenario, although both scenarios were equally plausible. Some deep-rooted opinions of team members were disproved: their dream scenarios appeared to be so unlikely that nothing needed to be done with them. At the same time, the scenarios indicated some extreme risks and uncertainties that should be closely monitored by DuSoleil. For example, by using new technologies, Asian competition was able to offer a much lower cost price than DuSoleil. If this competition increased significantly, the consequences would have such an impact that a strategic change would be imperative. For many, the scenario workshop led to the first actual integral business insight, which DuSoleil had lacked so far. Thanks to the inspirational atmosphere in the workshop, mutual relationships with the customer and supplier in the value chain and between DuSoleil and the Saudi Arabians were positively stimulated by the three-day workshop.

Once they had returned to the United States, the team looked again at the outcomes of the first workshop in the searchlight step. The vision and mission statement remained valid, though the business scope could now be specified in more detail with regard to services, products and customer segments. The steering committee was very much impressed with the findings in the outside-in step. For all, it became apparent what the world wanted from DuSoleil. But when the chairman of the board of their parent company asked Henri and Will Jr if DuSoleil had what it took to deliver on these demands, the brothers knew they had some homework to do.

To be continued...

06 The 8 steps to strategic success
what are our capabilities?

 Step 3: Inside-out: analysis

Objective and results

In order to determine the strategic opportunities, it is important to look at the organization itself. What can the organization do better than its competition? Where is the revenue created? But also: What are the constraints? What could the organization easily do that it doesn't do yet?

The objective of *Step 3: Inside-out: analysis* is to define strategic options based on the organization's strengths and constraints. The inside-out approach looks into the possibilities and impossibilities of the organization and links them to possibilities (and threats) in the market and the organization's environment. This identifies the strategic options for the organization: what can you already do that is in demand or will be in demand in the near future? Also, this inside-out approach allows the organization's weaknesses to be linked to the changes and demands of the environment, making the need for change visible. Together with a clear view of the organization's potential ability to change, feasible and realistic strategic options can be defined that state not only the opportunities but also the changes required to seize them and whether the organization is able to realize these changes.

THE RESULTS OF STEP 3: INSIDE-OUT: ANALYSIS ARE:

- an overview of the company's strengths (capabilities) and weaknesses (lack of capabilities);
- insight into the company's existing (core) competences;
- insight into the efficiency and effectiveness of the business processes;
- insight into the company's financial position;
- insight into the power and value of offline and online networks;
- insight into the company's distinctiveness;
- insight into the current business model;
- insight into the strategic options of the organization;
- insight into the necessary improvements;
- insight into the need for change, and into the potential for change.

Scope and content

An analysis of the strengths and constraints of the organization is the most important part of this step. There are numerous analyses which are appropriate. The objective is to identify the organization's power and constraints, keeping in mind that these are always relative to competitors, and that the customer's perception is all-important. In these analyses, important questions are:

- *What are our core competences?* Essential criteria of core competences are that they exceed the business unit, single department or product group; that they are essentially distinctive from competitors; and that they are sustainable. Because organizations increasingly act within a network of partners, it is important to look at the correlation between the core competences of the organization and those of its network partners.

- *What is our authentic value? What is our identity?* An identity is only perceived as authentic if the company is able to deliver what it promises. Is the company truly able to foster its identity and stay true to it? When organizations do not keep their promises or when they do not act according to the values and norms they propagate, customers will be dissatisfied and corporate reputations severely damaged.

- *What is the strength and value of our current network?* In Step 3, mapping out where within the network the centres of knowledge, resources and status are located and with which the company should be associated is a valuable exercise.

- *What is our distinctiveness?* In the inside-out step it should become clear where the company adds value for its customers by determining the company's truly unique elements and by defining what distinguishes the company from its competitors.

- *How are we organized?* This not only involves the organizational structure, but also the degree of compatibility between the organizational structure and organizational governance and control: are we 'lean and mean' enough? And it involves the degree of compatibility between the organizational structure and the organization's core activities given the nature of the industry it operates in: are we agile enough?

- *What does our business model look like?* A business model describes the way in which an organization creates, delivers and preserves value. How does your organization create and deliver value for its customers and itself? Is the way you have organized your partnerships in line with how you want to serve your customers? Are there other ways to make money from your activities? A useful strategy model to use could be the business model canvas, first introduced by Alex Osterwalder (see Part 3).

- *What are and aren't our sources of revenue?* After an assessment of your business model, an analysis of all product groups and markets served, and thus the whole portfolio, including aspects such as turnover, profit and margin contribution, will help to answer this question.

- *What are we doing relatively well and where can we improve?* An analysis of the effectiveness and efficiency of the organization's activities, preferably based on a benchmark against relevant peers, can give insight into the organization's current relative performance and its improvement potential.

From this analysis and assessment of the organization's strengths and constraints, strategic options can be defined. Linking the possibilities of the organization to possibilities in the market and the organization's environment will provide insights into new options, such as entering a new market that hadn't previously been known to be interested in the company's existing products. And by linking the organization's weaknesses in the face of new demands from developments in the market or external environment, the need for change becomes apparent. This need for change could also arise, however, from the organization's ambitions: maybe you're not performing up to your own standards.

But besides an analysis and assessment of the organization's strengths and constraints, it is also important to look at the organization's potential ability for change. Ultimately, the ability to change is what determines the real strategic possibilities of the organization. The factors governing the ability to change arise from the company's financial opportunities and the risks it is prepared to take, and from the flexibility, learning capabilities, development potential and willingness of the people in the organization to accept change. The potential ability for change should match the need for change, in order to arrive at realistic and feasible strategic options. If the need for change driven by demands from external developments is high, you might want to put more emphasis on meeting those demands in your strategic options and less on the pursuit of new, different possibilities for the organization. If your ambitions are overstretching the organization's abilities, you might even want to reconsider your ambitions.

Recommended models

In the inside-out step, several strategy models can be used to help analyse current performance and assess (future) possibilities. We recommend (see Part 3):

- profitability analysis: DuPont scheme
- financial ratios analysis;
- (social) network analysis;
- value propositions analysis;
- core competences;

- Kotler's 4 Ps of marketing;
- the business model canvas.

The process

Based on the business scope and ambition defined in the searchlight step, the scope for the analyses in Step 3 is known. Given the variety and diversity of analyses, it is appropriate to organize several teams to perform them. It is an obvious choice to compose these groups based on their functional expertise, such as finance, HR, IT, technology, marketing, logistics, procurement or other functional areas. Nevertheless, it is important that groups' assignments are as specific as possible and that each group is free to go into their functional field in depth without having to hold back because of personal involvement or interests. The analysis must provide insights which, if necessary, help to break with traditional mental models. Each team must thus be as open minded and objective as possible. To achieve this, it could be helpful to use predetermined templates, which also allows the analyses of the various groups to be compared easily.

The different groups present their results in a joint meeting. Based on the subsequent discussion (and any additional analysis), a shared overall picture of the internal situation of the organization is drafted. At this stage it is extremely important to be very critical of any excuses or unsubstantiated explanations of analysis outcomes, benchmark scores or organizational constraints. Ultimately, this stage leads to a definition of multiple strategic options based on the strengths and constraints of the organization.

Taking into account the three main characteristics of this step (participative, analytical and committing; see next paragraph), potential methods are benchmarking and (internal) crowdsourcing (see Part 4). Benchmarking helps you to evaluate the analysis of your own organization objectively. Productivity, flexibility, quality and reliability are terms that often appear on the agenda. Crowdsourcing – either internal or external – is an intensive way of gathering knowledge and ideas from outside or inside the organization. These methods will lead to additional activities in this step.

The lead-time of this step depends on the amount of time that employees have available. Often, much of the data is incorporated in regular management reports, which limits the amount of time needed to create an overview. However, extensive and time-consuming editing of available information is sometimes needed: usually a sign that the administration does not provide the relevant management information. In reality, the lead-time of this step – a few weeks – is hardly ever a serious problem because the outside-in step usually takes more time and both steps are mostly performed in parallel, with iteration and alignment where necessary (see the section on the strategic dialogue sequence).

Characteristics

As the name of this step suggests, this is pre-eminently an *analytical* step; see also Figure 6.1. It is about analysing and assessing the facts regarding the organization's internal situation and its performance. The goal is to identify the company's strengths and constraints. The level of participation is high, although mainly internally. The cooperation of the organization's members is crucial to being able to conduct the analysis. All departments within the organization (eg finance, production, logistics, sales) play a role in providing the information needed for the various analyses. In many cases, this phase is supported by analysis teams per functional area, as many analyses involving considerable detail are to be conducted.

FIGURE 6.1   Characteristics of the inside-out step

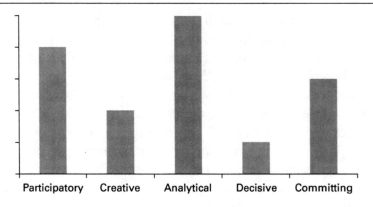

The degree of decision making in this step is limited. It is important, though, that the results of this diagnostic step are seen to be transparent and logical, so that they will not be up for discussion at a later stage. This also involves commitment: people need to fully support the diagnosis of the organization's internal condition.

The people involved

An important characteristic of Step 3 is the involvement of more people than just the management team. The step is highly participatory. Information needs to be collected and gathered from multiple departments in the organization. The involvement of key individuals within these departments is of crucial importance if timely and accurate information is to be provided. As already stated in the above paragraphs, it is important in this step, in spite of the focus on an inside-out approach, also to take the environment into account. The performance of the organization is, for example, largely determined by the perception of customers. Thus they too can be consulted in this step.

The inside-out step in the strategic dialogue sequence

The analyses needed in Step 3 depend on the scope set in Step 1 (Searchlight). Usually the inside-out step follows the searchlight step (see Figure 1.1 on page 19).

Step 3 can be carried out simultaneously with Step 2 (Outside-in). The inside-out step mainly provides opportunities based on the organization's own core competences and authenticity. The outside-in step mainly provides market-driven options based on, among other things, customer questions, technical possibilities, new knowledge, expected competitor actions, and regulation. Because the inside-out and outside-in steps both require extensive analyses and because these analyses in some cases overlap (in terms of the topic and/or the stakeholders to consult) and thus are carried out simultaneously, it is possible and sometimes sensible to incorporate the (preliminary) results of both analyses in each other's workshops. As a result, the perspectives from the outside-in analysis will give more meaning to those from the inside-out analysis and vice versa.

The results of Step 3 consist of strategic options for the organization based on the organization's possibilities, the weaknesses that need to be faced (need to be changed) and insights into the potential ability of the organization to change. These results are input for Step 4 (Options), in which strategic options are created or selected based on the input of both the inside-out and outside-in steps. Step 4 also identifies where the strategic possibilities of the outside-in and inside-out steps converge, as that is where new strategic options emerge.

Apart from following the searchlight step, there are also situations where one starts with Step 3. There might be a situation where the organization states that the current ambition is still valid but that the organization is not pulling its weight in seizing all the opportunities, or a situation in which the possibilities in the external environment are very limited and the organization should either come up with creative ways to make money from its activities or should cease these activities. In both situations, new internal analyses are needed in order to come up with new strategic options with higher potential.

Dos and don'ts

✔ Make sure that the inside-out step involves iteration with the outside-in step. It is true that the inside-out step revolves around providing insights about the organization. However, the organization's performance and possible improvements are relative to external developments and relative to the perception of customers, the performance of competitors and the experiences of partners and suppliers.

✔ Consider the effect of time intervals in financial analyses. Some organizations are seasonally dependent. This should be taken into account in the financial analyses. Trends and patterns are more interesting than the actual figures.

✘ Watch out for 'paralysis by analysis'. There is a risk of over-analysis owing to the stimulation caused by having too much expertise and information available. The internal analysis is not meant to detect and act on every single improvement. It is also meant as a blame game. With each analysis you must keep in mind and consider the effect of the outcome of the analysis on the strategic choices to be made and the ambitions of the organization as determined in the searchlight step.

CASE STUDY   DuSoleil

Previously...

In their quest to turn DuSoleil into a profitable company once again, Henri and Will Jr had started the strategy process. The strategy team had already presented a new mission statement and some 'quick wins' to the steering committee and had made a good impression with the insights gained from the scenario-analysis workshops. It had become apparent that DuSoleil had been fast asleep while the world was changing drastically. The outside-in step and the resulting scenarios had been very much needed for DuSoleil to understand what the world now wanted from them. But now the question had arisen as to whether DuSoleil had what it took to deliver on these demands. It was time for an inside-out analysis.

Do you know what we are good at?

The strategy team started by filling out the business model canvas to indicate the current situation. By following customer needs, the service and the business model, the team was provided with surprising insights and new ideas about the company's position. Also, the current organizational structure and governance mechanisms were brought into sharper focus. Each department was asked to draw up lists describing DuSoleil's core competences. With the use of industry benchmarks the consultancy firm showed and explained where the organization and its supply chain partners were falling short in terms of efficiency and performance in their way of working. One of the most critical problems uncovered was that, despite the presence of high technical expertise, DuSoleil failed to translate this knowledge into innovations that could affect the market. After a presentation to the steering committee, the explosive conclusions from these internal analyses were shared with all heads of departments and with the workers' council in each country. This initially led to emotional finger pointing between individuals and departments, but also identified the presence of narrow mental models and the need for change. The people in the factory blamed the head of the R&D department, but he in turn immediately pointed the finger at sales: they were people with little or no knowledge of what they were selling or what customers really wanted and who were in no sense contributing to formulating and introducing marketing concepts. 'In the beginning there was sales, and that's how it should have stayed' had been a popular quotation of Will Sr about the marketing discipline. Sales, however, pointed to the production department: they were saying 'no' to everything, never delivered on time, and delivered products at too expensive a cost price while also having quality problems. Tensions were very high, but the pain was being expressed for the first time. And as the points for improvement unravelled, the strategy team got a clear understanding of what improvements were needed in both the short and long term and of what was possible and impossible for DuSoleil in terms of its future.

During this inside-out analysis, the quick intervention team in their 'war room' identified a number of 'quick wins' for the internal organization. But the internal analysis also led to direct behavioural changes. The qualifications of internal islands and external kingdoms became a popular topic within the organization and created serious discussions on the intranet and at the coffee machine, and were the object of many canteen jokes. This resulted in people starting to confront each other and the management when they spotted any 'old' behaviour. Despite the still unclear strategic direction, the remaining threat of closure or reorganization and the heated discussions during presentations of the internal analysis, the brothers DuSoleil were surprised to notice that the atmosphere and teamwork in the weeks thereafter improved. Employees of the sales and R&D departments were meeting up more often to brainstorm how specific products and services could meet specific customer needs. Country managers started exchanging local market reports. And a number of sales people had even taken the initiative to contact their local gyms and discuss how the new DuSoleil concept could be of interest to them.

Towards financial insight

Most of the work in the internal analyses involved improving the transparency of the company's finances. A financial ratio analysis showed that, even though the short-term ratios were negative, the long-term ratios (including solvency) were still reasonably intact. However, the company's administrative and financial systems were unable to provide reliable insights into profitability per customer and per product. Although it caused a delay of several weeks in the strategy process, the company decided to gain structured insights into the financial situation of the company with the help of the company's accountant and the consultancy firm. They found that cost/price calculations were made at three locations within the organization. They also discovered that the allocation of fixed and indirect costs was not differentiated – the company was allocating a generic overhead that was sometimes as much as 30 per cent of the cost price of a sunbed.

The former accountant, a family friend who had been appointed to the job of financial director years ago by Will Sr, felt so much pressure that he concluded that the financial complexity of DuSoleil was such that he was in over his head and that setting the strategic direction towards further growth and the process that accompanied this was too much of a challenge for him. He went off to enjoy an early retirement and was replaced by a chief financial officer (CFO) appointed by Al-Flous, the Saudi parent company. Henri felt personally responsible for the company's not-so-rosy situation and decided to resign his position as CEO. His brother, Will Jr, did not follow him, but wanted to take on the challenge of sorting things out. He became the new CEO and handed over the leading of the strategy team to a senior staff member as Will himself joined the steering committee. Together, the new CEO and CFO finally managed to get a grip on the company's administration. Their appointment and the improved financial insight gave the strategy process a boost.

The findings of the internal analyses were supported by the steering committee and they recommended that the new CEO and CFO also present the situation to the banks and the Saudi investor: an open approach would certainly provide some goodwill to improve their relations and might help to secure future financing and investment. It turned out that they were correct about this: the banks agreed to give conditional support for future funding and Al-Flous, the Saudi-Arabian parent company, agreed to give guarantees for future investment. Subject to quick recovery of the financial results, it became apparent that in the long run there actually were some rationale and room for investments. This gave the team flexibility to generate alternative strategic options. The question now was: what alternatives should DuSoleil consider?

To be continued...

The 8 steps to strategic success what are realistic options?

 Step 4: Options

Objective and results

Step 4: Options brings together all the insights obtained in the previous three steps and translates them into strategic options. By bringing together the insights from the outside-in and inside-out perspectives, multiple strategic options can be developed. The different options developed in the outside-in and inside-out steps can be regarded as a 'long list' of strategic options. In the options step the options on this 'long list' are assessed, supplemented if need be and finally curtailed to come to a 'short list' of the most promising options. This is done by checking the options against the business scope and ambition, which were formulated in the searchlight step.

It is important to keep multiple options at hand, as the organization should be able to perform well in different possible futures. There is no single strategy and proposition that is the best option for each scenario. It is therefore useful to have several back-up options available if the chosen option does not prove to be successful; this could happen, for example, if market conditions change.

It should be easy to weigh up these options, so that in Step 5 (Choice) the new strategy can eventually be chosen from the 'short list' of options. In order to do so, the options should be developed in a systematic and thorough manner.

THE RESULTS OF STEP 4: OPTIONS ARE:

- a clear picture of realistic combinations of external opportunities and internal competences;
- insight into the opportunities to build distinctiveness or a unique position;
- a 'short list' of strategic options in order to be successful in various scenarios;
- options that are described in sufficient detail to make them a good foundation from which to choose the strategy.

Scope and content

To which market and customer needs can the organization respond by using its current competences? What competences are missing? Which competences need to be strengthened? What new businesses can the organization develop by using its available knowledge and technology, and in which markets can they be introduced? On what aspects is the organization unique (or can be so in the future)? The answers to these questions will lead to strategic options, which are developed in the outside-in step based on external analysis and in the inside-out step based on the strengths and constraints of the organization. The options are brought together in the options step. It is important not to have any unrealistic options formulated, for example responding to specific market demands in which the company lacks the required skills. However, an identified constraint does not necessarily mean that it cannot be part of a strategic option: there might be possibilities to develop competences through alliances or an acquisition.

Strategic options should contribute to the realization of the ambition of the organization and should thus be checked against the mission statement and vision and business scope, which were formulated in the searchlight step. This check can result in adjustments at both ends: it might turn out that some adaptation of the mission statement and vision is needed. The market may shift or the organization appears to be able to cope with more than initially assumed. Or it might turn out that some of the options on the 'long list' do not contribute (enough) and should be either adjusted or disregarded. There are some minimum requirements for option descriptions:

- *Proposition.* Which products and services can answer to which market and customer needs?

- *Market and market potential.* What is the purchasing power of customers, to what extent and how will it develop (growth potential)?

- *Competition.* Who else is active in this market and in what ways are they competing?

- *Differentiation.* How does the option create sustainable distinctiveness? Does it strengthen your authenticity, flexibility and interaction?

- *Option risks.* How far off is the option from the organization's current activities, customer base, product portfolio? Is the company able to overcome this stretch?

- *Required investments.* What are the required financial investments of the option and is the company able to make these investments?

- *Cooperation.* Are alliances or acquisitions necessary in order to realize the strategic option?

- *Global indication of internal consequences for the organization.* What effect does the option have on the staff budget, IT, operating processes and management?

- *Global business case including financial return analysis.* What effect does the option have in terms of return versus required investments?

- *Relation with mission statement, vision and business scope.* How does the option support the realization of the mission statement and vision and to what extent does the option relate to the core activities?

Once these issues are described, a good consideration between the options can be made. This leads to a 'short list' of options, from which eventually the new strategy will be chosen (in Step 5). The chosen strategic option (to be more specific: the chosen strategy) will then be worked out in more detail in Step 6 (Operationalization) by drawing up an implementation and action plan, and a detailed business case.

This step provides answers to the following questions:

- What are the strategic options to realize the mission statement and vision?
- What are the benefits, risks, preconditions and implications of the options?
- How do we take into account our own capabilities and our own conditions (eg targeted return or market share)?
- Should the mission statement and vision be adjusted?
- What options should we consider in choosing our strategy?

Recommended models

In the options step, strategy models can be used to help compare and weigh the different strategic options. We recommend (see Part 3):

- SWOT analysis;
- Porter's generic strategies;
- Tracey and Wiersema's value disciplines.

The process

In the options step, the outcomes of the outside-in step and the inside-out step are combined. This combination must lead to something meaningful in a very creative manner: there is no mathematical or algebraic solution to assess the different options and to select the most promising ones from a 'short list'. The process therefore starts off in an exploratory manner by collecting the strategic options formulated in Steps 2 and 3 and then supplementing them with all the possible strategic options you can think of (enter new markets, develop new products, design new business models). Tracy and Wiersema's value disciplines model and Porter's generic strategies model (see Part 3) can be useful in guiding this process. Next, it is important to formulate clear and realistic options that meet the minimum requirements introduced earlier. By defining all potential strategic options in this systematic and thorough manner, the greater part can be eliminated swiftly as they will prove to be unrealistic.

The steps in this phase are:

- Determine strategic options based on the mission statement, vision and ambition (the searchlight step), the outcomes of the outside-in step, the outcomes of the inside-out step and from your own creativity or inspiration (success cases, gurus or with the help of strategy models like the ones mentioned).
- Describe the options thoroughly, covering the minimally required elements already mentioned.
- Choose the most promising options based on the contribution they make to the company's stated ambition.
- If necessary, adjust the mission statement, vision and ambition.

The determination of strategic options is based on the outcomes of the outside-in and inside-out steps. The scenarios in Step 2 will, inter alia, reveal what customer demands and needs will disappear or be strengthened and what issues the stakeholders bring forward in each of the scenarios. Combining these with insights gained into the company's strengths and constraints, it becomes clear which customer needs the company can and can't serve. Usually workshops are organized to combine the outcomes of both steps. In these workshops, it is crucial to be consistent in terminology: often participants have very different interpretations of topics such as customer satisfaction or customer needs. This needlessly complicates discussions and results in confusion about the conclusions drawn.

Another point of attention in these workshops is to ensure that there is a rational and logical link between the outcomes of the analyses from Step 3 and the conclusions of the workshop: there can be a big temptation to draw conclusions based on individual interests even if the results of the analyses do not support this reasoning.

The formulation of options is a creative process. It is important to reflect the outcomes of the analysis from Step 3 (though in a creative manner), not to avoid new combinations (perhaps by the use of appropriate strategy models) and not to feel limited in your formulation. Participants should be able to step outside their comfort zones and feel free to explore extreme standpoints and perspectives, but the options formulated must always achieve a balance between the outside-in and inside-out perspectives. For instance, strategic options driven solely by customer needs should always take into account the company's capabilities and techno-logy, if they are not to become unrealistic options.

In a final check of the strategic options formulated and gathered on a 'long list', in conjunction with the mission statement and vision, the following questions are answered once again (see also the searchlight step): What customers and markets can we serve? What functions should or can we provide? Which processes and technology can we use? What is the value we want to offer to our employees? It is mainly a funda-mental discussion about the future possibilities for the organization while remaining true to itself. Further, thorough detailing of the options is usually done by people who will eventually work with one or more options and then discussed in a plenary session with those who will be the decision makers in Step 5. This ensures that there is a shared and consistent view among all involved.

The lead-time of this stage is usually a few weeks. The exact duration of the options step depends on the complexity of the company and its business playing field and the complexity of the strategic options. The workshops for option generation and discussion can be planned in advance so that they can take place in quick succession. However, it is often necessary to take some time to elaborate and evaluate the results in between the workshops. In this way, the danger that participants will change their minds after the decision has been made is minimized.

Characteristics

For the generation of strategic options, creativity is needed in order to explore new perspectives and new paths (Figure 7.1). In this step there is therefore strong emphasis on this characteristic. There is also strong emphasis on the analytical characteristic, as the combining and checking of the options requires a lot of understanding and comprehension.

There is some emphasis on the participatory character of the process in this step, as apart from the management team and/or the core strategy team, others will also participate. Often some of the key participants from Steps 2 and 3 are invited, as they can give more information about the why and how of the outcomes of their respective steps. For detailing the options, key staff and middle management are invited, to ensure that

FIGURE 7.1   Characteristics of the options step

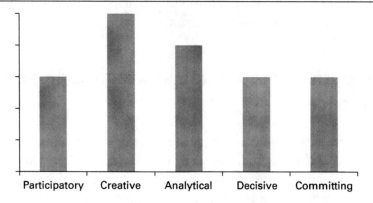

definitions are shared and consistent among both the eventual decision makers and those who will have to work with one or more of the strategic options. Overall, in this options step participation is less than in Steps 2 and 3. Nevertheless, involving more people in detailing the options is also beneficial to the analytical nature of that activity: broad participation will provide the necessary capacity and skills needed to secure the process.

The reduction of the long list of options to a short list is to some degree decisive in nature. A certain level of commitment is also required at this stage: options on the short list should not lack adequate substantiation, even if they contain good ideas. So by selecting strategic options for the short list you find those good enough to be chosen as the new strategy and so you commit yourself to each of them.

The people involved

The stakeholders in this step are usually the management team and the employees who participated in the formulation of the scenarios in the outside-in step and in performing the internal analyses in the inside-out step. It is all about mobilizing creative minds who have a clear perception of the possibilities in the outside world and who can link this perspective to insights into the internal possibilities. Any discussion about adjustment to the mission statement and vision must take place in the presence of the management team.

For the detailing of the options, as a preparation for the choice step, you might want also to involve employees of various (staff) departments, such as the business development, finance, marketing and R&D departments.

The options step in the strategic dialogue sequence

The options step follows the outside-in and inside-out steps (see Figure 1.1 on page 19). All results from these steps are integrated into realistic strategic options during the options step. The quality of the previous steps therefore determines the quality of the options. The less clear the picture created in the internal analyses about where the company makes profit and is/ isn't competitive and/or the less quality the formulated scenarios have, the less the strategic options are substantiated. And thus the harder it is to develop options that promote confidence that the company is heading towards a successful future.

The mission statement and vision, the results of the searchlight step, are important guidelines in formulating the options. This is iterative: on the one hand the mission statement and vision provide a framework in which to assess the strategic options; on the other, it might well be that interesting options that emerge from the scenarios and/or internal analyses give rise to a need to reconsider the mission statement and vision.

For the next step, the choice step, it is important that options are formulated in such a way that it is possible to compare them and to identify any mutual correlations. This also enables the organization to have alternative options still available when a particular option turns out to be insufficient to realize the organization's ambitions. The organization is thus able to adjust faster than it would if the process of analysing and developing options first needed to be conducted all over again.

Dos and don'ts

✔ Develop options for each of the scenarios. In this way, the company is prepared for different situations and can better deal with uncertainty.

✔ Be creative and do not compartmentalize. Also, let employees participate who would not normally do so. Invite cross-thinkers and do not be afraid of deviating insights.

✔ Formulate realistic options, in line with the company's opportunities or competences and capabilities that it might be possible to improve or acquire, involving technology, knowledge or funding. Taking on a challenge is good, recklessness is not.

✗ Do not allow any further brainstorming about the environment or about the strengths and constraints of the company. The purpose of the options step is to converge towards options, not to create more data.

✗ Do not let the person highest in rank express his or her opinion about the vision and mission statement after the analysis. This blocks the discussion, because we have found that people find it difficult to challenge and confront the leader about his or her statements. The results of a careful analysis are often set aside in favour of the leader's belief. It shows great spirit if the leader first decides to listen and only expresses his or her opinion at a later stage.

✗ Try not to stick to old insights and past performances. Choosing a familiar and safe approach is a typical human reaction. It is about strategy, the long-term course of action. This is different from minor adjustments to a business plan. An external facilitator or an external consultant can provide support for the removal of any such barriers.

✗ Do not let personal interests play a more important role than organizational interests. Participants may tend to deny or refuse support for specific insights that have implications for their own position. This should be openly discussed.

CASE STUDY   DuSoleil

Previously...

In their quest to turn DuSoleil into a profitable company once again, Henri and Will Jr had started a strategy process. After a promising start, with the strategy team having presented a new mission statement and some 'quick wins' to the steering committee, and having formed a thorough understanding of contemporary market dynamics and the possible futures for the market, the strategy process already had some serious implications for DuSoleil. The internal analysis proved that the company's administration had been a mess and the financial situation was not only unclear, but turned out to be not so promising. This had led to the resignation of the CFO and of Henri as CEO, with his brother Will Jr succeeding him. As the new CEO and CFO sorted out the financials, the steering committee had given them a valuable tip to engage in an open talk with the banks and the parent company Al-Flous to secure the likelihood of future investment. This had indeed led to some possibilities for a bright future for DuSoleil. Owing to the participation of many employees in both the outside-in and inside-out steps, some changes in behaviour were already apparent in the organization. It was now time to channel this new-found positive energy and to set a new strategic direction.

Growing anxiety

The strategy team had set a preliminary scope for the business at the start of the strategy process and the outside-in and inside-out steps had shown what opportunities and threats had priority, and what the strengths and weaknesses of DuSoleil were. Both the outside-in and the inside-out perspectives had provided some strategic options for the future course of DuSoleil, but real choices had not yet been made. Time was running out, however, for the strategy team. Despite the 'quick wins' and the need to change that were created in the organization by the strategy process, DuSoleil still had a negative result on its profit and loss account every month. The patience of the Saudi-Arabian parent company was decreasing and Will DuSoleil Jr was visiting Saudi Arabia with increasing frequency to explain that positive results would come, but that they still needed a bit more time.

Internal anxiety was also growing. Everyone knew that making strategic choices indicated changes within the organization. This increased the alertness of the unions and workers' councils in the different countries, and the steering committee had confronted the strategy team many times with direct and indirect pressure to respond by giving answers to the many questions raised by employees and by expressing the consequences of a new strategy. The euphoria about progress suddenly seemed to have disappeared.

The pressure increases with more at stake

The strategy team, overwhelmed with their regular daily activities and pressure from colleagues, were somewhat doubtful as they began the workshop in which they would determine the strategic options and make a provisional decision that would be submitted to the steering committee. Armed with the facts from the internal analyses, the PESTLE analysis and the scenario workshop, they conducted a SWOT analysis. The strengths and weaknesses were related to the opportunities and threats. On the one hand, this indicated for each opportunity which strengths could be used to seize the opportunity and which weaknesses would have to be improved so as not to miss out on the opportunity. On the other, it indicated what strengths could be used to respond to which threats, and what weaknesses made DuSoleil very vulnerable to specific threats. For the main opportunities and threats, the workshop also indicated the return required from a given input. To this end, the main opportunities and threats were made more concrete by formulating a number of strategic 'must-do' actions: what is the minimal effort the company should make and what minimum resources are needed to respond to the opportunity or threat? Now it became more specific: the company's technological knowledge had to be closely linked to market information to counter the threat of the new technologies of Asian competitors; marketing and sales activities needed investments in modern-day information and intelligence systems to secure up-to-date information on customer demands; and production facilities had to become more efficient.

While working on the SWOT analysis, the strategy team suddenly started acting less as a team and more from their individual functional interests. Until this moment the team members had been very pleased to be part of the team that would determine the course of action, but now the responsibility and tension of being a member of the team were experienced as a burden. The members also felt pressure from their managers and other stakeholders: individual team members learned in all kind of ways of these people's expectations that they would be the ones who would lead the company in the new strategic direction but would most definitely not be the ones who had to reorganize or restructure. For the members of the strategy team identified as having high potential this was a valuable lesson in management responsibility, stakeholder diplomacy and power politics. The personal requirements and political pressure came into full bloom when the strategic options had to be formulated.

What options do we have?

The team subsequently tried to define realistic options for the scenarios formulated in the outside-in step, based on the possibilities and constraints found in the inside-out step. But the departments' mindsets and the pressure from the team members' managers threatened to frustrate these workshops. After several sessions, in which the consultancy firm had a mediating role as an independent third party, a number of possible strategic directions were formulated, including growth in the wellness market, growth in markets in Europe outside the EU, and growth in the high-end market through new product development. These strategic options were in line with the requirements and conditions that were found in the external analysis and they seemed plausible and feasible, given the internal strengths and weaknesses. The 'must-do' actions, such as improving the company's knowledge in the field of cosmetic tanning and the recruitment and training of tanning consultants in the domestic market, already appeared to provide a good direction and starting point for determining the overall strategy. There was much discussion about the financial and political viability of the options and, at a particular moment, individual interests started to reappear. That was the moment to stop the workshop and head for the pub.

To be continued...

The 8 steps to strategic success

what is my preferred strategic option?

 Step 5: Choice

Objective and results

The objective of *Step 5: Choice* is to make a realistic choice from the strategic options selected in Step 4. These strategic options follow from the analysis of the organization's strengths and constraints and of the environment in which the organization operates. The short list of strategic options based on these analyses will be evaluated in this step in order to make a final choice. This choice is made by using criteria defined upfront.

The strategic direction involves a main choice of one of the alternatives, that is, the dominant strategic option. In this step it is not just about making a choice, but also about keeping open other options that might become relevant in the future. Strategy is about anticipating uncertainties. So besides making a main choice, a back-up choice is also made. Some of the other options, or elements of these options, are kept available so that the company can quickly switch to them if needed. The step is complete when a realistic and supported choice has been made for the main and back-up strategies.

THE RESULTS OF STEP 5: CHOICE ARE:

- an assessment of the strategic options, ranked on degree of importance and with a clear substantiation;
- a clear primary choice of strategic direction that the organization will pursue, based on the chosen main strategic option;
- a set of alternative strategies, with insight into when to switch to them;
- the basic structure of the chosen strategy, including a strategic plan with priorities and objectives.

Scope and content

The choice step is about making a choice of the main strategic direction from a 'short list' of options. For this, and prior to choosing among the strategic options, more 'feel' is created for each alternative. Through experiencing the options intensively (for example by means of a simulation, see Part 4), a clear picture can be formed of the implications and requirements of the 'short listed' strategic options. Next, based on the strategy process framework set up in the searchlight step, it must be decided:

- who is involved and who makes the final choice (process);
- which stakeholder should give consent or probe further;
- how we choose (procedure) and on what criteria? How are these criteria weighed and which scoring methodology do we apply?

So, before choosing any of the strategic options, we must decide what the selection process looks like. That is, the steps to take, the procedure to follow, which internal and external stakeholders to involve and who makes final decisions must all be decided upfront. Also, it must be clear what criteria will be used in evaluating the options. In the choice step, the different options are scored based on these criteria. The most common and relevant criteria are:

- *Return.* What are the option's expected costs and returns? What are the potential risks in choosing this option?

- *Acceptance.* In weighing the options, the degree of acceptance of the option by both the internal organization (management and staff) and external stakeholders (suppliers, customers, financiers and network partners) must be taken into account.

- *Feasibility.* What is the financial and technical feasibility of the option? To what extent is the option feasible given the current staff composition? In addition, organizational aspects, such as organizational structure, management and business model, are included in the assessment.

- *Contribution to the ambition.* To what extent do the options fit the organization's mission statement and ambition? Are they sufficiently in line with the expected opportunities and threats from the market?

- *Distinctive power.* Does the strategic option help make the organization sufficiently distinctive? How does the option make the organization sufficiently authentic and transparent? To what extent does the option differ from competitors' strategies and the organization's current course of action?

- *Sustainability.* To what extent does the option add to sustainable competitiveness? Does the option generate sufficient flexibility and capacity to take action? What are the option's implications and contributions within the area of corporate social responsibility?

- *Risk.* What risks for the company does the option imply and how does this influence the choice? Companies differ in their willingness to take risks. Is there an option that generates the highest profit, but also the entails the highest risk? Or will we be satisfied with less return, but lower risk?

In the choice step, the following questions are answered:

- *What is or are our preferred option(s) and what is their ranking? And what combination of options do we choose?* Both questions relate to the eventual outcome of this step, that is, the choice of a main direction, a back-up direction, or a combination of options that combines characteristics from different back-up options with the main option. Options can be implemented in succession or even simultaneously. To illustrate: internationalization can take place country by country, but a product can be introduced simultaneously in several countries.

- *Do we still need more information? And what do we choose considering our risk?* This question has to do with making the final choice. Have we collected enough information to make a well-informed and solid decision or are we still missing important information? An organization may choose a particular direction that eliminates other directions. Or, a less extreme variant might be chosen that can be applied in numerous scenarios.

- *How many resources do we use?* This concerns the amount of money and the number of resources and people that the organization wants to (and can) use. One option might require a major investment in new machinery, another might require employee training and education.

- *When would another option be preferable?* This question becomes important when consideration of a back-up strategy (one of the other strategic options) becomes likely. For instance, when industry dynamics change faster than anticipated or when (new) competitors respond to your initial strategy. Monitoring developments (such as market growth or competitor behaviour) is of great importance to any organization. By being able to determine early on which developments are the most important, the organization is able to respond quickly by anticipating or choosing a different course of action.

Recommended models

In the choice step some strategy models can be used. Models that help evaluate options and that facilitate making choices are particularly useful in this step. We recommend (see Part 3):

- strategy assessment matrix;
- risk–reward analysis;
- MABA analysis.

The process

In a feasible and transparent way, a choice must be made from a number of alternative strategic options. First, the process, procedure and methodology, and criteria are decided. Often this is done in a meeting of the core strategy and/or management team.

Next, the options are assessed and looked at from different perspectives by being weighed against the different criteria. To be able to give meaning to both the rational and irrational considerations with each of the strategic alternatives, participants should experience (and internalize) all eligible strategic options. For this purpose, methods such as simulation (see Part 4) can be used. When all participants have an adequate understanding of the options, they are ready to assess them. This can be done during a workshop, which varies in duration from half a day to a full day. A useful strategy model to include multiple perspectives and criteria might be a strategy assessment matrix (see Part 3). Each option and each combination of options identified as promising is given a score on each criterion. This score may be quantitative in nature (such as the rates of return that an option yields) or qualitative. The risk that an option entails may be denoted as low, medium or high. For degree of acceptance, scores are defined as insurmountable, problematic or fully accepted. Often plus and minus signs are used. Then the score for each option is multiplied by the weight given to each criterion. This results in a weighted score per criterion per option, which can be summed to give a total score for that option. The option that scores highest forms the main choice. In addition, it is determined whether there are options that should remain open in case they are needed to respond to specific scenarios. Scoring options is not as complicated as mathematics. The option with the most promising results, the most solid foundation and which best suits the mission statement, ambitions and the group's beliefs and inspiration wins.

Then, before embarking on the new strategic course, it is important to reflect on the chosen options. During the next workshop (also taking half or a full day), the outcomes of the selection process can be settled and verified again against the mission statement, vision, ambition and possible key figures. The participants look to see which powerful elements of other options can be combined with the main option, and which combinations are possible given the investment and funding. The 'strategic stretch' created due to recruitment and competence development is taken into account as well. Eventually a definite choice is made on the main option and back-up option. These options will be developed in full detail in a strategic plan with strategic priorities (required breakthroughs) and objectives established by the strategy team. This strategic plan sets the course for the organization and forms the basis for a successful future.

The lead-time of this step is approximately two weeks, provided the option step is properly completed. There is a chance that gaps are identified in the options or in the way that decision making should take place. This will then cause some delay as iteration with Step 4 (Options) or Step 1 (Searchlight) is necessary.

Characteristics

The choice step – what's in a name – has strong emphasis on the decisive and committing characteristics; see Figure 8.1.

FIGURE 8.1   Characteristics of the choice step

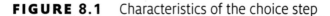

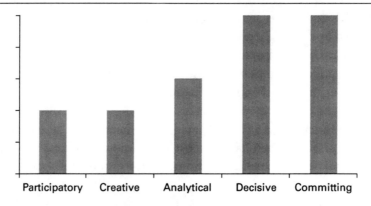

Participatory   Creative   Analytical   Decisive   Committing

The valuation of options is an activity that takes place within the group. The groups or individuals who have made the assessments present and communicate their recommendations in a manner agreed upfront. The discussion about the value and risks of the options should clarify the arguments against or in favour of the different options. It is a step based on convergence, which reduces the number of options to one single most promising option. In this process it is possible to incorporate the most valuable parts of the various options into this main option. Assessing the feasibility of the different options is an important part. But in this step it is also important to have open discussion, where all options are given a fair chance, including the options that might seem difficult or controversial at first sight. Good guidance of the conversation is essential, because in this step intuitive preferences, which were already present before starting the strategic dialogue, can easily take the lead.

The activities in this step have, at least to some extent, an analytical character. The option scores on each of the criteria must be properly interpreted in order to make a good decision. The participatory and creative characteristics have less emphasis in this step, as the options have already been created. The challenge now is to make the right choice.

The people involved

The stakeholders in this step are primarily members of the core strategy team and/or the management team. Optionally, other key stakeholders (both external and internal) are consulted about the choice of the main and back-up strategy. The purpose of this engagement is confirmation of the choice. Finally it is submitted to the board of directors and, if there is one, the shareholders' meeting.

The choice step in the strategic dialogue sequence

The choice step forms the heart of the strategy process: it connects the formulation of strategy with the starting point for implementing the strategy. The strategic dialogue model, see Figure 1.1 on page 19, therefore places Step 5 in the middle, connecting the left-hand cycle (the part that is about 'doing the right things') with the right-hand cycle in the model (the part that is about 'doing things right'). In the choice step, strategic options, which are based on the analyses from the inside-out step and the scenarios from the outside-in step, are assessed and selected. They reflect the possibilities and impossibilities of the organization vis-à-vis its environment and capabilities and its mission statement, vision and ambition. The options were formulated, combined and 'short listed' in the options step, paving the way for a well-informed and substantiated choice in the choice step. The choice step is thus closely linked to the options step, almost inseparably so.

When the main strategic direction has been chosen, it is detailed in a strategic plan. This strategic plan should also make clear what needs to be done in order to execute the new strategy successfully. It should indicate what needs to be implemented and changed in the organzation. This is the basis for Step 6 (Operationalization), in which the main strategic course is further detailed and translated into specific action plans.

Dos and don'ts

- ✔ Enter discussions with an open mind and give all strategic options a fair chance. This includes options which, at first sight, might seem difficult or controversial. Make use of proper and independent process guidance.
- ✔ Incorporate the possible reactions of competitors or other key stakeholders in the considerations.
- ✔ Investigate any relationships with business partners or other business units. This might give rise to additional options or obstacles.
- ✘ Do not try to come up with new options or re-try options that have already been eliminated in the process.
- ✘ Do not forget to learn from the past: options that lacked effectiveness in the past should – after reassessment – again be eliminated. Don't waste your time on them.

CASE STUDY   DuSoleil

Previously...

The strategy process that was set out to turn DuSoleil into a profitable company once again had now been under way for a long time and had already impacted the company. The outside-in step was a wake-up call on the lack of factual market knowledge, while the inside-out step proved the company's administration to be quite obscure and had led to the resignation of Henri as CEO and also of the CFO. The newly appointed CFO and Will Jr now formed the management team and had secured likely future investments with banks and the parent company Al-Flous for DuSoleil. The strategy team had then carried out a SWOT analysis and found some appealing strategic options for DuSoleil, including growth in the wellness market, growth in markets in Europe outside the EU, and growth in the high-end market through new product development. But with actual decision making coming closer, internal politics took over and 'hobby horses' and individual interests came to the fore in discussions. How could the strategy team get the steering committee to decide what strategic direction to take and would the organization support this direction and accept all its possible implications?

First have a closer look at the strategic options

In the workshop in the options step the strategy team had defined some clear potential strategic directions. The team realized that no decisions could be expected from the steering committee without further elaboration on the attractiveness and consequences of these strategic options. First, a joint MABA analysis was performed. The current and possible new product–market combinations (PMCs) for DuSoleil were derived from the different strategic options and mapped to the factors that determine the attractiveness of the market (size, growth, competition) and that of the business (competences, portfolio) for each of the PMCs. This highlighted some surprising suggestions. For example, it appeared that the retail market for sunbeds in Eastern Europe, which DuSoleil saw as a potential growth market, also had many characteristics of a market that would shortly (within a 1–3-year time frame) enter into severe price competition, treating sunbeds as mere commodities. The products currently offered in these markets increasingly lacked a distinctive character, making the lowest price the decision criterion of customers. So the strategy team learned that if DuSoleil was to see growth in Europe outside the EU as a potential strategic option, it had to factor in the likelihood that it would face price competition within a few years.

Another market that was identified as attractive in the options step was growth in the wellness market. In particular, private label production for the large fitness chains in North America seemed to be very appealing. The strategy team hadn't thought about this, but Al-Flous America, a subsidiary of Al-Flous in North America, had stumbled across it earlier in one of their strategy discussions and thought it might be an opportunity. By using the existing distribution channels and contacts of Al-Flous America, DuSoleil could have relatively easy access to this growth market, even though it would need considerable R&D to adapt the product range (including a 110-volt socket connection), plus Will Jr still had some difficulty with the idea of entering a new market under a different brand name. When estimating the business's attractiveness, the internal resistance to interference by the parent company in Saudi Arabia formed a contrast to the significant economies of scale that would be created when cooperating in the field of procurement, production, distribution and R&D.

It also appeared that the high-end and highly specialized retail market, which was given a great deal of internal attention at the time because of technical problems at some SME (small and medium-sized enterprises) customers in the Benelux countries, was of much less importance in terms of money than previously expected.

Then make real choices…?

Based on the MABA analysis and the group assessment which had incorporated criteria such as usability, feasibility and sustainability, the team made preliminary decisions to emphasize certain PMCs ('what'). The detailed actions resulting from the scenario analysis served as the basis for further development of the consequences of that choice ('how'). But how much investment and time would be required to make a success of those PMCs? How big would this success be? What were the risks of paying less attention to, or rejecting, other PMCs? In this discussion, emotions and personal interests took the lead again. Thanks to a risk–reward analysis led by the consultancy firm, the team managed to objectify this discussion and to assess the different choices with the help of a strategy assessment matrix that included the various criteria.

Most of the breaks, drinks and dinners that are traditionally part of strategy workshops were now devoted to the question of how support for these provi-sional decisions could be gained from the steering committee, the board of the parent company, the unions, the workers' councils in the various countries and the employees. The acceptance criterion now dominated the discussion. Part of the team felt the story was too abstract and argued for further study and substantiation. They wanted to build business cases and details of organiza-tional consequences for each option. Another part of the team, however, made an appeal to the entrepreneurship of DuSoleil and wanted the choices to be based on business plans and no more than general outlines of the organizational consequences. It was decided that the steering committee would be the first to be presented with the possible choices.

The steering committee then asked the strategy team for some time for consideration and invited the strategy team meanwhile to consult the unions, the workers' councils and delegations of employees on how they saw the different options and what benefits and implications they could foresee. After an intensive, two-week road-show with multiple consultative meetings, 'canteen sessions' and talks with key customers and key suppliers, the strategy team took another two weeks to conduct further analyses and calculations while keeping in mind the specific questions and concerns they had gathered during the consultations. Eventually, the strategy team again presented their findings to the steering committee for a final decision.

However, the steering committee turned out to be divided, with members holding one or two standpoints, where the organizational consequences of the options completely dominated the discussion about the strategic choice. The CFO preferred the strategic choice that would likely lead to relocation of production from Boston to the (also understaffed) factory in Antwerp, while the unions supported the choice that guaranteed the preservation of jobs in the United States. Will Jr realized that one day he found himself trying to persuade the chairman of the board of their parent company to support the choices that made it possible for his former R&D department to maintain a prominent role, while the next day he tended to support the options that gave him personal short-term security and created less trouble. The strategy team was overloaded with requests for more information from the steering committee members, while the deadline (making a decision before the holidays) was already very close.

Let's agree not to disagree

Ultimately, this game was decided in what later internally became known as 'The agreement at the Meuse'. During a dinner in Rotterdam organized by the consultancy firm, Will Jr, the CFO, the chairman of the board of the parent company and the union leader came to an agreement: the future prosperity of DuSoleil would best be served when all acted as one and individual preferences were subordinate to the objectified assessment of the strategic options which the strategy team had presented in the last steering committee meeting. Additional information would change those outcomes hardly or not at all. The factual preliminary work performed, the realistic scenarios and the properly analysed consequences of other options were solid ground for decision making. The proposed strategy to go for sustainable and profitable growth by moving into the high-end wellness sector and seizing economies of scale by working more closely with Al-Flous America were to be accepted by all, including all the organizational consequences of this strategy. Only the decision on possible reallocation of production facilities was postponed for another year: this required specific in-depth analysis of both facilities and detailed assessment of future market demands.

The strategy team went on holiday with a good feeling about the agreement, but a not so good feeling about the actual support for it. During the holiday everybody enjoyed their free time but there were also many Skype conversations, calls and e-mails, even late at night, which continued the discussion about this issue.

To be continued...

The 8 steps to strategic success

how do we implement?

 Step 6: Operationalization

Objective and results

Step 6: Operationalization is about implementing the chosen strategy effectively by drafting the plans on how it can successfully be realized. It marks the end of strategy formulation and the beginning of strategy implementation. In the operationalization step, the strategic choice is translated into plans for the organization on how to execute the new strategy. The actual execution of the plans is carried out in Step 7 (Execution).

On the one hand, the plans made in the operationalization step can be characterized as business plans, but on the other, they look like change plans. The plans must generate, for each business unit, department and eventually each employee and stakeholder, insight into what measures are to be taken to (help) realize the chosen strategy and deal with its implications and consequences. These plans should include measurable and verifiable objectives with a defined time frame. The objectives relate to both the (market) success of executing the new strategy and the speed and effectiveness of the changes realized in the organization (milestones) to enable it to be successful in the longer term.

Furthermore, a communication plan for all stakeholders is prepared in this step. When strategic options have been weighed and a choice made, that is the end of the strategy process for many top executives. But without explaining its consequences for people, resources, structures and systems, even the best strategy is doomed to fail. Many managers struggle with this issue. By giving explicit attention to the operationalization of the strategy, you can prepare and enable your organization to execute the strategy. Even though the demarcation between detailing the plans and working according to these plans is fluid and sometimes iterations are required, the operationalization step ends when the emphasis and attention shift to the execution of the change plans and the realization of the new strategy.

THE RESULTS OF STEP 6: OPERATIONALIZATION ARE:

- a business plan for each business unit (measurements and targets);
- a derived strategy and corresponding policies for each functional area (HR, finance, IT, R&D, purchasing, logistics etc);
- an established organization and business model;
- a detailed financial business case;
- breakthrough plans and change strategy;
- an implementation and action plan;
- a communication plan;
- key performance indicators (KPIs) for the purpose of steering the strategy and implementation.

Scope and content

In the operationalization step, the following questions are answered:

- What is our business model?
- What is our organizational model?
- What are our functional strategies, business unit strategies, and policy?
- What is our change strategy?
- What is our implementation plan?

At this stage, a new strategy is already fact. The objectives of the chosen strategic options are known and described in a strategic plan. In the options step (the results of which were also used in the choice step), for each of the strategic options, including the one chosen as the new strategy, a thorough and structured description was made; now, in the operationalization step, a business plan can be made for the new strategy. This business plan should state what the new strategy requires of the organization. This implies that strategic objectives are translated into objectives for each part of the organization and for each functional area. With this approach you could say that a new world, that of the new strategy, is described. Part of this is a detailed business case or detailed investment plan in order to ensure that the desired return is achieved. This requires a description of the market approach, selection of the pricing and distribution channels, and new product or service launch plans (or plans for expanding them). In short, based on all the aspects discussed in the inside-out step, new activities and necessary changes are identified. Strategy models, such as the business model canvas (see Part 3), which were used for these aspects in the inside-out step, can be used again at this stage to describe the desired future situation.

The operationalization step is also the first step that implements the strategy, by capturing 'quick wins' (ie measures that are easy to implement and to follow up on, and which produce immediate results in line with the new strategy, for instance the discontinuation of R&D projects). This can be done simultaneously with converting the strategy into action plans. Keep in mind also that much of the strategic direction will be unconsciously operationalized into daily practice. So you should harness the enthusiasm that comes with having a new strategy, either by pointing out potential 'quick wins' or by involving people in the elaboration of the strategy into new business plans and functional strategies which they will be using in their daily activities.

Next, by comparing the desired future performance on these objectives to the current performance, you can establish the changes needed in the organization's composition (inter alia, the structure, working processes or culture) to achieve the strategic objectives. The final phase of the operationalization step is to describe how the organization can develop from the current situation to the desired situation.

Based on this overall change approach, the implementation and action plans describe the most effective and efficient way to change the organization where needed and enable it to reach the desired performance. To conclude the operationalization step, these plans are complemented with a communication plan to keep all relevant stakeholders informed and involved.

Recommended models

A multitude of strategy models can be used in the operationalization step. Models that help detail the strategy for different components (such as business units or functional areas) and/or aspects are particularly useful, as are those that help provide an approach and framework for change management and change communication. We recommend (see Part 3):

- the business model canvas (if this model was used for the description of the current situation during the inside-out step, it may now serve as a model for redesign);
- the 7-S framework;
- project management;
- socially engineered change;
- change quadrants model;
- change communication model.

The process

Step 6 begins by creating an overview of what the new strategy requires of the organization. An important first action is to make the strategy and ambition more specific. In other words, the strategic objectives should be formulated as SMART (specific, measurable, acceptable, realistic, time-based) and 'broken down' into objectives for each part of the organization and every functional area. Therefore, once the strategy has been chosen, schedule a meeting as soon as possible and ensure that it is attended by the company's key officials and the core strategy team and/or the management team. This group has the task of creating an overview of the most important consequences of the new strategy. This results in business plans with SMART objectives and a financial business case.

After this meeting, you can work out what changes are needed in the organization's composition (inter alia, the structure, working processes or culture) in order to achieve the strategic objectives. The elements identified to be in need of change are then further detailed. This can be done in a workshop attended by representatives of all organizational entities (business units and/or (staff) departments), or – as in most organizations owing to their size and complexity – in multiple parallel workshops. In the latter, the detailing can be considered as preparation for a closing workshop with the core strategy team and/or management team. A proven way to do this preparation is to let each parallel group first formulate, in qualitative terms, the five most important consequences of the chosen strategy for their (appointed) field of interest. This works even better when group members do this individually, present their top five consequences to each other, and then, in critical and joint consultations, come to a group conclusion on the main consequences and requirements of the new strategy for their particular area of focus. For each of these a proposal is then made on how to realize the needed change – a change plan. Working in parallel teams does, however, require more strict process guidance.

The closing workshop is aimed at bringing the proposals (change plans) of each of the teams together. The implementation of a new strategy will sometimes require only small changes, though it usually brings about quite fundamental and significant ones. Changes often consist of many different aspects, and so do the corresponding change plans. By making use of a structured, uniform format for outlining how the changes should be realized, in this closing workshop all different aspects can be mapped out and eventually grouped into strategic projects that transcend individual business units or departments. This structured, uniform format contains six aspects which each proposed change plan should cover:

- well-substantiated and clearly defined steps (with milestones);
- a clear time frame (desired speed of change);
- a plan for participation (engaging key stakeholders);
- a plan for communication (informing all stakeholders);
- the role of management (and procedures for decision making);
- the role of the change (project) team (and the way of working).

Together, these aspects outline the path of strategy implementation and organizational change. After the closing workshop, the change and action plans are disseminated to, and discussed with, a wider group of stakeholders. This allows them to adopt the plans and act as enthusiastic pioneers during implementation.

The operationalization step finishes by identifying what (key) performance indicators should be monitored to ensure that the organization is still on the chosen strategic course. Sometimes the regular, operational key performance indicators (KPIs) can be used, with only small adjustments to the required scores on these indicators. And sometimes completely new ones are defined. The latter is then – naturally – also organized as change project, like all other required changes in the organization related to the new strategy. The performance indicators will be used in Step 8 (Monitoring), where you periodically check the organization's performance against the desired performance, and where you eventually take corrective measures to keep the organization on track.

The capturing of 'quick wins' in the operationalization step can be done simultaneously with detailing the strategy into change and action plans. The 'quick wins' or breakthrough projects should be identified right at the start of the operationalization step. This can be done immediately after the inventory of the consequences and requirements of the new strategy is made. Consequences and changes that are more time-consuming or require more investment can then be discussed later on, while the 'quick wins' are taken on board straight away. This has the advantage that during a relatively rapid deployment, the company can benefit from the new strategy at a very early stage. In Figure 9.1, the generic course of a strategy implementation process is depicted. It also shows that by having a simultaneous focus on change and results, that is, by capturing 'quick wins' at the beginning of the operationalization step, the start-up phase of strategy implementation does not require investment alone but can also produce some – albeit small – results (see Figure 9.1). Focusing on simultaneously realizing changes and getting results also prevents the strategy implementation becoming an obstacle to the organization remaining a 'going concern'.

In many change projects, not all objectives are achieved, or achieved on time. However, much can be done to prevent this. This starts in the

FIGURE 9.1 Simultaneous attention for realizing change and getting results

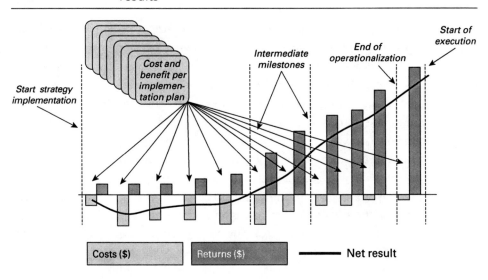

strategy formulation process: by forming the strategy in dialogue with key internal and external stakeholders, not only is the foundation of the new strategy improved, but it is also continuously tested on feasibility. This dialogue lets stakeholders estimate what is needed to realize the strategy and whether (and how) the organization can realize these changes. By engaging these key stakeholders again in the operationalization step, the proposed actual changes are again assessed on their feasibility and perhaps even on how to convince the organization to actively pursue the changes proposed. This engagement also serves to obtain consent and buy-in to the proposed changes and the way the changes are to be realized. This will help mobilize the stakeholders involved, allowing them to promote the changes and letting directors and the management team get a grip on the realization of the change plans and the implementation of the new strategy.

Another way to keep the change projects on track is to organize them as a change programme. The choice to go for a programme approach is usually made at this stage, based on the complexity and not just the content – but it is also process oriented. Moreover, it is often possible to assign responsibilities such that they align with the programme. The advantage of a change programme is that both the continuing activities and the change projects are used for the purposes of supporting the change process. It is also easier to move in a certain direction when you are not focused on a specific project result, but instead on the effect.

If all implementation and change plans are eventually aligned and approved, and with so many people having been intensively involved in the process so far, it is sometimes forgotten that not all employees have experienced this (level of) involvement. Sufficient communication is often lacking. Corridors are subsequently alive with rumours, often containing hardly any truth. It is therefore important to submit a centrally coordinated communication plan, and to update it as the realization of the change plans progresses. The communication plan should specify what will be communicated to employees, customers and other stakeholders by whom and when. The method of communicating the strategic choices and their consequences requires great care and a good balance between form and content. Besides providing information, there is also the goal of convincing the employees of the logic, urgency and accuracy of the choice made, so as to stimulate their willingness to change. Outwardly, the communication method must create (renewed) confidence in the current course and thus the continuity of the organization in the chain partners, shareholders and other stakeholders. Having completed the implementation programme, execution can start with a clear conscience. And needless to point out: communication is always two-way.

The time needed for the operationalization step depends entirely on the strategy to be operationalized. Where the consequences for the organization are relatively straightforward and manageable, operationalization can be performed quite quickly, especially when it concerns only a small part of the organization. Usually, however, this is not the case, so at least two months should be factored in for the operationalization step.

Characteristics

The operationalization step is a pretty straightforward process. The strategy and direction are fixed, but how to proceed in practice can be a more difficult question to answer. By involving many others and by using communication as a strategic instrument, this step is significantly different in character from the previous steps. As depicted in Figure 9.2, this step is mostly a participatory and committing process. Not only should it determine how the strategy implementation is to be realized, but it should also be broadly supported.

FIGURE 9.2 Characteristics of the operationalization step

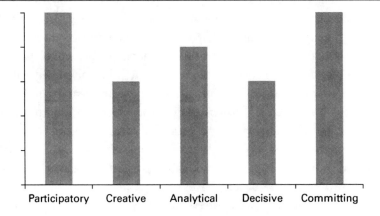

Participatory   Creative   Analytical   Decisive   Committing

So far, this is not very different from the choice step. In the operationalization step, however, there are much higher levels of participation, as key stakeholders who will be involved in executing the strategy are also involved in creating the implementation and change plans that will enable them to realize the strategy.

The operationalization step also has much stronger emphasis on the analytical characteristic. Analyses must be performed because a snapshot of the organization is to be created, for both the present and the future situation. This requires a lot of insight into the organization's driving forces. In contrast, this step has less emphasis on the creative and decisive characteristics. These play a less important role in this step, because the framework has already been outlined.

The people involved

In the steps in the left-hand part of the strategic dialogue, involvement was focused around the core strategy team and the management team. Obviously, other parties were regularly involved as well, especially when performing analyses (eg in the outside-in and inside-out steps). But the focus remained with those responsible for the new strategy and for the organization as a whole (the directors and management team).

In the operationalization step, this is very different. The role of the core strategy team and the management team shifts to that of a commissioning client 'for a programme' or 'for a number of projects', which are mentioned in the business plan or in subsequent implementation and change plans. Line and staff managers (or a selection of them based on their having a direct relationship to the new strategy) are invited to participate in the workshops. For the different parts of the organizational design, (employees of) the respective departments will be involved. For example, developments in competences will be completed with the assistance of the HR department. In the measurement of indicators, the control units and ICT often play a role. Finance is important in calculating the business case, and in identifying indicators to measure the performance of the organization's working processes. In some cases it is useful to invite people from outside (eg essential network partners, strategic suppliers, and others) to participate, especially when changes affect their activities as well. After the workshops, a small team with delegates from the different business units and competences involved in the workshops is charged with writing the actual implementation and change plans.

These plans are then handed over to a programme manager who takes control of the change programme and all its underlying projects. This manager then forms a team of project managers to bring the programme to fruition. Individual project managers are responsible for the underlying (sub-) projects and the required results. Strict management by a highly committed programme manager is essential in strategy implementation. This programme manager can also invite key external stakeholders to participate in the change projects, and is also the person who manages the execution of the communication plan.

At the same time as installing a programme manager, new objectives and performance targets will be set for the business. These should be assigned individually to members of the board and the management team, especially those responsible for the divisions, business units, market segments or regions of the business. New objectives will also be set for the commercial departments, such as sales, marketing and R&D, and for the operational departments, such as purchasing, production, logistics and customer service. Since these departments run the primary processes of the organization and deliver the (new) products and services, they should contribute to the new strategic objectives from day one.

The operationalization step in the strategic dialogue sequence

Prior to operationalizing anything, it must be made clear what it is that has to be operationalized. In the choice step, the main features of the chosen strategy are defined. This strategy is described in a strategic plan with strategic priorities and objectives. The operationalization step takes the strategic plan as a starting point by making its strategic objectives more specific. In other words, in the operationalization step, the strategic plan is worked out in more depth and prepared for execution.

Execution of the new strategy and realization of all change plans follow the operationalization step. The new strategy is implemented as described in the implementation and action plans formulated in the operationalization step. Therefore Step 6 is decisive for the path to take in Step 7 (Execution). This is depicted in the strategic dialogue model (see Figure 1.1 on page 19) by the direction of the arrows between the operationalization step and the execution step. It is a one-way relation. It also shows that the operationalization step has a similar one-way relation to the monitoring step. Operationalization is an important step because it not only describes the optimal way of realizing the strategy, but also determines the success criteria. Regular monitoring of the organization's performance and operational results will always take place. To keep track of performance against the new strategic objectives, it may be necessary to supplement this monitoring with additional indicators to determine whether the performance of the organization meets the expectations of the new strategy or whether it needs adjustment. The (additional) indicators required to perform Step 8 are part of the outcome of the operationalization step. This also holds for indicators to monitor the progress of implementation during the execution step: these indicators are defined in the change plans laid down in the operationalization step. In other words, the operationalization step not only determines the best way to achieve the strategy, but also defines what 'the best' actually entails.

However, the operationalization step need not always be preceded by the choice of a new strategy or by a choice step. The operationalization step might be started as a consequence of the monitoring step. Results from the monitoring step may lead to changes in the business plan or in the implementation and change plans. This indicates going back to the operationalization step or even a reassessment of the new strategy, and thus completing the right-hand cycle in the strategic dialogue model (see Figure 1.1). If the monitoring of the organization's performance shows that the strategic objectives are insufficiently realized, investigation into the cause is needed. If it is a structural deviation (ie consistent for a long period of time), the question arises as to whether the strategy needs to be reassessed. If the deviation in performance is the result of insufficient progress in the implementation of the strategy (lack of progress in one or more change projects), this triggers the question of whether the change approach should be adjusted. If such is the case, there will be an update of the implementation plan which clearly defines which projects are to be added or stopped, what further activities are needed, and what consequences this has for the business case. Such a review of the implementation plans usually requires a shorter lead-time, from two weeks to a month.

Dos and don'ts

✔ Operationalize from an outside, moving towards an inside perspective. Start with the market, followed by the customer and then the products. Delve deep into the organization: after the products, consider the processes, then management, structure, information, resources, employees, competences, leadership, behaviour and culture.

✔ Communicate often, even when the only message is that the change programme is 'work in progress'. Continue the strategic dialogue and engage stakeholders.

✔ Make sure that you have clear and concise leadership by individuals who carry the final responsibility (a small core group).

✔ Create highly decentralized responsibilities for answering the question 'How do we get there?' You set the direction and goals; let the 'workforce' choose its own path to glory.

✘ Do not operate from too high a level of abstraction. The strategic objectives should be SMART enough to result in real changes and new organizational design.

✘ Be careful not to make the operationalization step too detailed and specific. With too few individual choices remaining, plans might be considered as 'not invented here', and you have missed out on the opportunity to mobilize the right people to realize the necessary changes to make the new strategy a success.

✗ There is no point in putting any effort into changing the organization or its activities if you do not involve all key stakeholders.

CASE STUDY   DuSoleil

Previously...

The strategy process set out to turn DuSoleil into a profitable company once again had now been under way for a long time and had already made an impact on the company. Shaken by the lack of market knowledge and the new insights into where the market was heading, and shocked by the findings on the company's finances and the subsequent resignations of both Henri as CEO and the CFO, the strategy team had worked hard to present attractive strategic options for DuSoleil to the steering committee, including growth in the wellness market, growth in markets in Europe outside the EU, and growth in the high-end market through new product development. With a real 'Treaty at the Meuse', the internal divisions in the steering committee, which had been fired up by internal politics which took over decision-making discussions, were bridged. And a decision on the future focus had been made and was broadly supported. But was that truly the case? The strategy team noticed that even though it was the holiday season, their e-mail and telephones were constantly active.

Breaking free of internal politics

In the last week of the holidays, the strategy team decided to come back early and meet. They felt it was time to take back the initiative and act on the many signals that the 'Treaty at the Meuse' needed following up on to prevent it from going down in history as a 'paper tiger'. The strategy team felt they had done the right things in the strategy process so far: having come up with an inspiring mission statement, with realistic scenarios that outlined possible futures, and having carried out extensive analyses that got to the bottom of the capabilities of DuSoleil, they had presented multiple strategic options. And as a result of their ongoing engagement with key internal and external stakeholders throughout the strategy process, with specific attention paid in every step to ensuring the participation and inclusion of different points of view, and – in particular – based on the additional consultation round in the options step, the strategy team was of the opinion that the strategic option they recommended to the steering committee was not only the best but also the one that was best supported. The strategy to go for sustainable and profitable growth by moving into the high-end wellness sector and seizing economies of scale by working more closely together with Al-Flous America had organizational consequences, of course, but it also put DuSoleil ahead again in the market. So the strategy team decided that they shouldn't wait for an eruption of emotion but that they should guide the decision-making process to a close. They invited the steering committee to a meeting, which they had prepared with the consultancy firm. In this meeting, the steering committee was once again presented with the different options and the opinions of the key stakeholders on these options; it was also presented again with the objectified assessment of the options. The presentation concluded with a single question: what strategic direction do we decide to take? Only then were the steering committee members allowed to react to the strategy team and answer the question. There was intentionally no room for discussion. The result: the steering committee admitted to the strategy team that their recommendation was the correct one, well substantiated and with thorough investigation of support from key stakeholders.

Towards action: 'canteen sessions' and breakthrough projects

During drinks after the shareholders' meeting, in which the proposed new strategy had been affirmed by the Saudi parent company, the members of the steering committee and the strategy team jokingly told themselves that technically the choice step had taken them a bit longer as it had been expected that decisions would be made before the holidays. But now, with the final decision made, it was full speed ahead for the strategy process.

Three weeks after the shareholders' meeting, 'canteen sessions' were organized in all subsidiaries of DuSoleil in all countries; via a videoconferencing facility, Will DuSoleil Jr presented the strategic choices to local employees simultaneously. Prior to the real-time presentation by the CEO, local management had been informed of the new strategy and had received specific training for this occasion, to enable them to answer questions and handle responses to the CEO's presentation, as laid down in the communication plan. They answered questions where possible, gave additional background information and presented the overall implications of the new strategy to the local site. The reactions to the presentation were mixed. The majority was happy that a decision had finally been made; they were glad to see some light at the end of the tunnel and pleased that the uncertainty had finally come to an end, and that DuSoleil had a bright future ahead. Employees of the factory in Boston were relieved, as were the employees in Antwerp: both factories were to remain open for at least another year. However, at other sites some employees saw many obstacles ahead: the 'what' was clear, but the 'how' had yet to be completed, and that could affect them personally.

After this communication offensive, the strategy team went into action again. In order to move from strategic intentions to strategic action as soon as possible, five breakthrough projects were defined. These projects covered many of the actions required to operationalize the new strategy:

1 *Business planning and control.* A new business planning and control cycle was to be determined for the whole company and each of its subsidiaries. Also, a balanced business scorecard was to be designed and implemented to further improve the monitoring and steering possibilities for management. If all went well, in time the balanced scorecard might also be used as a 'track and trace' system for monitoring progress during strategy implementation.

2 *Product roadmaps.* Each country manager, the production managers and the senior R&D staff had to come together to create roadmaps on how the current product portfolio could be optimized, further developed and extended with new products that incorporated state-of-the-art and future technologies. The roadmaps had to ensure that each product line kept R&D, production and marketing and sales aligned on the chosen strategic direction and enabled DuSoleil to enter the wellness market and beat off Asian competitors.

3 *Commercial strategies.* The new strategy particularly required new marketing and sales policies. These policies should include the integration of the North- and Latin-American marketing and sales departments of DuSoleil and Al-Flous America, and a new branding policy to improve the company's appeal in the high-end wellness market.

4 *Management and organization.* As a result of the strategy process, the management and organizational structure had already changed a bit, with the resignation of Henri and the CFO. With the new strategy chosen, now it was time to have a look at the management structure and reassess the organizational structure, including the functions and their corresponding composition (number of full-time equivalent (fte) staff).

5 *Process improvement.* As the new strategy directed DuSoleil into new markets for further growth, it still had to be efficient enough to be competitive in all markets in which it was active. To this end, standardization of the processes for the development of new products and market introductions was to be implemented and programmes fostering continuous improvement were to be started.

The steering committee was then asked to appoint project managers for each of the breakthrough projects, preferably all from different departments and with different backgrounds. These project managers were assigned the task of coming up with a project plan and a proposal for a project team. Meanwhile, all country managers were asked to further tailor the strategy to their local business and write a business plan and marketing plans for the new activities.

As it was clear what should happen, the new strategy could also be equipped with multi-year budgets (including per department and administrative entity) and be operationalized into functional strategies and policies for HR, IT, finance, purchasing etc. The strategy team asked experts from the consultancy firm in each respective field to take these on, while they focused on putting together an overview of all the implementation activities that were needed for the new strategy.

When all the implementation and project plans for the breakthrough projects had been developed, the strategy team was shocked by the workload and capacity that the implementation required. Therefore, together with the steering committee, they prioritized and phased the plans. This had implications for the budgets, but after some toing and froing and some reconsideration, there was finally an overall implementation plan that was feasible with regard to timing, people and resources, supported by those who had to carry it out, and that would lead to the intended strategic outcomes via specific identified actions.

Progress or problems

The role of the strategy team changed significantly during this period. Until recently the team had been in charge of the process, but now this was taken over by the heads of department, the country managers and the project managers of the breakthrough projects. An important issue for DuSoleil in this step was to keep the balance between daily operations and the breakthrough projects. Because there was more to be done with a smaller number of people, because the introduction of a new way of working and newly appointed managers would still require some acclimatization, and because the monthly results were still not what they should be, the organization would have to deal with great pressure if it took on too much at once. And when the launch of a new type of sunbed – with integrated light therapy, specifically aimed at the wellness market – resulted in a PR and media crisis when the sunbed's in-built batteries failed owing to a power outage during the launch presentation, the planning of the breakthrough projects and the functional strategies were again adjusted.

An important aspect in the company's progress was that 'cash and customer' became the primary focus; increasing attention was paid to daily operations, with regard to the available time and capacity of the organization, and less to the breakthrough projects. This raised many critical questions in Saudi Arabia and at the banks as progress on implementation would slow down, but Will Jr showed that both the internal organization and customers were very enthusiastic about this new focus on daily operations. It had created an enormous increase in support for the new strategy, even though its realization had to wait. Another important aspect was something that the strategy team stumbled across in a workshop with the project teams for the breakthrough projects that was aimed at setting an overall approach to change and implementation of the strategy. It turned out that there was a divide between 'blueprint' and 'evolutionary' thinkers. The 'blueprints' preferred to first make a solid framework for, and detailed design of, all functional policies, before actually implementing any changes to them. The 'evolutionaries', on the other hand, preferred to start right away, with only a generic outline and not too many restrictions upfront, and then learn by doing. Owing to the operational pressure on short-term results and the good experiences with 'quick wins' by the intervention team earlier in the strategy process, the 'evolutionaries' won. The overall change plan now stated that the project teams should develop only the strategic, financial organizational-critical actions in detail, as for example was the case for the redefinition of the core processes and the roles of line managers in the new organization; but for large investments, such as those outlined in the product roadmaps or investments for marketing and branding in new countries, detailed business cases were to be made. For the majority of the actions in the breakthrough plans and functional strategies, it was decided just to go forth and try them and see how things worked out. Adjustments could be made during implementation. Responsibility for the realization of implementation and change plans would be assigned to line management. The strategy team sometimes complained about this to Will Jr, fearing that their role would be over, but he simply pointed out to them that the strategy is not theirs, but the company's. In this way, during the second half of the year the strategy developed rapidly into specific actions and activities. The implementation step was about to start officially.

To be continued...

10

The 8 steps to strategic success how can we realize change?

 Step 7: Execution

Objective and results

Time for action! In the execution step, the new strategy and the proposed changes will drive implementation. These plans include various change and action plans (by market, PMC, customer segment, product group, department, functional area etc) and a subsequently drawn up communication plan. The objective of the execution step is to carry out these plans and let the organization realize the objectives of the new strategy.

To execute the plans, all kind of actions needed for the future positioning of the company are carried out. Examples include: developing products, creating marketing campaigns, building shops and opening physical stores. It is also important that activities that no longer belong to the company's core activities are discontinued, for example by closing offices, eliminating overcapacity and selling businesses. Most of the activities of the implementation plan are focused on implementing the operational plans and proposed organizational adjustments. The desired changes also need to be incorporated in the administrative systems and reporting systems of the organization. And, not least, they should be introduced to, and adopted by, external stakeholders. This implementation of the strategy is thus a matter of accurate management of an appropriate change programme. At this stage, the execution of the communication plan is aimed at informing the stakeholders involved about the intended and necessary changes (benefits, urgency and approach) and progress (milestones and successes). Remember, good communication is a two-way street.

THE RESULTS OF STEP 7: EXECUTION ARE:

- execution of the business plan;
- execution of the implementation plan and subsequent change and action plans;
- execution of the communication plan, including its continuous updating;
- realization of the new strategy and the strategic objectives.

Scope and content

A change can be established in various ways. Implementing a strategic choice is a feasible change when there are clear goals (such as those described in the choice step), when it is clear what needs to change (as detailed in the operationalization step) and what the approach for change is (defined in the implementation plan in the operationalization step).

The execution step does not answer questions, but creates results. In this step there are the following points to keep an eye on:

- Are we effectively and efficiently carrying out our change programme?
- Are we following our script from the implementation plan, or is there a need to adjust our activities or to revise the plan?
- Are we actually implementing our strategy: do we realize the desired changes in performance?

Recommended models

In the execution step some strategy models can be used to facilitate change programme management. We recommend (see Part 3):

- stakeholder management;
- Kotter's eight phases of change;
- the seven forces for effective change model.

The process

After the operationalization of the strategy into strategic objectives and the necessary changes to enable the organization to realize them, and the discussion on the change process's main issues and related decision making, three processes start in parallel:

- start of the execution of the business plans by top management, business unit and division managers, sales and marketing, R&D and the operational departments;
- start of the execution of the implementation plan and subsequent change and action plans by the programme manager responsible for the change programme, and his or her team consisting of heads of department, project managers and interim managers;
- start of the execution of the communication plan, most likely by the communication (staff) department and under the responsibility of the programme manager. The content of the message is now complete, as the intended course of action and the major changes foreseen at each level and for each process are identified in the change and action plans.

The company must get ready for these three processes, so employees in various disciplines should take action and get to work. Many activities will first be taken on by the decision makers, but later they will trickle down to the workplace. This can be in the form of projects, all under the management of the change programme manager. Also, the company's partners will need to be – or even better, to feel – committed to the new strategy. Knowledge partners must provide expertise for the new products. Contracts with suppliers should be adapted or drawn up based on the provision of new materials and components. Distribution partners must be prepared to deliver new services or products, and existing distribution partners may face new competition, such as from online distributors. At the same time, subcontractors may no longer need to deliver particular parts or raw materials. This means that many contracts will be ended, plus real estate might be purchased, rented or sold, and new systems might be implemented. Ultimately, the organization should perform to the new strategic objectives in the market, and this should result in the desired return, growth and profit. There is no discipline that should just sit and watch, and if things go well successes will be achieved. And celebrated!

The execution of the implementation plan and the design of all change projects must be initiated in a central and top-down manner. Top management is responsible. In order to maintain an overview of the progress made in the various change projects during implementation, preferably a programme manager is appointed to oversee the complete change programme and all its (sub-) projects, for example to coordinate a similar change within different departments. Another possibility is appointing a steering committee or another change programme group, who coordinates and monitors the progress of the total group of change projects.

The execution step begins with a discussion with the most important internal stakeholders about the implementation plan. This discussion assesses whether there is sufficient clarity on the implementation plan and whether it is properly developed. Subsequently, the group discusses the intended and needed changes. This process is performed, for example, through a 'from the past to the future' workshop. This spreading of knowledge is aimed at those involved, so they understand the necessity and urgency of the changes, and to inform them about the approach and their (possible) role in it. It is all about adopting the changes. Often strategy models, such as Kotter's 'eight phases of change', are used in the execution step (see Part 3).

Most changes concern the actions of people in the organization, and require the management and staff to change their behaviour, or to obtain new knowledge and skills. Here strategy models, such as the 'seven forces for effective change' model (see Part 3), can provide useful guidelines. A practical way to realize change is through the use of an experience-and-learn programme (action learning). In practice, this appears to have a big effect in creating faster change and increased enthusiasm not only at the senior management level, but also at the middle management level. Indeed, at the latter level, the direct management of daily work activities and the guiding of employees in their behavioural development converge. Paying attention to and supporting middle management in this step, as the linchpin in the change process, enables the company to keep running in times of significant change.

The execution of the communication plan is performed entirely in parallel with the execution of the implementation plan. The only thing that is known throughout the organization is that a new strategic choice is to be developed. After operationalizing the strategic choice, more specific communication, about the intended and necessary changes and the proposed approach to achieve them, can take place with stakeholders and other interested parties. The communication must be in line with the chosen change approach, using for example strategy models such as the change communication model (see Part 3). Good communication brings calmness into the organization: it prevents rumours from developing. It creates a perspective for all individuals: everyone knows where they stand, what is coming (and why) and what is expected of them. It is important to organize two-way communication: not just communicate via a memo or canteen session ('Any questions? Please do not ask!'), but be open to comments and suggestions. There are often very practical suggestions within the lower organizational levels that can greatly increase employee willingness to change and accept the strategic choice. This can easily be facilitated, for instance by the use of internal digital platforms. The better its fit with the stakeholder targeted, the better the message comes across, the faster the change can occur and the more effectively the strategic choice is implemented.

The process of this step is largely linear: the implementation plan is based on steps and is executed accordingly. The more clearly the plan describes the steps and milestones, the easier it is to manage progress and to celebrate and reward it. Milestones are usually ambitious, but they can become acceptable by discussing them with stakeholders. Not all changes are accepted immediately by those in the organization. It helps to know which parts will encounter more resistance, so that adequate attention can be paid whenever needed. This calls for proper internal and external stakeholder management. When the execution step goes well, markets and customers will notice the changes realized. The company will deliver new services or products, change their promotion and advertisements, change the service or change the product's point of sale.

Also, there may be relatively small changes that can quickly lead to success. Once the first successes have been achieved, no matter how small, it is very useful to exaggerate the extent of them. This has a positive effect on the shared views on change within the rest of the organization and on the organization's partners: success creates belief.

Characteristics

The step is characterized as a participatory and committing process. Here the power of engagement indeed pays off. There is little creativity, analysis or decision, as it is foremost about carrying out the implementation and communication plan, which are drawn up in the operationalization step, see Figure 10.1.

FIGURE 10.1   Characteristics of the execution step

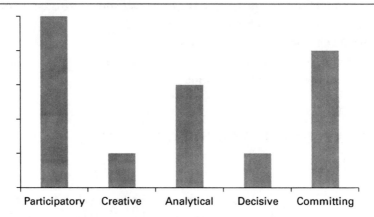

| Participatory | Creative | Analytical | Decisive | Committing |

Implementation is difficult. The excitement and newness of the strategy process have largely disappeared. People want to get back to their routines. These are the circumstances in which the changes actually have to be realized and results produced. There will also be disappointments. Brands or products are discontinued, locations may be closed or a subsidiary company sold. Leadership, communication and consistency (by sticking to agreements) are of crucial importance. In fact, implementation benefits from the involvement of stakeholders and other interested parties: letting them help to achieve the results will commit them to the necessary changes and the intended change process.

Implementation is also fun. There are new things, there will be successes! In this step, there will be new customers, new locations opened in new countries, new distributors found, new products developed or even an acquisition made. Of course there will also be failures, as in order to achieve something you must first make sacrifices. And if it really doesn't work, there are other options available that have already been developed in the various scenarios.

The people involved

In this step, everyone in the organization must be involved! The aim is to activate everybody to realize the new strategy: everyone should help implement necessary changes in such a way that all can contribute to the realization of the chosen strategy, and everyone should be invited to participate in the necessary adjustments within the organization itself or in its activities.

The key stakeholders outside the organization should also be involved, including customers, suppliers, unions, regulators and other network partners. The purpose of the involvement of these parties is to inform them of the success of the new strategy, the underlying progress of change, and to let them feel committed and participative.

The execution step in the strategic dialogue sequence

The execution step is preceded by the operationalization step (see Figure 1.1 on page 19). Where the operationalization step focuses on preparing the implementation plan with all the associated templates and measurement instruments, the focus of the execution step is to actually run the plan; the actual implementation. In the execution step, the mission statement and ambition from the searchlight step should become reality. A precondition of starting the execution step is that the implementation plan contains tangible objectives and a clear description of the approach needed to achieve each objective. Feasibility should also be checked: are the required competences and staffing resources available (or able to be made so) in order to execute the implementation plan? The execution step thus begins with an examination of these preconditions and cannot start without the operationalization step having been completed first. When the execution step is completed, the monitoring step starts; its function is to monitor to what extent the organization is on track to achieve its strategic objectives.

Dos and don'ts

✔ Celebrate success!

✔ Make sure that innovations are introduced in the market in a flawless manner in line with the organization's authenticity.

✔ Invest in knowledge and experience and take on the right competences, whatever the position may be: product developer, merging manager, marketer or web specialist.

✔ Ensure that those in charge of the programme or projects and all others involved outside the line management report directly to the management team or steering committee. Assign clear responsibilities and avoid any evasion of responsibility.

✔ Take on interim managers. This can be very effective in the realization of changes that exceed the existing capabilities of the department.

✔ Communicate, communicate, communicate! Guarantee the continuity of change communication in the (project) organization. Assign responsibility for communication to a member of the top management or steering committee and always put communication on the agenda, even when there is little progress to communicate. Even just an announcement when progress is expected can be effective communication. Besides, there can never be too much time spent on careful communication.

✖ Do not expect line managers also to be change managers: they are responsible for the *going concern* and often they are themselves also part of the change. Coach and train them in order to let them lead their department in getting good results from the changes.

✖ Do not be shocked by the degree of resistance: not everyone feels equally enthusiastic about the changes. Good change managers know how to deal with resistance and find advocates of change.

✘ Do not use change communication separately from the change-related content you want to communicate. The effectiveness of the communication is greater when it is not the moment of communication but the content of the change that dominates.

CASE STUDY DuSoleil

Previously...

DuSoleil had set out on a new strategic direction. Under the guidance of Will DuSoleil Jr, the recently appointed CEO, the company was heading for a bright future. Although the strategy process had rocked the boat somewhat, especially with the resignation of Henri DuSoleil, the company now knew where it wanted to go and what it had to do to be successful. Breakthrough projects had been formulated to get the organization focused on the new growth markets, including the upper-end wellness market, and new products, based on the latest technology. These breakthrough projects also addressed the necessary improvements, including those in aligning marketing and sales with R&D and production, and getting finance and management reporting up to standard. Multi-year budgets and functional strategies and policies had also been formulated. The strategy team had collected, prioritized and phased all implementation and change plans and completed them with a structured communication plan. The 'evolutionary' vision of change was set out as the overall approach, and responsibility for the realization of the implementation and change plans had been assigned to line management. It was time to set out on the new strategic course and reap some first successes. Things were about to change at DuSoleil.

From intention to action

After the chosen strategic direction had been operationalized in the five breakthrough plans, budgets, new functional policies and an overall change plan, the strategy implementation could officially start. Of course, during the strategy process some changes had already occurred: a new management team had been put in place, renewed attention was given to 'cash and customer' in operations, and the overall atmosphere was revitalized and refreshed, leading to new exchanges between departments and countries.

The strategy team now changed its role to overall programme management in support of the CFO, CEO and line management, letting the heads of departments, the other line managers and the project teams for the breakthrough projects take responsibility for the realization of the implementation and change plans. Just as the operationalization step was completed, the strategy team had come up with a thorough communication plan, which would help to ensure that changes would 'land smoothly' and there would be no surprises for employees nor for key customers and key suppliers.

Looking at the PDCA cycle, DuSoleil now was at 'Do': the time for talking and discussion was over; it was time for action and getting results. By making this very explicit in every management meeting he attended, Will Jr prevented any delaying techniques taking root. There was no room for 'we must first elaborate on this in further detail', a phrase used by some line managers who still felt resistance to particular aspects of the plan or felt insecure about having the responsibility. The steering committee therefore prioritized breakthrough project 4, mobilizing all the other project teams and line managers to help the project 4 team to complete the restructuring and formation of the management and organization structure; as a result, by 1 November all management positions had been filled and those affected knew they would lose their jobs. Speed, accuracy and communication played a crucial role in the success of this breakthrough project. Will Jr spent a lot of time on his people, the unions and the workers' councils in the various countries. Because customers also faced many changes, he had to divide his time and attention between external stakeholders and internal staff. However, the 'management and organization' breakthrough plan stated that the HR director had the explicit task of advising the CEO on these matters, and the communication plan that the strategy team had formulated was of great support in this. Within the steering committee, to which the progress of the breakthrough plans was reported fortnightly, the communication and change aspects received the same attention as the new product roadmap or the new brand positioning.

Time to take the lead

As the 'quick wins' had been undertaken by the intervention team from the beginning, and during the strategy process stakeholders had been regularly informed of the findings and had even participated in some of the activities, the overall response to the start of the execution step was: 'Hey, didn't we start already?' Will Jr was happy with this response as it demonstrated that there had indeed been some evidential change in behaviour within the organization. What a difference from the old days, when the strategy process was a management issue developed in isolation and in which the departments had little interest. Yet, Will Jr was still not fully at ease with the implementation. Subconsciously the traditional perspectives were still there: the objections and the hidden agendas of the managers who were against the plan but who said yes even though they still had to prove this 'yes' by acting accordingly. The organization and the processes were described on paper, but Will Jr noticed that some people experienced problems in coping with their new role. It was now time for him as CEO to call upon his management team to stand up and take the lead.

Keeping all on board: well informed and enthusiastic

In order to carefully monitor (by listening), coordinate and persevere with actions (by telling), a stepwise communication structure was developed in line with the communication plan drawn up by the strategy team. At each site, plenary monthly meetings ('canteen sessions') were organized, as they had seemed to be a highly valued method of direct communication in the earlier steps of the strategy process. During this period, all employees were kept informed about progress in the implementation and change plans through the DuSoleil Newspaper. Furthermore, relevant aspects from the breakthrough projects and from the implementation and change plans became fixed items on the agenda of each operational work meeting, as was an overall progress update. Topics that could not be solved by the teams were passed on to the strategy team, who in turn looked for additional assistance on this topic from other parts of the organization. As Will Jr noticed signals that his subconscious feeling was more than just a feeling, he asked the strategy team to step in and assign a coach from the consultancy firm to the managers who seemed to be falling back into old behaviour. Also, training, coaching and meetings for the managers who experienced difficulties with their new role were initiated by the strategy team.

Successes were widely reported and teams who achieved something extra-ordinary were shown special appreciation. The Christmas meeting was a big event, despite the still tight financial situation, and represented the end of a difficult period and the beginning of better times. The 'Sunny Business Award' was presented for the first time to a joint DuSoleil/Al-Flous team, the team that had made a success of entering into the US market. It marked the beginning of a new tradition of internal business improvement competitions.

Rise and fall, and rise again

Although great successes were achieved, implementation was not easy. For example, when defining the first innovation project from the product roadmaps the old discussion between the R&D and marketing and sales departments arose again. The R&D department sat back and waited, as according to the new rules of the game they should not start until the marketing and sales department had come up with a market-driven business plan and had defined an overall concept. The marketing and sales department, however, while facing many operational problems in sales, was also busy with the integration of the North- and Latin-American marketing and sales departments with those of Al-Flous America and was still lacking the necessary market intelligence data on future consumer requirements. Besides, they had never before written a good project briefing for an innovation project. This delayed the start of the innovation project and also blocked other implementation projects in progress in the marketing and sales department. The creative, market-driven input that was expected was not delivered. When the new Saudi-Arabian manager of the integrated DuSoleil/ Al-Flous marketing and sales department resigned after no more than nine months, people looked to Will DuSoleil Jr to take action. It was clear that both the capacity and competences in marketing and sales were inadequate and created a bottle-neck in the strategy implementation. An interim director was appointed and half the people were fired and replaced by 'real' marketers from outside the company. The internal communication group was halved in order to make way for the expertise and fresh ideas of new blood. Via an agency, temporary capacity was hired in order to clear the internal backlog. Besides the fact that this blast of fresh air boosted market orientation, these corrective actions were also a clear signal to the rest of the company: there is no way back. 'Lead, follow, or get the hell out of here', as Will Jr said (quoting Jack Welch) in one of his interviews with the DuSoleil Newspaper.

That interview, as well as measures taken within the marketing and sales department, made Will Jr appear tougher than he actually felt himself to be. In the evenings he often lay awake worrying about pressure from the Saudi investor, concerns regarding the transition of his company, and especially the consequences this whole process had caused within the family. His coaching conversations with the consultancy firm had prevented him from wanting to do too much himself in one case while at the same time taking on too much in other cases, and in all cases requiring too much of himself. 'Leading a change is not something you do just like that,' he learned. 'And that's why those leading change should take good care of themselves.' Before he fell asleep, Will Jr comforted himself with something he had picked up from two staff members at the coffee machine earlier that day: 'Little Will has really developed from the R&D underdog to a CEO in charge. Our CEO', they had said to each other. With a smile on his face, Will finally fell asleep.

To be continued...

11

The 8 steps to strategic success are we performing on target?

 Step 8: Monitoring

Objective and results

In *Step 8: Monitoring*, the performance of the organization is carefully followed and the degree to which the organization, after the implementation of changes, actually manages to achieve its strategic goals is periodically reviewed. This is what the monitoring step is about: the continual reviewing of progress on your strategic goals. The objective of this step is to exercise control over the organization's performance in relation to the strategic goals. The performance is measured based on performance indicators formulated in the operationalization step. This evaluation will take place periodically, for example every month, within the management team.

Parallel to the monitoring of results, developments evolving from the strategic choice must be monitored. They should be noticed early, thanks to the early-warning signals identified in the option and choice steps. Are the assumptions made then still valid? Is the outcome different from the one expected, and is there any reason to reconsider the choice?

The monitoring step is the last step in the strategic dialogue model (see Figure 1.1): this step ensures that the organization is acting in line with the strategic choice. But it can also be the start of new steps if adjustment is needed.

THE RESULTS OF STEP 8: MONITORING ARE:

- Are we still on the right track or do we need to intervene?
- Are there environmental signals that indicate that the current course of action is no longer the right one?
- What adjustment is required?

Scope and content

The monitoring step provides an answer to the following questions:

- *Are we achieving (or have we achieved) the desired strategic position? Have we realized our strategic objectives?* These questions are answered by monitoring the performance of the organization. Performance indicators developed in the operationalization step measure organizational performance. Based on the PDCA cycle, those responsible are encouraged to make adjustments whenever performance is inadequate.

- *How can we continue to actively monitor trends and developments? And are our assumptions still valid?* These questions are answered by continuous review of the strategic choice and underlying assumptions. On the basis of early-warning signals, the organization can monitor the scenarios, trends and developments in the organization and environment. Periodically you may also seek to find developments that were not identified earlier and that might provoke a reassessment of the strategic choice.

- *Can we continue, or is there a need for any adjustment or strategic reorientation? How should we adjust?*

Recommended models

In the monitoring step several strategy models can be used. Models that help collect and interpret information on the organization's performance in a structured manner and models that help measure progress and identify steering measures are particularly useful in this step. We recommend (see Part 3):

- the PDCA (or Deming) cycle;
- the EFQM model;
- the balanced scorecard.

The process

After implementation of the new strategy, it is important to monitor the performance of the organization against the strategic objectives. In order to do so, performance indicators must be available (preferably formulated in the operationalization step). The monitoring step includes the following activities:

- Define SMART performance indicators.
- Identify dependencies between performance indicators.
- Determine the objectives (ie the required scores) for each indicator.
- Appoint those responsible for supplying correct information for each indicator.
- Determine – together with the line manager responsible for performance – the manner and frequency of reporting on the performance of each indicator.

The monitoring process consists of two parts: first, a short phase in which performance management is designed; that is, the choice of performance indicators and objectives, assignment of responsibilities, setting up reporting cycles and establishing decision-making procedures for intervention. Many organizations use the balanced scorecard in this phase (see Part 3). Then follows a long phase in which the performance of the organization is monitored, adjustments are made if there are any deviations, and the organization should realize (most of) the objectives of the new strategy. This phase will not be completed until new objectives are formulated or a new strategy is chosen.

Similar phasing takes place for monitoring developments in the environment and testing the assumptions underlying the strategic choice. First, the information system is designed. Then follows a (long) period of actually monitoring developments, reviewing the performance of the organization against the strategic objectives and the influence or effect of these developments on deviating performances. Only when structural abnormalities or early warnings of deviating developments are identified are adjustments made and the question arises as to whether the chosen strategy should be reconsidered.

The results of the monitoring step consist mainly of an information system with reports on the organization's performance and the strategic developments of both the organization and its environment. Based on these reports, the organization must make adjustments if deviations in performance warrant it.

To this end, the manager responsible should be asked how he or she will discuss the reports with stakeholders within the department and consider the possibilities for adjustment. In other words, every manager should formulate a reporting and subsequent action cycle for their department. Here, a strategy model like the Deming cycle or the plan–do–check–act cycle (the PDCA cycle; see Part 3) will prove useful.

Naturally, it takes time for the company to benefit from the strategic changes made in the execution step. The first performance reports will often not lead directly to any adjustments, even if strong deviations are identified, as the recently implemented changes often do not have an immediate effect. This is no excuse for the lack of success of improperly implemented changes, but adjustments should not become monthly routines, mainly to prevent those involved getting tired of constant change and thus reduce its effectiveness.

Characteristics

Monitoring is an intensive process. It might come across as no more than watching the activities of others, but monitoring performance requires not only reporting, but also making adjustments. And that is, by definition, very action oriented and requires much interaction. The step is therefore characterized as both highly analytical (in reporting) and decisive (in making adjustments); see Figure 11.1.

FIGURE 11.1   Characteristics of the monitoring step

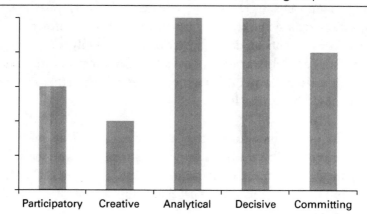

It is clear that it is not only important to spot signals and make decisions, but also to actually act. But without the commitment of the organization, corrective action will be undertaken either very late or not at all. The activities can thus be characterized to a certain extent as committing and also as somewhat participatory; it is important for decision makers not only to monitor (and act) themselves, but also to take responsibility and continuously monitor their own performance at all levels within the different departments. The monitoring step doesn't require much creativity.

The people involved

In the monitoring step, the management team and the managers responsible for the realization of performance in a particular area are directly involved. In addition, managers and employees who are responsible for providing information about performance will be involved, albeit in a different role and with less intensity. In practice, this often concerns those involved in the operationalization step. The aim of involving all these people is to gain commitment to measuring the organization's performance and to focus decision making about performance and any adjustments required in those parts of the organization that best suit this responsibility (which means that these activities are often very decentralized within the organization).

For monitoring developments in the organizational environment, key stakeholders are directly or indirectly involved. For example, the main customers, alliance partners and suppliers can be periodically asked to give their views on trends and developments. The purpose of involving external stakeholders is to broaden the information sources in order to increase the ability to spot important environmental developments.

The monitoring step in the strategic dialogue sequence

The monitoring step is preceded by the execution step in the strategic dialogue model (see Figure 1.1 on page 19). In the execution step, all intended and necessary changes are implemented. Actual completion means that the organization has been designed to operate according to the chosen strategy. In Step 8, the focus is on 'checking that everything is going well'. This can be done using the performance indicators drawn up in the operationalization step or by using the early-warning signals set out in the option and choice steps.

Should there be structural deviations or abnormalities in performance and/or developments that turn out differently from expected when choosing the strategy, the monitoring step is not the final step. This is because there might be reason to revise the chosen strategy. In that case, the monitoring step is followed by Step 5: is the choice made still the best one or are there other strategic options that have a better fit? In Figure 1.1 this is depicted as the one-way arrow completing the right-hand cycle in the figure.

An active and vigorous monitoring step proves the value of the strategic dialogue model: strategy remains a (periodic) item on the management agenda. Strategy is an ongoing process!

Dos and don'ts

✔ Use the same design for all the organization's performance reports in order to be able to elaborate on and communicate them in a consistent way, and in order to align them to all individual and organizational initiatives. That makes it easier to achieve a shared goal.

✔ Choose indicators that enable careful monitoring of performance. There are many different indicators, but there are only few KPIs that really measure what you need to know or that indicate whether you should make adjustments.

✔ Make sure the responsibilities are clearly defined. Correlations between the indicators must be defined and for each indicator you must determine who is responsible for the provision of information for measuring performance, and who is responsible for actual performance on the indicator.

✘ Computerized performance systems often contain a large collection of indicators (so-called libraries). The design of performance management cannot be universal: it depends on the chosen strategy of the organization. Use those libraries merely for inspiration.

✘ Do not misjudge the need for investment for designing adequate business intelligence systems. Benefiting from 'Big Data' often means big investments upfront. Ideally, you will be able to access the required information and databases from these business intelligence (BI) systems for making reports.

✘ In designing strategic intelligence systems to monitor developments in the environment, make sure that these will not be ignored or only used occasionally: systematic monitoring helps to prevent surprises and gives you the ability to spot developments at an early stage and anticipate them, which truly provides a competitive advantage.

CASE STUDY   DuSoleil

Previously...

DuSoleil was back on track. The transition of the organization had been guided carefully and the chosen strategic direction made very specific. With new spirit and leadership Will DuSoleil Jr, the recently appointed CEO, had taken the lead in changing the company and setting it on course for a bright future. Although the strategy process had rocked the boat somewhat, especially with the resignation of his brother Henri DuSoleil, the company now knew where it wanted to go and what it had to do to be successful. Breakthrough projects had been formulated and executed, lay-offs had been necessary, and integration with the North- and Latin-American marketing and sales departments of Al-Flous had been realized. Things had changed at DuSoleil. But the Saudi-Arabian parent company wanted to be certain that these changes were there to stay and that DuSoleil would deliver the promised returns on their investments.

When a plan comes together...

It was 18 months since Will DuSoleil entered the strategy process. After a turbulent first year in which DuSoleil's new strategic direction was determined, the plans had been operationalized and executed and the organization had undergone serious changes. Will could now look back at a successful transition. Sales volumes were, after a dip created by eliminating loss-making activities, back on the old level. The new business initiatives promised substantial growth. The investments in people, innovations and branding were substantial and it had been quite difficult to negotiate with the banks and the Saudi Arabians to gain their financial support. Because the strategic plan offered a clear perspective, owing to the clear focus and the well-informed choices made, because Will Jr could point to significant cost reductions already realized, and especially because the profitability and cash flow of the business were tremendously improved, DuSoleil did receive the financial investments in the end. Will Jr was, however, most proud of his people. In the past, DuSoleil had been an introverted, product-oriented family business; now it had been transformed into a market-oriented, business-driven partner for fitness and wellness centres. 'From a family business to a business family', he had said in one of the recent editions of the DuSoleil Newspaper.

Check and take action!

However, all this had not happened automatically. After a promising start to the strategy implementation, various assumptions proved to be incorrect. A new lighting technology was developing much faster than expected, for example, and the 'home tanning' trend increased against all expectations, thereby attracting too much interest from the retail channel. The main benefit, however, was that this time DuSoleil realized what was happening at an early stage. The balanced business scorecard not only showed the top-line financials, but also warned if the underlying scores on customers, processes and innovations threatened to go south. This allowed the management team to intervene in time. The scorecards were introduced in all departments and at all sites, so that monitoring performance on multiple perspectives had become second nature in the entire company. All managers and heads of departments had undergone thorough training in performance management and in creating conditions for continuous improvement in their department or in their team. Everyone with a managerial function (or ambition) knew about the plan–do–check–act approach. Each department and team periodically checked its performance against the plan, evaluated its activities and acted upon any deviation. DuSoleil was very much alive again and continuously challenged itself to perform up to, or exceed, its own new high standards.

The strategic dialogue as a continuous process

Intensive monitoring of the change process, the operational business performance and their underlying forces had contributed significantly to the transition of DuSoleil. Will Jr, however, wanted to actively monitor the strategic direction too. Before being dismissed, the strategy team was asked to come up with a way to do this. Will Jr had learned from the shock he received from the findings in the outside-in step and wanted never again to be surprised by market developments that the company did not know about. To him, strategy was no longer an annual ritual dance performed during the isolated management team's weekends. The strategy was now a living element. The strategy team recommended to Will Jr that he should make sure that engagement with stakeholders took place throughout the year, and that – at least once or twice a year – all developments should be collected to evaluate and assess the strategic course in a structured manner. Will Jr conferred with his CFO and agreed to install this proposed permanent monitoring of the strategy. From now on, through continuous internal and external engagements DuSoleil would be stimulated to maintain focus. Internally, business improvement competitions, internal meetings and feet-on-the-table discussions would keep managers focused and very much alert to new developments and ideas. Externally, managers would be encouraged to visit the boards of their key customers and key suppliers once every quarter to check and discuss business affairs. In these conversations, not only should operational progress be evaluated, but the partners should also look forward together in order to identify any trends and developments in the market.

In a very intense year, DuSoleil had turned around and had embarked on its new strategic direction. The steps of the strategic dialogue had guided DuSoleil to strategic success. At a specially organized company event Will Jr thanked the strategy team profusely, as they had done a great job in facilitating this strategy process.

Decisive, authentic and flexible

DuSoleil now knew how to shorten the strategic loops. New opportunities, for example, were not saved until the annual budgeting cycle was complete, but instead were assessed in accordance with the strategic frameworks during rapid selection workshops, and thereafter implemented immediately. Although there were some initiatives that failed, this decisive way of working greatly stimulated DuSoleil's effectiveness. The strategy process within the strategic dialogue model had meant a lot for the DuSoleil brand. The transition had helped to shift the perception of DuSoleil in markets all over the world from being a 'supplier of sunbeds' to a 'partner in wellness'.

But there had also been sustainable change in the culture of the company. The organization had consciously said goodbye to the former family culture and leadership style. There was now an organization in which people represented the core values of innovation, entrepreneurship and team spirit. This authenticity was appreciated by the customers and also gave DuSoleil a strong image in the labour market.

Finally, it was proved that the strategic dialogue had ensured that the company's agility, something that had always been regarded as a core characteristic of the company of which it was very proud, was now actually realized in full. It had responded quickly to requests from distributors for new products, although they were not always getting it entirely their own way. Problems with products experienced by customers were usually resolved within two days, and the production department was able to anticipate the varying sizes of orders quickly and perfectly. DuSoleil was back on top of the world and there to stay. The Saudi Arabians would certainly receive their return on investment.

Standing in the boardroom overlooking the city from the 26th floor, Will DuSoleil Jr thought once more about that afternoon long ago, when his father took him to the first tanning studio in Boston. Now he himself, after such an intense strategic learning experience, stood here to start the next chapter of the story of DuSoleil. With strong self-confidence, he turned around and opened the meeting of the board of directors.

The end

This concludes Part 2, the core of the book: the strategic dialogue model and its 8 steps for strategic success. The next two parts are intended to be used as an additional reference and guide either to each step (the strategy models presented in Part 3) or to a specific characteristic of the strategy process as a whole (the methods of engagement presented in Part 4). We recommend that you read and go through the next two parts not from beginning to end, but selectively: looking up a specific strategy model or a specific method of engagement. You can use Parts 1 and 2 for referrals. Let the strategic dialogue model and its 8 steps thus be your guide!

In the concluding Part 5 you will find some suggestions and points of attention for applying the strategic dialogue yourself.

PART 3
Key strategy models

In Part 2, for each of the 8 steps of the strategy process with the strategic dialogue model, we recommended a number of strategy models for you to use. These strategy models help to:

- keep an overview of what data and information are relevant to gather;
- interpret and analyse data and information;
- diagnose trends and developments;
- give meaning to findings and gain new insights;
- design new strategies;
- operationalize strategy;
- implement strategy; and/or
- monitor performance.

In Part 3, we present a selection of methods, models, theories and frameworks that can assist you in your strategy process. Some of them are useful in a particular step of the strategic dialogue, and some can be used in two or more steps.

The selection of strategy models presented here is based on our consulting experience. Many of the models are very well known and very popular. Some are lesser known but very useful, and have been proven to work in strategy processes with the strategic dialogue. For us, some of the models are essential for the strategy process and (thus) closely linked to one of the 8 steps, for instance the scenario planning model with Step 2. Therefore we provide more detail on these models in this part. We are well aware that some of the models are not so well known and/or are relatively new. A few of these have their origins in the Dutch and European tradition of consultation. However, these models, for example the socially engineered change model, do fit in with a general shift in strategy processes to be more participative and inclusive. It is certainly not our claim to be exhaustive or exclusive, nor that all of these models have to be used. There are many more models and methods available than those described in this book, which you can find on numerous websites or in anthologies on key management models. In the end, you should pick the models that most appeal to your situation and that best suit you in your strategy process.

This part provides a selection of key strategy models that correspond to each of the 8 steps of the strategic dialogue model. For each model we provide a brief introduction and a recommendation on how to use it, with diagrams of the models. We have included references to the model, either direct references where you can find the original model or references on which we based the model as presented in this part. These latter references can also be used as recommendations for further reading.

The models are grouped around each of the 8 steps, based on where the model is recommended. This way, you can look up which strategy model you might want to consider using according to which step of the strategy process you are in.

Models for Step 1: Searchlight

 Step 1: Searchlight

Step 1: Searchlight is about setting the scope of the strategy process: both content-wise and process-wise (see Part 2). In this step several strategy models can be used, particularly those that help express ambitions or a vision and mission statement, or models that help define the company's business playing field and business scope.

MODELS THAT CAN BE USED IN STEP 1: SEARCHLIGHT ARE:

- Strategy 3.0;
- BHAG;
- Abell's business definition model;
- Key market characteristics.

Strategy 3.0

FIGURE 12.1   Strategy 3.0

	Strategy 1.0	*Strategy 2.0*	*Strategy 3.0*
Spirit of the age	Industrial era	Information age	Network era
Mission statement	Value for shareholders (profitability)	Value for stakeholders (yield)	Lifetime value (sustainability)
Values	Be better ('Mind')	Be different ('Heart')	Make a difference ('Soul')
Intent	Superior product	Superior business	Superior network
Strategy formulation process characteristics	• Top-down • Linear • Hierarchical (1:many)	• Participative • Linear • Dialogue (1:1)	• Participative • Iterative • Sharing (many:many)

Essence

The Strategy 3.0 model gives companies a conceptual framework about how their strategy formulation process can evolve with changing times. Organizations are often used to a top-down strategy formulation process, which basically aims at making profits for the shareholder. Modern times call for a more participative and iterative strategy formulation, which allows organizations and network partners with whom they share important values to aim for a higher purpose.

Usefulness

This model is particularly useful as a mental framework in Step 1. It allows companies to think about who they are and what they stand for in the world. It leads to fundamental discussions on the DNA of the company and how it fits into the world of tomorrow (regarding trends in the environment, development with customers and owners, values of employees etc). By explicitly discussing the 'raison d'être' and values (passion and purpose) of the organization, the process for formulating strategy is shaped.

Execution

In some organizations, it is deeply embedded in the organization's DNA that the main aim is to satisfy customers and shareholders, through their processes, innovation, services and/or by being better than the competition. This is good as long as strategic choices reflect these core values. To keep pace with the (digital) network economy in the world of today, organizations may find that they should change the way they regard people, culture, management or leadership. Organizations will feel a shift to a new perspective on strategy that challenges them to reveal their true feelings and to take positions openly. Organizations that have it in their DNA to really share with partners, and whose highest inner motive is to work together to bring about something special, can use the Strategy 3.0 model to make their values explicit and use them as an anchor in the rest of the strategy formulation process. This includes discussions on how to encompass the risks and disadvantages of these values: Is this what a customer wants? Is this how the strategy team thinks? Will everyone in the organization agree? What would it take to achieve this ambition?

These discussions should be recorded, so they can be addressed later in the strategy process. When strategic options are being assessed in Step 4 (Options), this model could return as an anchor: Are we just keeping up appearances with these strategic options? Do our options truly reflect who we think and/or say we are? Also, in the operationalization of the strategy in Step 6, you should check whether the chosen actions are in line with the outcomes of the discussion using the Strategy 3.0 model: Are the actions in line with what we have formulated as our core values or have we strayed? The Strategy 3.0 model thus helps to ensure the authenticity of the company throughout the strategy process. And it helps to shape the strategy formulation process itself: the way you organize discussions on new strategies must reflect the way you think about your organization as whole.

Verdict

The Strategy 3.0 model is a valuable eye-opener and a useful stepping stone for organizations to discuss their authenticity (the core of their DNA) and their place in the world in a structured way, early on in the strategy formulation process. It does, however, require some empathy and representational power on the participants' part. For the more digital thinkers in particular, the model and its added value can appear to be a bit vague.

Literature

The Strategy 3.0 model is based on the following sources:

- Kotler, P, Kartajaya, H and Setiawan, I (2010) *Marketing 3.0: From products to customers to human spirit*, John Wiley & Sons Inc, Hoboken, NJ
- Kelly, K (1997) New rules for the new economy: twelve dependable principles for thriving in a turbulent world, *Wired*, Issue 5.09, September
- Sisodia, R, Wolfe, D B and Seth, J (2007) *Firms of Endearment: How world class companies profit from passion and purpose*, Wharton School Publishing, Upper Saddle River, NJ
- Porter, M and Kramer, M (2011) Creating shared value: how to reinvent capitalism – and unleash a wave of innovation and growth, *Harvard Business Review*, 89 (1/2), pp 62–77

BHAG

FIGURE 12.2   BHAG

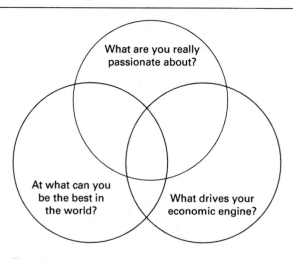

SOURCE: after Collins and Porras (1994)

Essence

A BHAG (or: Big Hairy Audacious Goal) gives a statement that helps focus an organization on a single medium- to long-term organization-wide goal.

The BHAG – first introduced by James Collins and Jerry Porras in their book *Built to Last* – poses three questions to an organization: What are you deeply passionate about? What can you be the best in the world at? What drives your economic engine? Your BHAG should be an answer to all three questions at once: it should give an inspiring direction for the organization's future.

Usefulness

Many organizations set goals that describe what they hope to accomplish over the coming years. These goals help align employees of the business to work together more effectively, for instance increase margins by 5 per cent in two years' time. The BHAG revolves around the question of what the organization wants to achieve in the longer term by formulating the next great and inspiring purpose for the company. It has a longer time horizon: it gives an overview of the shared dream of the organization.

Execution

The BHAG poses three questions in parallel:

- *What are you deeply passionate about?* According to Collins and Porras, companies can only be really outstanding in areas where they are fully committed. The answer to this question should be formulated as 'a customer's problem that the company is going to resolve like no other'.

- *What can you be the best in the world at?* This question goes beyond one or two features or best-selling products. It is about identifying a core competence which others cannot match. It might be a patented technology, but it could also be the creativity of employees or the logistic competences of the company.

- *What drives the economic engine?* This could be the utilization rate of a plant, the price premium of the brand or the service offered or products sold. It is essential to keep this financial pillar in view.

By first answering each of the questions, possibly with multiple answers per question, and then comparing and combining those answers, the BHAG is shaped. Ultimately there will be a shared understanding of what the BHAG for the organization is. It is not necessary to formulate it as a catchy one-liner in the first instance – such a spin-off can be created later and perhaps by creative professionals. Often, however, during the process a certain phrase will linger and will form the basis for the inspiringly worded BHAG.

Verdict

The BHAG is very useful to (re-)state the 'raison d'être' of the organization and to create a single long-term focus. This will be especially useful when the strategy process needs some creative thinking or reconsideration of business models. Then the BHAG model will help to prepare fertile ground for reinventing your organization.

The BHAG is an inspiring and versatile instrument, but requires some creative flexibility on the part of participants. A BHAG exercise in a very old-fashioned, traditional company without any inspiration from outside or from the younger members of staff could result in a repetition of old truths.

Literature

For the BHAG model we refer to the following sources:

- Collins, J and Porras, J (1996) Building your company's vision, *Harvard Business Review*, 74 (5), pp 65–77
- Collins, J and Porras, J (1994) *Built to Last: Successful habits of visionary companies*, Harper Business, New York

Abell's business definition model

FIGURE 12.3   Abell's business definition model

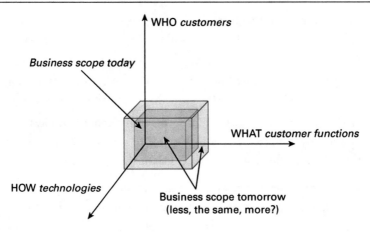

SOURCE: after Abell (1980)

Essence

The business definition model introduced by Derek Abell defines and considers a company on the basis of three dimensions: the customers (who), their needs (what) and the technology and competences the company dedicates to serving those needs (how). The model is used to gain insight into the company and its proposition to the market and into the company's possibilities for development in each of the three dimensions. Using this model, the current and future potential of the company can be mapped.

Usefulness

Abell's business definition model can be used to:

- define the business scope of a company: giving insight into the current position of the company in its market(s);
- describe the business domain of a company: giving insight into the positions the company could occupy in the market (its potential);
- obtain a picture of the (potential) market.

Execution

To determine the scope and domain of the business with Abell's business definition model, there are three questions to be answered:

- *Who*: determine the customer groups to which the company can deliver value. This question should be asked from the customer perspective.
- *What*: determine customers' needs in order to identify which of the company's activities offer added value to these customer groups.
- *How*: determine what technologies, competences and systems applied by the company will allow it to perform better (ie fulfil the needs of the customer better) than the competition.

By first answering each question for the current situation of the organization, a shared understanding is created, which could then serve as common point of reference in the strategy process. Then, by answering each question for the future of the organization, a shared understanding of the potential of the organization is created. In this way, Abell's business scope model can be useful in Step 1 to set the scope for the exploration of the future possibilities for the organization and (thus) set the scope for the strategy process: How ambitious should the organization be? Should it look into both new customer groups and new activities and technologies? And how radically new should those be?

Verdict

The model provides a clear framework for discussions about the current and potential business scope of the company. Besides extending the business scope, a discussion on limiting that scope can also lead to surprising insights. In particular, the How question often leads to a fundamental discussion about the business model of the company. For this discussion, Abell's business definition model is less suitable. Other models, for example the business model canvas, are more appropriate to this discussion.

Literature

For Abell's business definition model we refer to the following source:

- Abell, D F (1980) *Defining the Business: The starting point of strategic planning*, Prentice Hall, Englewood Cliffs, NJ

Key market characteristics

FIGURE 12.4   Key market characteristics

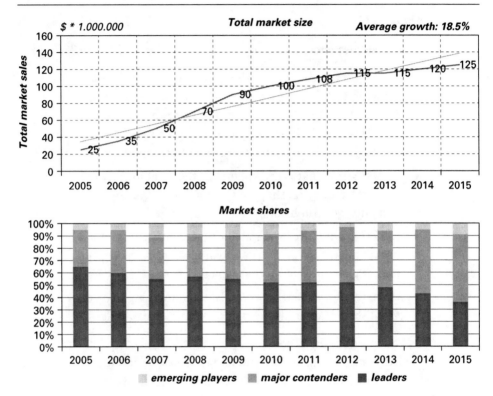

Essence

Market characteristics give a general impression of a market and its dynamics. Companies should have insight into the characteristics of the markets in which they (want to) operate.

Usefulness

Seriously studying the market(s) in which the company is active is of great value in deriving a first shared framework. In practice, this happens (all too) seldom. It seems so obvious and there is so much on the table that one forgets to check what knowledge is shared or whether there is still a (non-coherent) collection of individual opinions. The key market characteristics model helps to build a framework that sets the scope for analyses in the strategy process. This has particular added value if there is little or no quantitative information on the degree of concentration, market size and market growth.

Execution

The market characteristics that should at least be studied are:

- *Market structure.* What is the concentration of the market (number and size of providers, number of customers)? What can we say about the nature of the applicants and the homogeneity of the market (B2B or B2C, market segments)? What is the composition of the chain (number of links and type of outlets)?

- *Market size.* What is the volume of the total market in terms of units and money (perhaps subdivided into relevant customer segments, geographical areas, per capita)?

- *Market growth.* By how much (in percentage terms) has the market grown in the past five years? What is the expected future market growth? Are there seasonal effects?

- *Maturity of the (sub-) market.* Is it an emerging market or an established market? Is the market stable or dynamic?

This can be done in a plenary session, where participants state their knowledge and/or where they will find the information (eg 'I don't know by heart, but I know it is in a report somewhere on my desk'). Please keep in mind that it is not (yet) about the exact analysis of the market, but about coming to a shared understanding that can serve as a point of reference throughout the strategy process.

Verdict

By studying the market characteristics, shared insight is gained into some general characteristics of the market. Based on this shared understanding, further analyses can be performed, particularly in Step 2 (Outside-in).

The shared point of reference on the most important market data, found with the help of the key market characteristics model, also will be very useful in Step 1 when formulating the company's mission statement and vision.

Literature

The key market characteristics model is based on the following sources:

- Aaker, D A and McLoughlin, D (2010) *Strategic Market Management: Global perspectives*, John Wiley & Sons, Chichester
- Kotler, P and Armstrong, G (1967 and 2011) *Marketing Management*, Prentice Hall, Upper Saddle River, NJ (2011, 14th edn)
- Alsem, K J (2006) *Strategic Marketing: A practical approach*, McGraw-Hill, Maidenhead

13 Models for Step 2: Outside-in: Scenarios

 Step 2: Outside-in: scenarios

Step 2: Outside-in: scenarios aims to provide a comprehensive picture of the company's environment and the parties involved – which developments and stakeholders are most prominent in determining the future of the organization – and to provide options for the organization based on these insights. In this step, several strategy models can be useful, particularly those that help analyse and interpret developments in society and in the market, with competitors, with customers, and all other relevant developments in the environment. Models that help generate strategic options from an outside-in perspective are also useful.

> **MODELS THAT CAN BE USED IN STEP 2: OUTSIDE-IN: SCENARIOS ARE:**
>
> - PEST (or PESTLE) analysis model;
> - stakeholder analysis;
> - competitive analysis: Porter's five forces model;
> - customer analysis: Curry's pyramid;
> - scenario planning.

PEST (or PESTLE) analysis model

FIGURE 13.1   PEST (or PESTLE) analysis

Essence

The PEST analysis model helps to analyse the environment's main influences on a company. These influences are divided into different perspectives: Political (or legal), Economic, Socio-cultural and Technological. The model name is an acronym of these perspectives.

Often the model is extended with additional perspectives. Well-known alternative acronyms are PESTLE analysis, including Legal and Environmental perspectives, STEEPLE analysis, adding an Ethical perspective, and PESTED analysis, with Ecological/Environmental and Demographic perspectives.

Using the PEST (or PESTLE) analysis model is a structured way to obtain insight into the environmental factors and their impact on the company. It is not very important which perspectives are made explicit, as long as all relevant perspectives are included in the analysis of the environment. You can thus choose the acronym you like best.

Usefulness

The PEST (or PESTLE) analysis model provides a conceptual framework for a complete picture of the environment. Its use prevents you lingering too long on the environmental factors that are already known. The PEST (or PESTLE) analysis model forces people to think about a wide(r) range of factors that affect the success of their company, but that also affect their customers, suppliers, competitors, knowledge institutions etc.

In Step 2, the PEST (or PESTLE) analysis model provides a basis for exploring trends and uncertainties, as a complete picture of developments in the company's environment is painted.

Execution

In the use of the PEST (or PESTLE) analysis model, the different perspectives are used as stepping stones for analysis:

- *Politics.* Is there political stability in the regions in which the company is active? What is the position of supervisors and regulators? What government policies can be expected?

- *Economic.* What are the expected trends in economic factors (such as growth of gross national product (GNP), interest rate and inflation rate)? What are the economic trends in the industry and what is their impact on the company? To what extent is funding accessible? What is the purchasing power and investment capacity of target groups?

- *Socio-cultural/demographic.* What is the population density in the market? What is the composition of potential target groups, in terms of age, background, family size etc? What is the buying behaviour of current and potential customers? What are consumers' preferences? What changes in customers' lifestyles can be perceived and what are the consequences for the company?

- *Technological.* What are the important developments in technology and what are the consequences for the company? What technologies are likely to come to market in the next few years?

- *Legal.* What is the outlook in terms of laws and regulations? What constraints are to be expected from future legislation? What opportunities does future legislation offer?
- *Ecological.* What are the important developments in the field of ecology, such as nature preservation, carbon footprint minimization or emissions reduction, and what are the consequences for the organization's activities?

The PEST (or PESTLE) analysis model should be applied not only to the current business environment, but with a longer-term view in mind. Trends and uncertainties generally have a longer validity than just the current year. Where possible, it is important to quantify trends and base them on facts.

The model can be used to prepare questions for interviews with stakeholders, experts, customers and other parties. Or it could be useful as a guide during workshops or a brainstorming session. It can also be used for the purpose of scenario planning, making it possible to distinguish between uncertainties and trends. By discussing which are most relevant to the success of the company, scenarios can be mapped out.

Verdict

The PEST (or PESTLE) analysis model is a very useful framework for identifying the relevant factors in the environment. It provides a wide field of vision and can structure analysis. It also serves as a framework for discussions with (external) stakeholders who are consulted in the strategy formulation process. A PEST analysis is often considered fundamental to Step 2 in order to understand how the environment in which the organization is active is developing.

Literature

The PEST (or PESTLE) analysis model is based on the following sources:

- Johnson, G and Scholes, K (1998 and 2011) *Exploring Strategy*, Prentice Hall, Upper Saddle River, NJ (2011, 9th edn)

Stakeholder analysis

FIGURE 13.2   Stakeholder analysis

	Relation	Coalition	Interest	Power	Priority
Employees					
Customers					
Suppliers					
Competitors					
Regulators					
Trade unions					
Labour unions					
...					

Essence

A stakeholder analysis maps the interests of groups and individuals who are important to the company. These stakeholders can be external or internal. They can also be divided into those with primary interests (including shareholders, employees, creditors, suppliers, customers and competitors) and those with secondary interests (other authorities, social group, media and society).

Usefulness

With a stakeholder analysis, a company can form an idea of:

- which stakeholders are dominant;
- the relationship of the different stakeholders to each other;
- the various stakeholders' interests in their relationship with the company;

- the influencing power the stakeholders (should) have on the decision.

Execution

A stakeholder analysis consists of mapping out for each stakeholder:

- their current relationship with the organization;
- possible coalitions in which the stakeholder and other stakeholders might be involved;
- the stakeholder's position in the environment/market in which the organization is active;
- the stakeholder's power;
- the stakeholder's priorities.

Next, the organization should analyse the stakeholders and their potential influence (regarding both the impact and the interest of the stakeholder) and take the insights from this analysis into account in the rest of the strategy process and decision-making process.

Verdict

The stakeholder analysis model is an evergreen model that should always be applied in a strategy process. It is astonishing, however, how often in real businesses a structured analysis is not carried out. In a dynamic environment, a stakeholder analysis should be performed more frequently (preferably regularly). Relevant groups change quite rapidly, as do their power relations, interests and priorities. Companies must consider both their primary and secondary stakeholders. This last category is especially important for companies that are highly dependent on their image and public opinion.

Literature

The stakeholder analysis model is based on the following sources:

- Freeman, R E and Harrison, J S (2010) *Stakeholder Theory: The state of the art*, Cambridge University Press, Cambridge
- Freeman, R E (1984 and 2010) *Strategic Management: A stakeholder approach*, Cambridge University Press, Cambridge

Competitive analysis: Porter's five forces model

FIGURE 13.3   Competitive analysis: Porter's five forces

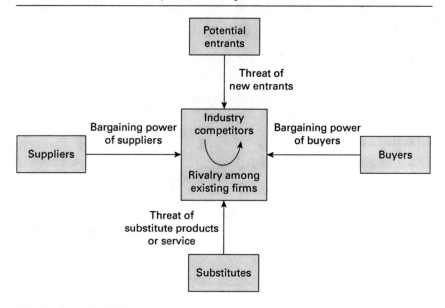

SOURCE: after Porter (1980)

Essence

The five forces model introduced by Michael Porter in his 1980 book *Competitive Strategy* is a tool to get a complete picture of the competitive situation of a company. It assesses the attractiveness of the industry in which the organization is active and provides insight into the operating range of the company, with regard to both suppliers and customers. This is determined by five competitive forces: industry competitors (rivalry among existing firms), threat of new entrants, threat of substitutes and the bargaining power of both buyers and suppliers. The weaker these forces are, the more attractive an industry or company becomes.

Sometimes the model is extended with additional forces: government, partners (next to competitors) and compatible products (next to substitutes). These might help in getting an even more complete picture.

Usefulness

Using Porter's five forces model results in:

- a summary of the relevant players and the development of their positions in the competitive field;
- insight into the factors that influence those positions and how the players interact and compete with each other;
- insight into current and future market attitudes;
- a clear picture of the trends and dynamics in the industry;
- a base for exploring changes in industry movements such as chain integration or specialization.

Using Porter's five forces model helps to obtain sought-after insights into the industry dynamics in Step 2, and is useful input for scenario planning.

Execution

Porter's five forces model clearly incorporates the total market, including potential new entrants and substitutes (the 'total size of the pie') and the way in which the total market is divided between customers, suppliers and competitors (the 'distribution of pieces of the pie'). In order not to be blinded by details, effective use of the model requires a clear definition of the level and depth of the analysis. The model provides real value as not only is the current industry situation charted, but also possible future developments.

In his book, Michael Porter presented, for each of the five forces, a list of topics to include in the analysis. This list, and the more elaborate ones developed over the years, can be used as a guideline for the analysis. Hence we refer to the book for these topic lists.

It is important that these analyses and assessments are properly carried out, based on as many data and facts as possible. Information such as financial statements about competitors, suppliers and other parties is usually readily available. However, information about reputation and innovations will be more difficult to come by, but it is important to question commercial colleagues on what they hear from their customers about what competitors offer.

The model can be used as a framework for document research, but also as a conceptual framework for discussions during a workshop. Or in combination: using the research as input for discussions.

Verdict

Porter's five forces model is ideally suited for insight into the dynamics of the industry and the interests of other parties. It thus offers results that are useful for scenario analyses and exploration of opportunities and threats facing the organization.

Literature

For Porter's five forces model we refer to the following source:

- Porter, M E (1980 and 1998) *Competitive Strategy: Techniques for analyzing industries and competitors*, Free Press, New York

Customer analysis: Curry's pyramid

FIGURE 13.4   Customer analysis: Curry's pyramid

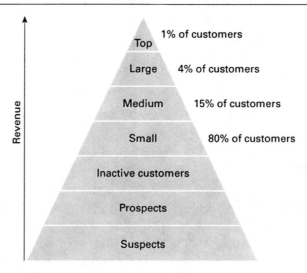

SOURCE: after Curry (1992)

Essence

A customer analysis helps to classify customers into groups. Based on this classification, good and bad customers can be identified and policies drawn up accordingly. Using a pyramid to depict the customer classification, with the most valuable group of customers at the top and a vast majority of less valuable customers at the bottom of the pyramid, the customer analysis is a mechanism for segmenting and, in so doing, visualizing and analysing customer behaviour, loyalty and value within each of those customer segments. Jay and Adam Curry (2000) revitalized this concept of the customer pyramid.

Usefulness

Based on several characteristics, the customer analysis assesses whether the customer base contains more or less homogeneous groups. Various quantitative data about customers are also collected, such as which products they purchase and what revenues each customer brings in. The goal is to map out what each customer contributes to the company results. The pyramid model provides a visually attractive display of this segmentation and analysis. It also helps to show that customers should be treated differently in each segment of the pyramid. In addition, the pyramid model provides an insight into cross-selling and up-selling opportunities (imagine customers 'moving up in the pyramid'; see Figure 13.4).

A customer analysis provides insight into:

- customer contribution to revenue and margins, and development(s) therein;
- which products are and/or will be bought by which customers in which amounts;
- the potential to sell to customers in each customer group.

Execution

A customer analysis starts with a definition of customer groups based on specific factors. These factors usually include, but are not limited to, turnover and profitability per customer. The segmentation reflects how an organization considers and treats a (future) customer, segments of customers, or the entire potential customer base.

Next, all current and potential customers are segmented into the (most) appropriate customer group. Then an analysis is made of attractiveness to the company per customer group, often expressed as contribution to revenue and margin and potential therein. Finally, an assessment is made of the attractiveness to the company of all customer groups: What would happen if certain groups were no longer served? What is required to serve potential customers in a very attractive customer group? The customer analysis also gives insights into the customers with whom the company is making (or losing) money, or which customers the company should strive for (and what that takes).

Verdict

The analysis of customers in general, as downstream activities in the supply chain, is covered in Porter's five forces model. However, a specific customer analysis gives many additional insights. When the customer base fluctuates significantly, this additional analysis is very desirable and should be performed periodically to keep insights up to date.

One of the indirect advantages of a customer analysis, especially when performed repetitively in a structured manner, is that the categorization of customers also allows for account management and/or targeted marketing policies.

Literature

For Curry's pyramid model we refer to the following sources:

- Curry, J and Curry, A (2000) *The Customer Marketing Method: How to implement and profit from customer relationship management*, Free Press, New York
- Curry, J (1992) *Know Your Customers: How customer marketing can increase profits*, Kogan Page, London

Scenario planning

FIGURE 13.5   Scenario planning

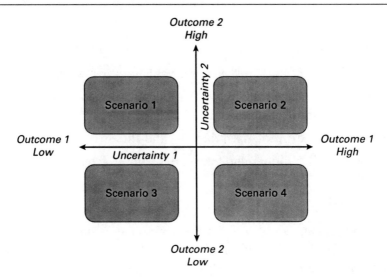

Essence

Scenarios are stories that describe possible futures. They contain exceptional events, the key players and their motivations, and depict the dynamics in the world. Scenarios help people to imagine the future and the challenges it poses to them. Scenario planning is a means of assessing a number of structurally quite different, but equally plausible, future models of the world. By seeing a range of possible futures, decision makers will be better informed, and intentions based on this knowledge will be more likely to succeed. By using scenarios, companies can handle uncertainty and move away from one-dimensional projections. Thus, the more strategic options are created, the better prepared the company is for situations which deviate from the expected, and the better it is able to respond proactively to future developments.

Usefulness

Many companies tend to focus on trends they see developing in the way in which the organization is active. Modern-day industries are, however, very dynamic and trends are not always predictable. Analysis of the environment and industry thus uncovers many uncertain and as yet poorly understood developments. Companies should keep those in focus when looking at their options for the future. Scenario planning offers a method for acknowledging and working with what is not known (in detail) yet or cannot exactly be predicted (yet). By using scenario planning, companies can:

- assess various certain and uncertain developments;
- obtain insight into multiple foreseeable future images;
- improve management creativity to identify options to respond to possible future changes;
- avoid compartmentalized thinking and entrenched beliefs;
- plan possible futures and take patterns into account.

Execution

Scenario planning starts with a systematic analysis on both the micro and macro levels of the environment in which the organization is active. Often one or more of the models recommended for Step 2 can be used (the PEST (or PESTLE) analysis model is often used). The analyses are preferably checked with, or carried out together with, external parties: business partners, but also scientists and scientific institutions, policy-makers, industry organizations, politicians, opinion leaders and other parties who can give relevant input on the future of the company. Including their views in the analysis ensures that the organization is challenged on its implicit assumptions about the future. In the analysis, trends and uncertainties are distinguished. Trends are high-probability developments that will lead to a specific outcome that is largely predictable. Uncertainties are developments that can go in different directions (no specific outcome) and that are uncertain (it is hard to predict which outcome is most likely).

Next, the relevant trends, developments and uncertainties are weighed on the degree of uncertainty of the direction of their outcome and on the degree of potential impact they will have on the future of the company. From this assessment, the two highest-scoring trends and developments are selected. They will form the scenarios. Usually they are depicted on two axes, forming a cross (see also Figure 13.5). The four squares formed by the axes represent the four scenarios that can be based on these two most important (uncertain) developments. As with Figure 13.5, scenario planning benefits from being visually displayed in order to create different scenarios. Then each of the scenarios is detailed. It helps to enrich them with, for instance, milestones for events on the timeline of the scenarios, descriptions of the market in which the company will then be active and the customers it will then serve, and/or dialogues between key stakeholders in this future.

Subsequently, the implications for the company of each of the scenarios are investigated. Developments in a scenario will be likely to have a certain impact and both the development and the impact may vary between scenarios. Then, with a clear understanding of the potential implications of each scenario for the organization, possible options for the organization in each possible future business environment (ie scenario) can be determined: how can the organization best respond to the developments and their impacts and implications? These options then serve as input for Step 4 (Options; see Part 2). With a possible positioning of the organization in each of the scenarios and multiple options available, scenario planning is then concluded with a recommendation on the options. This recommendation can vary from 'betting the farm' on one option that only works out well in one of the scenarios, to recommending certain options that are beneficial for the organization in all the scenarios.

Finally, the model identifies indicators that will show when a particular development is about to happen and which of the scenarios is to become reality. These indicators serve as so-called early-warning signals, and will be monitored (see Step 8 in Part 2).

Verdict

Scenario planning is an essential tool for developing strategic options and formulating a powerful strategy. Options are important not only to have a choice, but also to have alternatives if things turn out differently from expected. Scenarios are extremely useful when there are many uncertainties about the (long-term) future of a company. It is better to take into account different possible futures in which the company should be able to operate than to make a single unambiguous prediction.

The big challenge in scenario planning is in convincing decision makers to hold multiple futures possible and to overcome the urge to choose a single scenario (probably the one with the best-preferred outcomes). Only then will multiple options be at hand and a flexible and adaptive strategy can be set out.

Literature

For scenario planning we refer to the following sources:

- Van der Heijden, K (1998) *Scenarios: The art of strategic conversation*, John Wiley & Sons, Chichester
- Schwartz, P (1991) *The Art of the Long View: Planning for the future in an uncertain world*, Currency Doubleday, New York

Models for Step 3: Inside-out: Analysis

14

 Step 3: Inside-out: analysis

Step 3: Inside-out: analysis looks into the possibilities and impossibilities of the organization and links them to possibilities in the market and the organization's environment. This identifies the strategic options for the organization based on the organization's strengths and constraints. In this step several strategy models can be useful, particularly models that help analyse the organization's current performance and future potential.

MODELS THAT CAN BE USED IN STEP 3: INSIDE-OUT: ANALYSIS ARE:

- profitability analysis: DuPont scheme;
- financial ratio analysis;
- (social) network analysis;
- value propositions analysis;
- core competences;
- Kotler's 4 Ps of Marketing;
- The business model canvas.

Profitability analysis: DuPont scheme

Essence

The DuPont scheme can be used to illustrate how different factors influence financial performance indicators, such as return on capital employed (ROCE), return on assets (ROA) and return on equity (ROE). Although these ratios can be calculated with a simple formula, the model provides more value by giving insight into the underlying factors of those ratios. The model makes it possible to predict the effect of the variability of one or more variables.

Usefulness

The model can be used in several ways. First, it is a basic model to analyse the contribution of different activities to the company's overall profitability. Second, the model is used to study and predict the effect of possible management actions. Third, the model can be used for benchmarking, for example when different companies in an industry are compared to answer the question of why some companies achieve better returns than their peers. And finally, the model can be used for longitudinal benchmarking of the company's performance over time: do certain actions change the contribution to the overall firm's profitability?

The DuPont scheme shows significant differences between industries. Thus, a high score for ROE is caused by operational efficiency or capital efficiency. In the financial industry, for example, ROE is mainly determined by high leverage: large profits made with relatively few assets. During an investigation of the profitability of a specific company it is of great importance to choose its peers carefully (ie the companies that will be benchmarked).

Execution

The DuPont scheme consists of the following steps:

- Feed basic information into the model. Mostly these are accounting numbers related to revenue, interest-free liabilities, total cost, equity and current and non-current assets.
- Calculate the other parameters using the formulas in the figure. This provides initial insights into the current profitability.

FIGURE 14.1 Profitability analysis: DuPont scheme

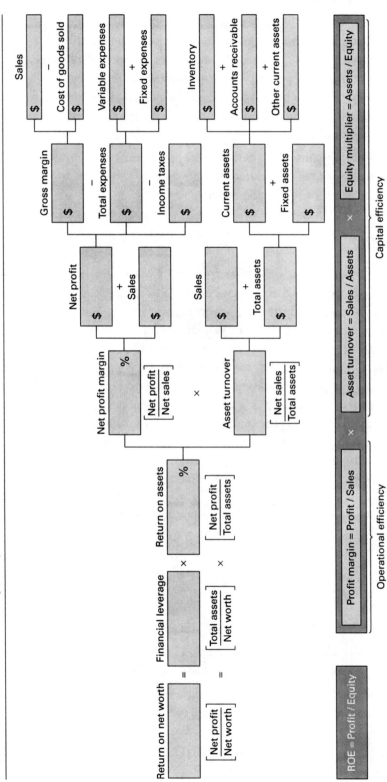

SOURCE: after Brown (1919)

- Determine which improvements are possible and what consequences they would have on costs, revenue and assets. The effect (of potential improvements) can either be calculated with the model or estimated on the side and then entered as new data input from which the model can show the effects on ROCE, ROA and ROE.

- Compare different alternative improvements on their effects and the investments required (in time, money or organizational capacity) to realize the improvement.

Verdict

The DuPont scheme originates from the work of F Donaldson Brown, who developed the scheme at DuPont in 1919. It has thus proven its value that it is still useful. It does, however, have its limitations. On the one hand, it lacks the capability to validate the numbers used, and it doesn't include all variables, such as cost of capital and return on financial assets. On the other hand, the DuPont scheme is often used not only for analysis, but also for deciding on actions. But taking appropriate actions to improve profitability is a challenging task, as the scheme does not give any insights into the underlying causes of a particular deviation or specific outcome in the scheme. Such insights are required to determine what actions are most appropriate. And finally, the DuPont scheme focuses exclusively on financial parameters and ignores other important factors such as employee motivation, even though non-financial factors are often very important. Other models, for instance the balanced score-card (see p 244), do include indicators to track a company's progress on non-financial key parameters.

Literature

The DuPont scheme is based on the following sources:

- Bodie, Z, Kane, A and Marcus, A J (2004) *Essentials of Investments*, Irwin/McGraw-Hill, New York

- Groppelli, A A and Nikbakht, E (2000) *Finance*, Barron's Educational Series, Hauppauge, NY

- Ross, S A, Westerfield, R and Jaffe, J (1999) *Corporate Finance*, McGraw-Hill, New York

Financial ratio analysis

FIGURE 14.2   Financial ratio analysis

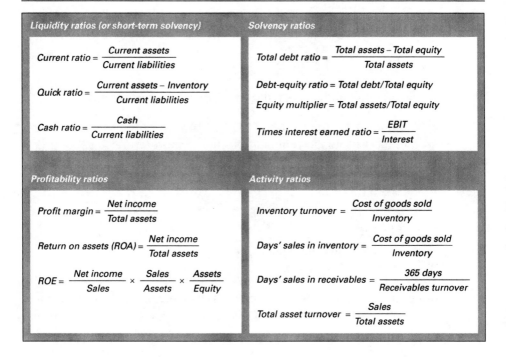

Liquidity ratios (or short-term solvency)	Solvency ratios
$\text{Current ratio} = \dfrac{\text{Current assets}}{\text{Current liabilities}}$	$\text{Total debt ratio} = \dfrac{\text{Total assets} - \text{Total equity}}{\text{Total assets}}$
$\text{Quick ratio} = \dfrac{\text{Current assets} - \text{Inventory}}{\text{Current liabilities}}$	$\text{Debt-equity ratio} = \text{Total debt/Total equity}$
	$\text{Equity multiplier} = \text{Total assets/Total equity}$
$\text{Cash ratio} = \dfrac{\text{Cash}}{\text{Current liabilities}}$	$\text{Times interest earned ratio} = \dfrac{EBIT}{Interest}$

Profitability ratios	Activity ratios
$\text{Profit margin} = \dfrac{\text{Net income}}{\text{Total assets}}$	$\text{Inventory turnover} = \dfrac{\text{Cost of goods sold}}{\text{Inventory}}$
$\text{Return on assets (ROA)} = \dfrac{\text{Net income}}{\text{Total assets}}$	$\text{Days' sales in inventory} = \dfrac{\text{Cost of goods sold}}{\text{Inventory}}$
$\text{ROE} = \dfrac{\text{Net income}}{\text{Sales}} \times \dfrac{\text{Sales}}{\text{Assets}} \times \dfrac{\text{Assets}}{\text{Equity}}$	$\text{Days' sales in receivables} = \dfrac{365 \ days}{\text{Receivables turnover}}$
	$\text{Total asset turnover} = \dfrac{\text{Sales}}{\text{Total assets}}$

Essence

The financial ratio analysis helps a company to analyse the financial performance of all its activities and products and services in all markets. Financial ratios are ratios based on the balance sheet and profit and loss account of the organization. This model can give two types of insight: on where the organization performs best and on what financial constraints and possibilities the company has when considering a new strategy.

Usefulness

Each organization considering a new strategy should perform a thorough financial analysis. The financial ratios analysis standardizes financial data, so that they are transparent and can be compared to those of competitors. Most of the ratios can also be calculated per product, per market, per business unit or any other company cross-section.

Financial ratio analysis provides a view of:

- the financial situation of the company;
- the extent to which the company will be able to pay its debts or attract investors;
- the possibilities to undertake more investments.

Execution

Financial ratio analysis includes four different types of ratio:

- Liquidity ratios indicate the extent to which the company is able to meet its financial obligations in the short term.
- Solvency ratios indicate the extent to which the company structurally meets all its financial obligations.
- Profitability ratios measure earnings capacity with the current capital.
- Activity ratios show the turnover periods.

To perform a financial ratio analysis, you simply collect the data mentioned in each of the formulas and then calculate the ratios. The required data are generally readily available as most ratios are part of regular management reports.

Verdict

A financial ratio analysis provides insights into the current state of affairs of an organization. It can also give an impression of the future financial situation if policies remained unchanged. However, financial ratio analysis should not be used in absolute terms. There is great risk in paying too much attention to the financial component in setting a new strategy: the results of the ratio analysis never set the direction for a new strategy, but only show the financial possibilities and limitations of the organization.

Literature

Financial ratio analysis is based on the following source:

- Keown, A J et al (1994) *Foundations of Finance: The logic and practice of financial management*, Prentice Hall, Englewood Cliffs, NJ

(Social) network analysis

FIGURE 14.3   (Social) network analysis

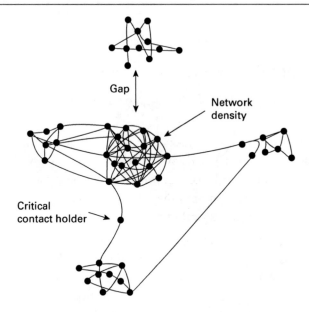

Essence

'It is not what you know, it's who you know.' For years, this was snobbish wisdom for those without knowledge, but in today's network economy this argument is gaining relevance. The essence of a network analysis is to see whether the company has a competitive advantage through its partners in offline and online networks. A (social) network analysis assesses the contacts of an organization's individual employees with individual stakeholders in the organization's business environment (for instance, contact with a supplier company's employee). These contacts are then depicted as a network consisting of nodes or points (representing individual actors within the network) and ties or lines (which represent relationships between individuals).

Usefulness

A network analysis revolves around the mapping of the contacts of individuals. This is obviously a snapshot and is often a complex and time-consuming task. It is a valuable exercise in the inside-out step to identify where the strength of the company's network lies (and potentially can be exploited). Mobilize and engage your network in the strategy process: most people find it an honour to be consulted or even considered an expert.

Execution

A network analysis follows a number of steps:

- Map the key players of your organization onto the organization chart.

- Map out the most important contacts of these individual key employees in the network of your organization (eg with suppliers, with customers, with competitors, with unions, with trade agencies etc). You can find these by asking your employees and/or analyse their online social network contacts.

- Cluster the contacts most relevant to the company: concentrate them around themes as 'information' (such as knowledge or customer networks), 'resources' (such as financial or funding networks) and 'status' (persons or institutions with which the organization would like to be associated).

- Assess the density of the network map. A dense network with many nodes (the dark spots in Figure 14.3) gives a good indication of how strongly your organization is embedded in that network. A dense network with many lines is also an indication that information will be shared rapidly and that mutual trust might be very strong within that group as there are so many relations within it. A dense network will – almost automatically – strengthen the ties between its nodes. By ensuring that the organization has more than one representative in that network, it could derive greater benefit from it. But be careful: the density says nothing about the quality of the network.

- Assess the gaps in the network. Where is there no connection? The lack of gaps is a proven indicator of a powerful network, which in turn benefits the company's strength, entrepreneurship and flexibility.

- Identify the critical contact holders in your organization. Who are the contact holders that link the organization to critical partners?

Make sure your organization looks for a back-up for these critical contact holders, as you don't want to jeopardize your network and the strengths you gain from it when an individual employee leaves the organization.

- Organize the network. Assign the management of networks to people who are explicitly responsible for that task. Go fetch, but more particularly – bring in. Don't transmit, but discuss and share. Nurture the critical contact holders: try to bind them to the company and build bridges across the gaps.

Verdict

Because most companies do not have a map of the organization's network nor of the strength that this network offers the organization, and because networks play a crucial role in the value creation and business models of modern-day companies, this exercise is highly recommended.

Literature

(Social) network analysis is based on the following sources:

- Burt, R S (2009) *Social Capital: Reaching out, reaching in*, Elgar Publishing, Northhampton, MA
- Surowiecki, J (2004) *The Wisdom of Crowds: Why the many are smarter than the few and how collective wisdom shapes business, economies, societies and nations*, Double Day, New York

Value propositions analysis

FIGURE 14.4 Value propositions analysis

	Customer needs						Customer needs			
WOW!						WOW!			★	
Good				•		Good	•		•	•
Average	•	•	•		•	Average		•		
Acceptable						Acceptable				
Below-par						Below-par				

Essence

A distinctive value proposition is the reason for a customer to choose a particular company. A value proposition that meets all customer needs but has a score equal to the value proposition of a competitor will not be interesting enough. It is about creating a 'wow!' factor that generates a unique customer experience. Not selected, not elected!

Usefulness

A value propositions analysis gives insights into the distinctiveness of the organization and shows the added value of the company's products and services as perceived by the customer. Customer perception is a crucial element in the analysis: most organizations overestimate themselves.

As well as being used in analysing the company's strengths and constraints in the inside-out step, the model can also be used in the operationalization step to test the distinctive character of the company's new strategy: it can serve as a stepping stone to defining new products or services.

Execution

This analysis of the value proposition will require interaction with customers and consists of several steps:

- Ask the customer what their needs really are and what they find authentic about your organization. Do this for all customers (if you have segmented your customers, do it for the most important segmented groups). After the overall questions, ask customers, for each phase in the sales process (for instance, the orientation, pre-selection, purchasing, use and after-sales phases), what they need and what they find authentic about your organization. These phases form the x-axis of the model (see Figure 14.4).

- Ask the customer (both overall and per segmented group) how the organization's approach to their needs compares with that of your main competitors. These scores form the y-axis of the model (see Figure 14.4).

- Determine the factors for which the organization can create a 'wow!' factor. These factors are what customers are willing to pay for and what make the organization stand out. What unique skills and characteristics must the company deliver to achieve that 'wow!' factor? Could they make the company unique tomorrow, too?

- Determine which factors and activities cost most. If these activities are less important in terms of the customers' experience, do not hesitate to reduce the organization's performance on these activities as long as there is a 'wow!' factor from other activities in return. If the highest costs are incurred for the most critical customer decision factors, you should identify how these costs can be reduced.

- Use the results of the analysis as input for the option step. If there is no 'wow!' factor and the costs of the crucial factors are structurally high, the organization needs more radical strategic options than just the optimization of existing value propositions. For example, it might need other business models or maybe a focus on another market.

Verdict

Insight into the distinctive character of the company is crucial in any strategy process: it helps to differentiate it and to build on its natural strengths. It also prevents possible pitfalls stemming from overconfidence. The model is interesting in several respects: it provides guidance for customer interaction and also gives insight into the actual value added by the company in relation to customer needs.

Literature

For value propositions analysis we refer to the following sources:

- Kaplan, R S and Norton, D P (2004) *Strategy Maps: Converting intangible assets into tangible outcomes*, Harvard Business Press, Cambridge, MA

- Barnes, C, Blake, H and Pinder, D (2009) *Creating and Delivering Your Value Proposition: Managing customer experience for profit*, Kogan Page, London

Core competences

FIGURE 14.5 Core competences

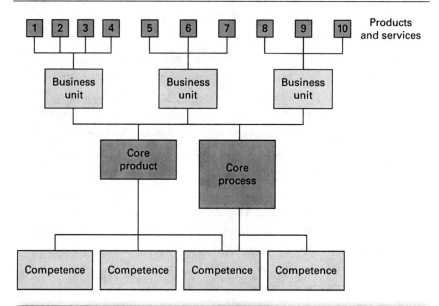

	Weak (1)	Average (3)	Strong (5)
Value for customer	Hardly visible	Translated into value added	New features and savings
Uniqueness	Generally available skills	State-of-the-art	Exclusivity is arguably distinctive
Leveragability	Fixed with existing products	Limited transmissability within the product or market group	Flexible availability throughout the organization gives competitive advantage
Inimitability	Some knowledge needed, but nothing proprietary	Long experience and extensive knowledge needed	Proprietary knowledge and specific expertise required
Internal level	Moderate. We do it sometimes	We can do this like our competitors can	Only we can do this at this level

SOURCE: after Hamel and Prahalad (1994)

Essence

Core competences are unique qualities of an organization that can be used to create value for customers. Such core competences enable an organization to access a wide variety of markets. Premiered by Prahalad and Hamel in their 1990 *Harvard Business Review* article (and their 1994 book), an assessment of an organization's core competences is now an essential element in formulating strategy. Giving proper attention to what your organization stands for and what makes it unique helps to answer the question as to what future possibilities your organization has. The process of stating the organization's core competences encourages management to think about strengths and properties which set the company apart from the competition.

Usefulness

To understand core competences, it must be understood that a company must have something special that makes it different from any other organization. When identifying core competences, you should look for what makes the organization unique. Ask yourself: what can your organization do that others cannot, or not as well as you can? Among the answers to this question you will find your core competences. Core competences can be the collective learning within an organization, the ability to integrate different skills and technologies, the power to offer resources and knowledge combined to provide superior products and services, or any other aspect that makes the organization stand out and makes it competitive. A core competence meets the following three conditions:

- It is valuable and provides benefits to buyers.
- Competitors cannot (easily) imitate it.
- It is rare and can be widely used in many products and markets.

A company which has identified and builds on its core competences can create long-term competitive advantage.

Execution

The starting point when analysing core competences is to ask yourself questions such as: What makes the organization different? What unique capabilities does the organization have? What can we successfully withstand competition on, 10 years from now? These types of question will reveal some of the strengths of your organization. Each of these can then be assessed individually to see if it is a core competence:

- Does this strength form the basis for competitive advantage?
- Does it characterize the company's uniqueness?
- Is it widespread in the organization?
- Is it difficult to copy?
- Is it difficult to identify as it seems to be a combination of technologies, processes and the way things are going in this organization?

If the above criteria are met, you can take it that you have identified your core competences. To make sure, you can rate the core competences (or putative core competences) on the following criteria:

- *Value for the customer.* Is the core competence visible to the customer? Does it provide added value or even new functionality or cost savings for the customer?
- *Uniqueness.* Is the company the only one with that competence in-house? Does the whole market have access to this competence?
- *Extensibility.* Is the competence related to only one product or market, or does the entire organization use this competence?
- *Thresholds.* Are there patents or licences to prevent other players acquiring this competence?
- *Internal level.* Is the company the best in this competence? Is it one of the better ones or is it not very good at it?

The higher the scores of the core competences, the firmer a foundation they can be for the organization to build on.

Verdict

In theory, the process of assessing core competences stimulates management to develop a strong understanding of the characteristics of their organization and of what distinguishes the company from its competitors. In practice, it is difficult to determine core competences. Even with the benefit of hindsight, it is difficult to point to the core competences underlying historical successes, let alone find pointers for the unknown future. Often core competences do not seem to be as unique or inimitable as management would like.

Nevertheless, the process of thinking about core competences makes management aware of what their organization is good at, where its uniqueness comes from, and how it can be sustained.

Literature

For core competences we refer to the following source:

- Hamel, G and Prahalad, C K (1994) *Competing for the Future: Breakthrough strategies for seizing control of your industry and creating the markets of tomorrow*, Harvard Business School Press, Cambridge, MA

Kotler's 4 Ps of marketing

FIGURE 14.6 Kotler's 4 Ps of marketing

SOURCE: after Kotler (1967)

Essence

Philip Kotler introduced what is commonly known as the 4 Ps of marketing: product, price, place and promotion. These four factors together form the marketing mix of an organization, enabling it to make deliberate and strategic decisions on the positioning in the marketplace of a product (or service), a group of products or even the organization as a whole. With an analysis of Kotler's 4 Ps of marketing, insight is created into the company's positioning and potential positioning.

Usefulness

Marketing (and sales) is the functional field in any organization that bridges the customer's perspective and the organizational perspective. An analysis of the elements that form the marketing mix of an organization, the 4 Ps introduced by Philip Kotler, gives insights into the company's current interactions with customers and the position the company has in the perception of its customers. These are valuable insights in the outside-in step. The analysis of Kotler's 4 Ps of marketing can be applied to the whole organization, or just to a product group or a specific product or market. This choice particularly depends on the homogeneity of the product portfolio and market.

This model can also be used in the operationalization step to formulate marketing strategies based on the new, overall strategic direction of the organization. In that step Kotler's 4 Ps of marketing help to:

- interpret the company's marketing policies, including use of digital technology and social media, and therefore the range of its desired (market) positioning;
- obtain insight into how important the target group is and how the use of the (marketing) tools fits with it;
- obtain insight into the effect of the marketing tools used.

Execution

In order to analyse the organization's position from the perspective of its customers in its (target) markets, the organization first has to gather information on each of the 4 Ps:

- *Product.* What functions does the product offer the customer? Does the range of products cover all customer needs? Should any products be adapted with regard to design, quality or functionality?
- *Price.* Does the price correspond with the value that the customer attaches to the product?
- *Place.* What do customers expect from us in terms of locations, availability (also online) and distribution? Are our products available in the right quantities, in the right place, at the right time?
- *Promotion.* Does our communication meet customers' expectations? Do we interact with our customers through the right channels and (social) media?

Next, an assessment is made of whether the 4 Ps are well enough aligned to each other (for instance, a low-price product group should not be exclusively available at a high-end retail store). This gives insights into what optimization can be done or what changes might be needed. It also serves as input for the operationalization step: based on the new, overall strategic direction a new interpretation, alignment and optimization can be given to the 4 Ps.

The analysis should also include the organization's activities and possibilities in the digital domain. Think, for instance, about crowdsourcing, internet-based discussion platforms or affiliate marketing (a type of performance-based marketing in which advertisers reward their partners (affiliates) for sales or leads that the affiliate has generated). And don't forget your online social media!

Verdict

Kotler's 4 Ps is particularly useful in highly competitive markets, where a company must be continuously aware of keeping its established position and market share, while maintaining margins. Small shifts in the market can have relatively large consequences for operations.

Over the years, the 4 Ps have become an institution. But there have also been countless suggestions to improve or enhance the model, by adding more Ps. Numerous articles and discussions suggest at least adding People as the fifth P. As with any model, the 4 Ps are just a conceptual framework to help structure information, so feel free to elaborate on them.

Literature

For Kotler's 4 Ps we refer to the following source:

- Kotler, P and Armstrong, G (1967 and 2011) *Marketing Management*, Prentice Hall, Upper Saddle River, NJ (2011, 14th edn)

The business model canvas

FIGURE 14.7   Business model canvas

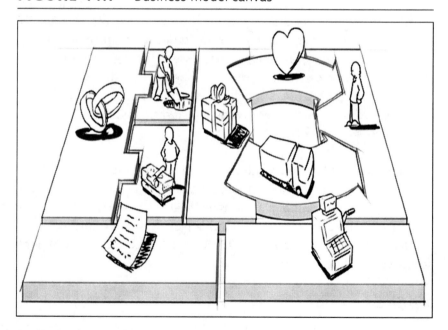

SOURCE: after Osterwalder (2004)

(continued on opposite page)

The Business Model Canvas

Designed for:

Designed by:

On: Day Month Year

Iteration: No

Key Partners

Who are our Key Partners?
Who are our key Suppliers?
Which Key Resources are we acquiring from partners?
Which Key Activities do partners perform?

motivations for partnerships:
Optimization and economy
Reduction of risk and uncertainty
Acquisition of particular resources and activities

Key Activities

What Key Activities do our Value Propositions require?
Our Distribution Channels?
Customer Relationships?
Revenue streams?

categories
Production
Problem Solving
Platform/Network

Key Resources

What Key Resources do our Value Propositions require?
Our Distribution Channels?
Customer Relationships?
Revenue Streams?

types of resources
Physical
Intellectual (brand patents, copyrights, data)
Human
Financial

Value Propositions

What value do we deliver to the customer?
Which one of our customer's problems are we helping to solve?
What bundles of products and services are we offering to each Customer Segment?
Which customer needs are we satisfying?

characteristics
Newness
Performance
Customization
"Getting the Job Done"
Design
Brand/Status
Price
Cost Reduction
Risk Reduction
Accessibility
Convenience/Usability

Customer Relationships

What type of relationship does each of our Customer Segments expect us to establish and maintain with them?
Which ones have we established?
How are they integrated with the rest of our business model?
How costly are they?

examples
Personal assistance
Dedicated Personal Assistance
Self-Service
Automated Services
Communities
Co-creation

Channels

Through which Channels do our Customer Segments want to be reached?
How are we reaching them now?
How are our Channels integrated?
Which ones work best?
Which ones are most cost-efficient?
How are we integrating them with customer routines?

channel phases:
1. Awareness – How do we raise awareness about our company's products and services?
2. Evaluation – How do we help customers evaluate our organization's Value Proposition?
3. Purchase – How do we allow customers to purchase specific products and services?
4. Delivery – How do we deliver a Value Proposition to customers?
5. After sales – How do we provide post-purchase customer support?

Customer Segments

For whom are we creating value?
Who are our most important customers?

Mass Market
Niche Market
Segmented
Diversified
Multi-sided Platform

Cost Structure

What are the most important costs inherent in our business model?
Which Key Resources are most expensive?
Which Key Activities are most expensive?

IS YOUR BUSINESS MORE:
Cost Driven (leanest cost structure, low price value proposition, maximum automation, extensive outsourcing)
Value Driven (focused on value creation, premium value proposition)

SAMPLE CHARACTERISTICS:
Fixed Costs (salaries, rents, utilities)
Variable costs
Economies of scale
Economies of scope

Revenue Streams

For what value are our customers really willing to pay?
For what do they currently pay?
How are they currently paying?
How would they prefer to pay?
How much does each Revenue Stream contribute to overall revenues?

types:
Asset sale/Usage fee
Subscription Fees
Lending/Renting/Leasing
Licensing
Brokerage fees
Advertising

FIXED PRICING
List Price
Product feature dependent
Customer segment dependent
Volume dependent

dynamic pricing
Negotiation(bargaining)
Yield Management
Real-time-Market

www.businessmodelgeneration.com

Essence

The business model canvas simply describes the rationale of how an organization creates, delivers and preserves value. It provides a common language to describe, visualize, develop and explore business models. On the basis of nine basic building blocks, one can see at a glance how a company does its business and earns money. The model is highly visual and shows how the building blocks interlock.

Usefulness

The business model canvas has quickly become popular thanks to its highly visual, integrated view, showing how a business is actually run. It is a perfect tool for analysis in the inside-out step. The business model canvas helps to generate new ideas, either by analysing your own company's business or by analysing your competitors' business.

The model can also be used in the choice step (or even the operationalization step) to make the strategic options under consideration (or the strategic option(s) chosen) more specific. With the business model canvas, alternative business models can be developed or even completely new business models invented which had not previously been considered.

Execution

The business model canvas consists of nine generic building blocks:

- *Customer segments*. For whom do we create value? Who are our most important customers?
- *Value proposition*. What value do we provide our customers? What customer problems do we solve?
- *Servicing model or channels*. How do we (want to) reach our customers? What works best, what is cost-effective?
- *Customer relationship*. What relationship do customers in each segment expect? Which service is required for which type of customer?
- *Revenues*. How do we make earnings from our customers: what do they pay for? How much do customers pay now or are willing to pay? How do we generate income with each transaction?
- *Key activities*. Which activities are needed to create and deliver the value proposition, to use the channels, to foster relationships and to reach the customers?

- *Key resources.* Which resources are necessary to create and deliver the value proposition, the channels and the customer relationship?

- *Key partners.* Who are our main partners? What resources do they have and what activities do they do (better than us) that enables us to deliver value to our customers?

- *Cost structure.* What are the costs to create and deliver our added value to our customers? Which of our (partners') important resources are the most expensive? Which main activities cost the most? How do we incur costs with each transaction?

Using the business model canvas starts with printing out the canvas on a large surface (see Figure 14.7). The canvas is then used as a drawing board on which groups of people can jointly start sketching and scribing, or paste Post-It notes on it. Each of the nine building blocks is to be considered and discussed. Many digital tools (an app for tablet computers, online toolbox and serious game) are available for the business model canvas.

Verdict

A pitfall of the business model canvas is that the analysis of its nine building blocks is often based on assumptions rather than on facts. In particular, poor knowledge about existing customers but also about new segments often leads to unsubstantiated assumptions. A second pitfall, certainly when used in the options step, is that substantiation of a strategic option is prematurely regarded as the best or only business model for that strategic option (too much detail and insufficient exploration). The business model canvas is particularly suitable for creating multiple, alternative models. It is a hands-on tool that fosters understanding and creativity.

Literature

For the business model canvas we refer to the following sources:

- Osterwalder, A and Pigneur, Y (2010) *Business Model Generation: A handbook for visionaries, game changers and challengers*, John Wiley & Sons, Chichester

- Osterwalder, A (2004) *The Business Model Ontology. A proposition in a design science approach*, University of Lausanne, Switzerland

15 Models for Step 4: Options

 ## Step 4: Options

Step 4: Options brings together the insights from the outside-in perspective and the inside-out perspective (see Steps 2 and 3 in Part 2) and translates them into strategic options. Multiple strategic options can be developed. In the options step the options on this 'long list' are assessed, supplemented if needed and finally curtailed to come to a 'short list' of the most promising options. In this step several strategy models can be useful, particularly models that help compare and weigh the different strategic options.

MODELS THAT CAN BE USED IN STEP 4: OPTIONS ARE:

- SWOT analysis;
- Porter's generic strategies;
- Treacy and Wiersema's value disciplines.

SWOT analysis

FIGURE 15.1   SWOT analysis

	Opportunities	Threats
Strengths	**SO strategies** use strengths to take advantage of opportunities	**ST strategies** take advantage of opportunities by overcoming weaknesses
Weaknesses	**WO strategies** use strengths to avoid threats	**WT strategies** minimize weaknesses to avoid threats

Essence

Any company undertaking strategic planning must, at some point, assess its strengths and weaknesses. When combined with an inventory of opportunities and threats within or beyond the company's environment, the company conducts a so-called SWOT analysis: establishing its current position in light of its Strengths, Weaknesses, Opportunities and Threats.

Usefulness

The SWOT analysis provides helpful information for matching resources and capabilities to the competitive environment in which the organization operates. The model can be used as a tool for devising and selecting strategy, and is equally applicable in any decision-making situation, provided the desired objective has been clearly defined.

Execution

A SWOT analysis starts with identifying the company's strengths, weaknesses, opportunities and threats. Strengths and weaknesses are internal factors. They are the skills and assets – or lack of them – that are intrinsic to the company and which add to, or detract from, the company's value relative to competitive forces. Strengths and weaknesses can be measured with the help of an internal analysis (see also Step 3 (Inside-out: analysis) in Part 2 and key strategic models for this step in Part 3). Technologies, skills, financial resources, capacity, ICT, management resources, and culture should then be examined on a company-wide scale. Opportunities and threats, however, are external factors: they are not created by the company, but emerge due to the activity of competitors and changes in the market dynamics. They occur due to external macro environmental forces, such as demographic, economic, technological, political, legal, social and cultural dynamics, as well as external industry-specific environmental forces, such as customers, competitors, distribution channels and suppliers. Opportunities and threats can be measured with the help of an external analysis (see also Step 2 (Outside-in: scenarios) in Part 2 and key strategic models for this step in Part 3).

Scans of the internal and external environment are therefore an important part of the SWOT analysis to identify:

- *Strengths (S).* What does the company do well? Does the company have a technological or knowledge advantage? Does it, for example, benefit from an experienced sales force? Does it have a state-of-the-art web shop? Note: external opportunities, such as a new market, are not strengths.
- *Weaknesses (W).* These are the things that a company lacks or does not do well. Does the company have enough capital to

invest? Or is there a lack of relevant knowledge or innovation power? Does the company have antiquated machinery? Note: do not identify threats as a weakness. A company's weaknesses should always be viewed in relation to its competitors: if everyone performs equally poorly, the poor performance is not a pronounced weakness.

- *Opportunities (O)*. Could the company benefit from any technological developments or demographic changes taking place, or could the demand for its products or services increase as a result of successful partnerships? Could assets be used in other ways? For example, existing products could be introduced in new markets, or R&D could be turned into cash by licensing concepts or technologies, or selling patents. There are many perceived opportunities: whether they are real depends on the extent and level of detail included in the market analysis.

- *Threats (T)*. One company's opportunity may well be another company's threat. Changes in regulation, substitute technologies and other forces in the competitive field may pose serious threats if, for example, they result in lower sales, higher cost of operations or capital, the inability to break even, shrinking margins, or if profitability and rates of return drop significantly below market expectations. Opportunities and threats can both be classified according to their potential impact as well as their actual probability.

The outcomes of the internal and external analyses can be placed in a so-called confrontation matrix (Figure 15.2). In this matrix, the strengths, weaknesses, opportunities and threats are listed and combined. Points are given for each of the combinations: the more important they are, the more points awarded. This confrontation leads to an identification of the organization's primary, and often urgent, strategic issues.

The next step is to evaluate the actions the firm should take based on its SWOT analysis. Should the company focus on using its strengths to capitalize on opportunities, or acquire strengths in order to seize opportunities? Moreover, should the company continue to actively try to minimize weaknesses and to avoid threats?

FIGURE 15.2   Confrontation matrix in the SWOT analysis

	O1	O2	O3	O4	O5	T1	T2	T3	T4	T5
S1										
S2										
S3										
S4										
S5										
W1										
W2										
W3										
W4										
W5										

SO and WT strategies are quite straightforward. A company should do what it is good at when the opportunity arises and avoid activities/businesses for which it does not have the competences. WO strategies are much less straightforward and much more risky. If a company decides to take on an opportunity despite not having the required strengths, it must:

- develop the required strengths; or
- buy or borrow the required strengths; or
- outmanoeuvre the competition.

In essence, companies that use ST strategies will 'buy or bust' their way out of trouble. This happens when big players fend off smaller players by means of expensive price wars, through enormous marketing budgets or multiple-channel promotions. Some companies use scenario planning (see Step 2) in an attempt to anticipate these types of threat.

Verdict

A SWOT analysis is a valuable self-assessment tool for management. The elements – strengths, weaknesses, opportunities and threats – seem deceptively simple, but in fact deciding the company's strengths and

weaknesses, and assessing the impact and probability of the opportunities and threats in the external environment, is far more complex
than it looks at first sight. Furthermore, beyond the classification of the
SWOT elements, the model offers no assistance with the tricky task of
translating the findings into strategic alternatives. The inherent risk of
making incorrect assumptions when assessing the SWOT elements
often causes management to dither when it comes to choosing between
various strategic alternatives, frequently resulting in unnecessary and/or
undesirable delay.

Literature

The SWOT analysis is based on the following sources:

- Abell, D F and Hammond, J S (1979) *Strategic Marketing Planning: Problems and analytical approaches*, Prentice Hall, Englewood Cliffs, NJ
- Hill, T and Westbrook, R (1997) SWOT analysis: it's time for a product recall, *Long Range Planning*, 30 (1), pp 46–52

Porter's generic strategies

FIGURE 15.3   Porter's generic strategies

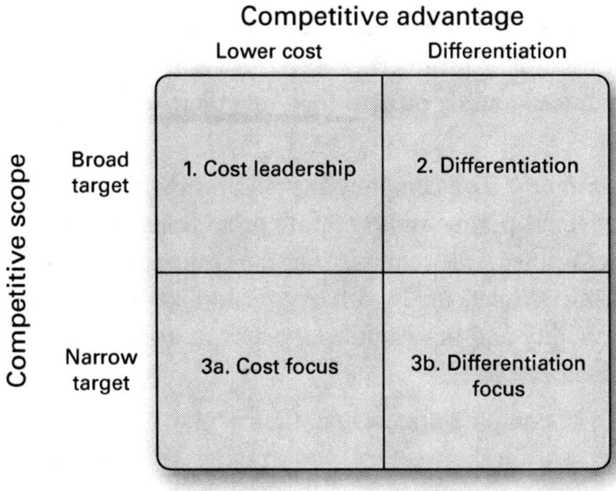

SOURCE: after Porter (1985)

Essence

In his 1980 book *Competitive Strategy*, Michael Porter identified three generic strategies by means of which companies can achieve a competitive advantage in a market. The strategies are divided into two dimensions: the strategic advantage that a company seeks to offer to the customer (price or specificity) and the degree of market segmentation (market as a whole or niche) the company uses within this context. The strategies are cost leadership, differentiation and focus.

Usefulness

Porter's generic strategies offer support when fleshing out the strategy. For all options generated, it should be clear to some degree to whom the strategy is directed (wide or limited market scope) and how it results in a competitive advantage (distinctive in value added or cost price). Using this model, the strategic options are classified and ranked. It can therefore be used when listing the options for the choice step. The model offers insight into the basis for the competitive advantage, possibly up to PMC level, and provides a starting point for discussion with regard to the corporate strategy pursued.

Execution

The three generic strategies are:

- *Cost leadership*. The company seeks cost advantage and supplies standard products at lower prices than its competitors. This requires, among other things, an efficient production process.
- *Differentiation*. The company supplies products with distinctive properties and therefore provides added value to the customer. This requires that the company distinguishes itself from competitors by offering customization, providing higher quality and innovation, or better customer service and convenience.
- *Focus*. The company focuses on a particular segment in the industry; within that segment the strategy is to achieve a cost or differentiation advantage.

There are many ways to implement the model. In its simplest form, the strategic options are placed in the model. A little more insight is provided when the strategies of competitors (for a given PMC) are also placed in the model. In this way it is immediately clear where market openings still exist and where market saturation seems to occur. Finally, the model becomes even more powerful when PMCs are shown within the model at a higher level of detail. This increases its effectiveness, because it becomes clear for which businesses the company should focus on a small group of customers and for which ones it should focus on a broader market. It also increases its efficiency, indicating which businesses are delivered at the lowest possible cost and which ones offer optimum added value.

Verdict

The model is extremely simple in its application but at the same time forces the participants in the process of formulating strategy to discuss the positioning of the company and its current portfolio: in what way does the company really distinguish itself from competitors? In the same way, potential future PMCs can be mapped. The model increases in value if the positions of competitors are also drawn up. Use of the model within the strategic dialogue is therefore highly recommended.

Literature

For Porter's generic strategies we refer to the following source:

- Porter, M E (1985) *Competitive Advantage*, Free Press, New York

Treacy and Wiersema's value disciplines

FIGURE 15.4   Treacy and Wiersema's value disciplines

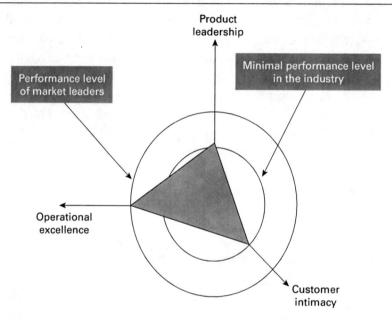

SOURCE: after Treacy and Wiersema (1995)

Essence

The basic idea of the model is that no company can be all things to all people. The key issues upon which a company will fail or succeed in delivering unique value to its customers by fulfilling their needs can be identified and discussed using the value disciplines model. Every good business should have a value proposition, an operating model (ie a specific business model) and a value discipline. According to Treacy and Wiersema, there are three generic value disciplines that enable an organization to deliver value to its customers: operational excellence, product leadership and customer intimacy.

Usefulness

Organizations constantly question the needs of their customers and the true value of what they offer. The value disciplines help to answer these questions. The use of this model often provides new insights, especially when an organization reflects on its 'raison d'être' and how it wants to serve its (desired) customers.

Execution

The three value disciplines are:

- *Operational excellence:* striving for optimal operational costs. These organizations are leaders in operational excellence, delivering relatively high-quality products at relatively low prices. But such organizations do not use the latest products or services. Instead, they look at the direction of the market and undertake activities that are recognized as critical success factors, and they do it well. Their attention is focused on efficiency, streamlining processes, integration within the supply chain, low inventories, no frills and the dynamics of the control volumes. It's about standardization of (modular) products and processes.

- *Product leadership:* the best product (in technical terms and using the latest technology) to offer. Product leaders are inventors and brand marketers. These organizations are constantly experimenting with new products, services or experiences. Their markets are unfamiliar. Margins may be high, simply because of the high risks. Research and development should therefore be focused on design and short lead-times in order to produce a few big-hit singles to offset the undoubtedly numerous failures. Technological innovation and product lifecycle management are essential.

- *Customer intimacy:* the best total solutions in order to be the most reliable and respond optimally to customer needs. Leaders in customer intimacy will do anything to keep their (small) circle of customers satisfied as long as they believe that the customer is worth it. They do not believe in one-off transactions and they invest time and money in a long-term relationship with a few customers. They want to know everything about their customers and work closely with them. They focus on exceeding expectations, as well as customer retention, lifetime value, reliability and 'always being nice'. It's all about customer relationship management (CRM).

Opting for a specific value proposition depends on matching the organization's capabilities with the requirements necessary to fulfil the customer's needs. Three rounds of discussions are usually needed to gain full understanding of the situation. In the first round the focus is explicitly on customers and competitors within the sector, in the second round the focus is on the company itself, and in the third round each option is further fleshed out.

Verdict

Treacy and Wiersema's value disciplines is highly regarded and widely accepted. However, too often the model is misused, for example when consultants and managers force an organization to choose and excel in only a single value proposition. In this way, the model leads to forced decision making. Such a one-dimensional choice is short-sighted and will focus too much on a single value proposition. True market leaders do not excel just in one (predetermined) value discipline, but also compete on all value disciplines or even initiate new ones, such as sustainability. In addition, market leaders try to raise industry standards.

Furthermore, the value disciplines focus on value for the customer, and inherently emphasize the natural tendency of organizations to keep in step with changing customer needs and market developments in an attempt to do everything possible to avoid losing a customer. However, over-focusing on customer needs will ultimately result in the organization paying less attention to its own competences and capabilities. Finally, the three value disciplines do not cover all possible strategic options. Strategic decisions such as 'make or buy?' and corporate branding versus product branding, for example, are not covered by this model. It is therefore recommended that you use the model in combination with other strategic models.

Literature

For Treacy and Wiersema's value disciplines we refer to the following source:

- Treacy, M and Wiersema, F (1995) *The Discipline of Market Leaders: Choose your customers, narrow your focus, dominate your market*, Perseus Books, New York

Models for Step 5: Choice

16

 Step 5: Choice

*S*tep 5: Choice is about making a realistic choice from the strategic options selected in Step 4. In this step, these options are evaluated and assessed in order to make a final choice. Several strategy models can be useful here, particularly models that help evaluate the different strategic options and that facilitate decision making.

MODELS THAT CAN BE USED IN STEP 5: CHOICE ARE:

- strategy assessment matrix;
- risk–reward analysis;
- MABA analysis.

Strategy assessment matrix

FIGURE 16.1 Strategy assessment matrix

	Strategic option 1	Strategic option 2	Strategic option 3
Usefulness • Concurs with mission statement • Matches ambitions • Meets turnover requirements • Fits with risk profile • ...			
Feasibility • Fits with room for investment • Fits with current capabilities • Right partners available • Level of complexity to implement •			
Acceptability • Employees • Shareholders • Customers • Suppliers •			
Reward • Profit increase • Turnover increase • Market share increase • Innovation increase • Av. return on investment • ...			

Essence

The strategy assessment matrix is a model that helps to assess and prioritize different strategic options. The model holds different criteria to weigh the different strategic options. It is a tool to objectify the assessment of strategic options and the subsequent choice of an option.

Usefulness

Using the strategy assessment matrix is a practical and convenient way to evaluate various strategic options. With this model a more broad evaluation can be made. It overcomes the pitfall of looking predominantly at financial returns when choosing a new strategic direction. When including more than the financial criterion in assessing options, the organization can make a more balanced judgement and include factors such as acceptability. The strategy assessment matrix enables options to be scored on multiple criteria, and thus enables priority to be assigned according to the weighted scores.

Execution

The strategy assessment matrix can be customized for each organization. It is in that sense more of a framework. Often in the searchlight step the criteria which the strategy has to meet have already been stated, for instance 'our new strategy must lead to an increase in turnover up to so many millions'. At the start of the choice step a final list of these criteria can be drawn up, with or without additions or alterations to the original set of criteria. The extent to which a strategic option meets the criteria which were originally set is referred to as the usefulness of an option: if it doesn't meet those criteria the option might not be useful to the organization's ambitions. The most common additional criteria, after usefulness, which is the first criterion chosen, are those concerning feasibility and acceptability. Feasibility relates, for instance, to the extent to which the required investment for a strategic option fits the financial capabilities of the organization, the extent to which the organization has the required competences and/or the extent to which the organization has the ability to find the right collaborative partners. The acceptability of a strategic option includes how different stakeholders relate to the option: positive, neutral or negative. And, if desired, other factors, such as those relating to specific scenarios (from the outside-in step), can be added.

After choosing the criteria, each criterion is broken down into more specific and measurable elements. For instance, usefulness is measured using elements such as 'meeting turnover requirement' or 'contribution to organization's ambition', while feasibility is measured using elements such as 'fits within the space for investments' or 'fits with current capabilities'. Acceptability is often broken down into a score per (group of) stakeholders.

The strategy assessment matrix is then set up by placing the various strategic alternatives in the columns of the matrix, and placing the criteria on which these are to be scored on the rows. The scoring method depends on the criterion and is to be agreed for each criterion beforehand. Scoring options can include the use of exact numbers, assigning pluses and minuses, or ranking the options. By scoring the various options on all criteria, a first attempt at prioritization can be made. It can sometimes be interesting to let a broader group score the options on the criteria rather than just those who are to make the final decision. By broadening the group, the assessment of the options is further objectified. The subsequent discussion then gives scope for exchanging arguments and reaching a consensus.

Verdict

This matrix can be used as a practical and convenient way to assess strategic options. Criteria can be customized and are easily added. Information from other steps in the strategy process can be used in preparing this matrix. However, the scores in the strategy assessment matrix are not enough in themselves: it is the reasoning behind the scores that leads to a (joint) decision. So try to preserve the arguments from the discussions (on the pluses and minuses), so they have not been lost if reconsideration of the choice is necessary in the future.

Literature

The strategy assessment matrix is based on the following source:

- Pietersma, P and Van den Berg, G J J B (2012) *The Grand Book on Strategy: In dialogue to strategic advantage* [translated from Dutch: *Het Groot Strategieboek: In dialoog naar een strategische voorsprong*], Academic Service, The Hague

Risk–reward analysis

FIGURE 16.2   Risk–reward analysis

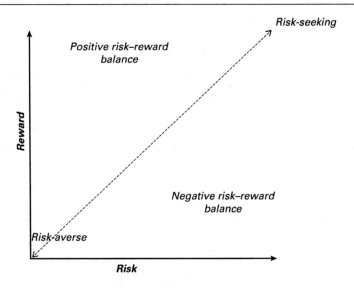

Essence

Risk–reward analysis compares the potential income (rewards) of strategic options with the associated risks. The result is an assessment of the attractiveness of strategic options, which serves as a basis for decision making. Risk–reward analysis works in the same way as a risk–return analysis for financial products, such as appreciating bonds and options.

Usefulness

Risk–reward analysis can be performed on every level of detail. The top manager could write it down on the back of a beer coaster or a team of analysts may perform an in-depth analysis, including extensive market research, ROI calculations, sensitivity analyses and scenario development. The basic steps for the analysis, however, remain the same.

Risk–reward analysis allows completely different options or combinations thereof to be compared. It sets the risk of an option against the rewards which the option could bring. This will rank the strategic options according to the trade-off between associated risk and expected reward.

Execution

A risk–reward analysis starts with a list of feasible strategic options. For each of the options the potential returns are assessed. This includes input from market analysis to determine market share increases and financial returns, and also information on investment requirements, cost-saving potential, possible yield etc. Often information on qualitative factors, such as a better image, completeness of product range, strategic expansion of capacities such as technology, is also included in assessing the potential return of a strategic option. The required input and information are potentially already available from the outside-in step, the inside-out step or the options step. Subsequently, for each strategic option the associated risks are assessed. Factors to be considered include industrial threats, effects on relationships in the supply chain and exit barriers, but also factors such as exclusion of other options and vulnerability from overstretching financial reserves. The options can then be plotted on a risk–reward analysis chart: risk on one axis and reward on the other. This chart is then the starting point for discussions, both on why the options are ranked in the given order and on finding ways to reduce the risk associated with options with the highest reward potential. Likewise, ways to increase potential reward for relatively safe options are discussed. These discussions result in prioritization of the different options. The ultimate goal of risk–reward analysis is to balance risks and rewards according to the company's desired optimum. This optimum often is based on the company's desired risk profile: risk-averse organizations will focus on the long-term survival of the organization and will therefore accept lower rewards, while more enterprising, risk-seeking companies will accept more risks as they pursue the highest rewards. In any case, the balance between the two must be positive.

An alternative to risk–reward analysis is risk–reward–resource analysis or RRR analysis. This alternative analysis includes the amount of resources required per option. In the chart the amount of resources required is then displayed as a bubble, which increases in size as resource requirements increase.

Verdict

One of the main pitfalls in strategic management is that decisions are taken on the basis of limited information and a few different perspectives.

Inaccurate, optimistic or unrealistic predictions about the possible rewards of strategic options relegate risk to the background. While rewards are often overestimated, risks are often underestimated. The result is that the strategic options are overstated. The disadvantage of risk–reward analysis is that the evaluation of the dimensions – risk, reward and possibly resources – is the result of a complex interaction of factors. The weight of each factor and the interrelationship between them are often influenced by emotion. To maximize the effect of using risk–reward analysis, all potential risks and rewards should be analysed in detail, with sufficient attention given to the underlying coherence and complexity of factors. This helps to overcome oversimplification.

Literature

Risk–reward analysis is based on the following sources:

- Van Assen, M F, Van den Berg, G J J B and Pietersma, P (2008) *Key Management Models: The 60+ models every manager needs to know*, 2nd edn, Prentice Hall, Upper Saddle River, NJ

- Sperandeo, V (1998) *Trader Vic II: Principles or professional speculation*, John Wiley & Sons, New York

MABA analysis

FIGURE 16.3   MABA analysis

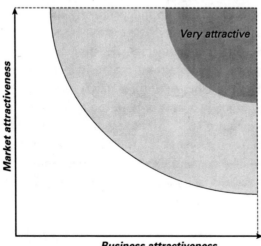

Essence

MABA analysis assesses the relative market attractiveness (MA) and business attractiveness (BA) of a strategic option. The strategic options with both high MA and high BA are those most preferred for an organization.

Usefulness

MABA analysis is used to assess strategic options and help determine which option is the most preferred one for the organization. MA is determined by external indicators such as profit margins, market size, market growth (expectations), concentration, stability and rivalry. BA is determined by internal indicators such as fit with current capabilities, building on the current product and services portfolio, allowing for an interesting value chain position and matching organizational ambitions.

Apart from use in the choice step to assess strategic options on their attractiveness, MABA analysis can also be useful in the operational-ization step to analyse and interpret the company's product or services portfolio and to make decisions about new business opportunities.

Execution

The first step in a MABA analysis is to decide which indicators are useful to the two dimensions of attractiveness and determine to what extent they are important (weighing). This will objectify the discussion on the options, and it is clear that an independently derived set of indicators leads to more objective results. The second step is scoring the strategic options on the different indicators. Because these are sometimes not mutually exclusive, it is important to consider the extent to which one option influences the other option's attractiveness. The final step is representing the options in a matrix with the dimensions of attractiveness on the axes (see Figure 16.3). Managers and advisers alike tend to place the most attractive options in the top left- or top right-hand corner of the matrix. To emphasize the most attractive options, some split the matrix into quadrants or multiple blocks or even use curved or diagonal lines as dividers (see Figure 16.3).

Verdict

MABA analysis is a powerful tool for companies to assess strategic options and business opportunities. In situations where financial resources or management time is scarce, the model offers a solution to decision making. Make sure that the model does not lose its main quality: simplifying a complex situation. MABA analysis is less powerful when it is applied to the existing activities of the organization.

The shortcoming of MABA analysis lies in the choosing and weighting of indicators. Different indicators and weights often lead to very different outcomes. There is a risk that a false sense of objectivity arises with the choice of some quantitative indicators. MABA analysis is limited to two or three artificially combined dimensions. Further analyses must be carried out with the aid of other indicators to compensate for this.

Literature

MABA analysis is based on the following source:

- Kotler, P and Armstrong, G (1967 and 2011) *Marketing Management*, Prentice Hall, Upper Saddle River, NJ (2011, 14th edn)

17

Models for Step 6: Operationalization

⇢⇢⇢Step 6: Operationalization

---

*S*tep 6: *Operationalization* marks the end of strategy formulation and the beginning of strategy implementation. In the operationalization step, the chosen strategic direction is translated into plans for the organization on how to execute the new strategy. Also, change plans are drawn up to show how the organization wants to get to where it aspires to be, including how it wants to engage internal and external stakeholders during the change.

A multitude of strategy models can be used in the operationalization step, particularly those that help detail the strategy for the different components (such as business units or functional areas) and/or aspects. Strategy models that help set an approach and framework for change management and change communication are also useful. In this step the business model canvas (see also p 184) can be used again to design new business models for the organization or to redesign existing ones. If the model has already been used in the inside-out step, that input can now be used as the basis for redesign.

MODELS THAT CAN BE USED IN STEP 6: OPERATIONALIZATION ARE:

- the 7-S framework;
- project management;
- socially engineered change;
- change quadrants model;
- change communication model.

The 7-S framework

FIGURE 17.1 7-S framework

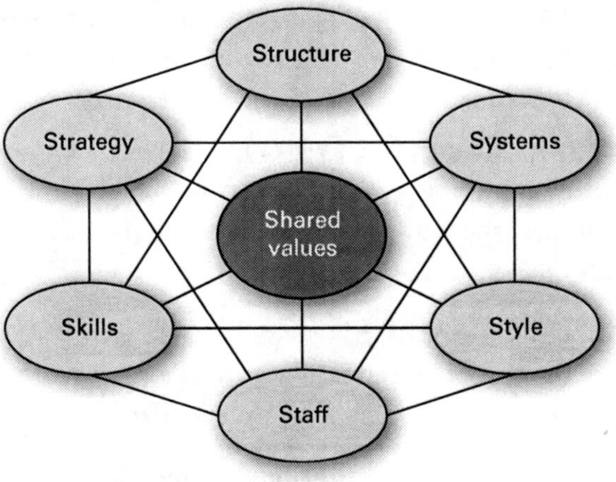

SOURCE: after Ragiel and Friga (2001)

Essence

The 7-S framework is a diagnostic model used to organize a company effectively. Strategy implementation needs to consider how a strategy can work in conjunction with seven key elements: strategy, structure, systems, shared values, style, staff and skills. The premise of the model is that these seven elements have to be aligned, because they mutually reinforce each other.

Usefulness

The 7-S framework is an appropriate model for defining and analysing the most important elements of an organization. The framework can be used to design a new organization or to identify gaps and inconsistencies in the current organization. The seven 'S's' that make up the 7-S framework are as follows:

- *Strategy* refers to the chosen strategic direction of the organization (the starting point for the operationalization step).

- *Structure* refers to organizational structure, hierarchy and coordination, including the division of labour and the integration of tasks and activities.

- *Systems* are the primary and secondary processes that the organization employs to get things done, such as manufacturing systems, supply planning and order-taking processes.

- *Shared values* include the core beliefs and expectations that employees have of their company and are those values that underlie the company's very reason for existence. They are therefore placed at the centre of the framework.

- *Style* refers to the unwritten yet tangible evidence of how the organization really sets priorities and spends its time. Symbolic behaviour and the way management relate to their workers are exemplary indicators of the organization's style.

- *Staff* comprises the people in the organization.

- *Skills* are the distinctive capabilities of the total workforce and the organization as a whole, and are independent of individuals.

The seven interdependent organizational elements may be classified as either 'hard' or 'soft'. Hard (rational, tangible) elements are strategy, structure and systems. Soft (emotional) elements are shared values, style, staff and skills. A well-designed organization has a proper balance between the hard and soft elements.

Execution

The 7-S framework can best be used as a matrix or table for assessing the impact of the organization's proposed strategy. Construct a matrix in which conflicts and possible solutions or combinations of the seven S's are listed. Then either decide how to adjust the strategy, or change the organization to adapt to the strategy.

Verdict

The 7-S framework is a clear and robust diagnostic model. However, the 'soft' elements present a challenge because it is hard to define them in a measurable way. Consequently, the 7-S framework is often used in a stripped-down manner: listing issues against a checklist. Used in this way, it does not provide improvement suggestions. After all, the development of a new organizational capability requires more than an understanding of why the current capabilities are insufficient. However, there are plenty of additional models that operate on the level of the individual S's and may unlock unforeseen potential.

Literature

For the 7-S framework we refer to the following source:

- Ragiel, E M and Friga, P N (2001) *The McKinsey Mind: Understanding and implementing the problem solving tools and management techniques*, McGraw-Hill, New York

Project management

Essence

Most change plans consist of multiple projects. The project management model helps to bring a project to successful completion. It includes those aspects that are of importance for completing a project on time and within budget and with the intended objectives. It is a complex process.

Usefulness

A project is a clear collective action with a clear objective, aimed at achieving a single, non-routine process. Managing a project is a complex process. The project management model shows which factors are important in managing a project.

Execution

Four major themes are important for a good project:

- *Result of the project and the steps involved.* This indicates which steps must be completed. Dividing a project into steps, also called phasing, is typical of project management.

- *Project hierarchy.* This indicates how the project relates to other projects in the organization. Often change projects run alongside improvement or other projects. The project hierarchy stems from the fact that almost every project is part of a larger project.

- *Basic project documentation.* This contains a summary of the project definition, project organization and project management approach. It is used to control projects and keep them on schedule. It is also used to check that the project meets all requirements and that all aspects have been considered.

- *Project management cycle.* This aims to achieve results in each phase. Setting up and progressing through the management cycle is the responsibility of the project manager.

The skills and competences that a project manager must possess are not always specified in detail, including in this model, but they are nevertheless crucial to the success of the project together with the four themes listed above.

FIGURE 17.2 Project management

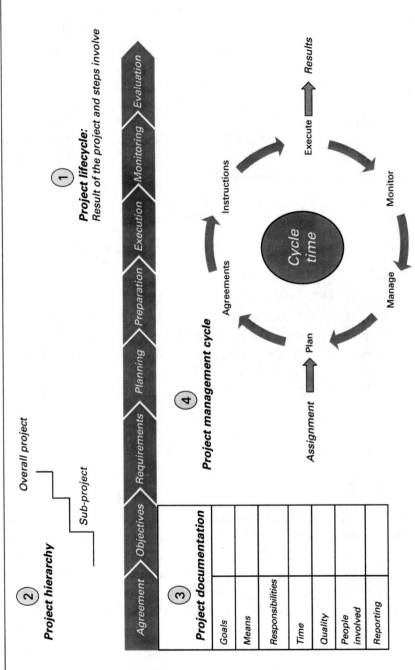

② **Project hierarchy**

Overall project

Sub-project

① **Project lifecycle:**
Result of the project and steps involve

Agreement | Objectives | Requirements | Planning | Preparation | Execution | Monitoring | Evaluation

③ **Project documentation**

Goals	
Means	
Responsibilities	
Time	
Quality	
People involved	
Reporting	

④ **Project management cycle**

Assignment — Plan

Agreements

Instructions

Execute — Results

Monitor

Manage

Cycle time

Verdict

If the implementation of the strategy is organized as a project or a series of projects, the project management model is useful to ensure that the specified outcomes are delivered and that the required capacities for the project have been made available. Before the start of a project, a clear and realistic plan is made. Operating funds for the project must be made available because projects often involve activities beyond the basic operations. This can create bottlenecks. A clear scope and end result ensure that milestones are achieved, without deviating from the final product and without unnoticed project creep occurring because 'other cases also need to be considered'.

Literature

For project management we refer to the following sources:

- Maylor, H (2002) *Project Management*, 3rd edn, Financial Times/Pitman, London
- Moussault, A, Baardman, E and Brave, F (2006 and 2011) *International Project Management Association Anthology of Methods in Project Management* [translated from Dutch: *IPMA Wegwijzer voor methoden bij Projectmanagement*], Van Haren Publishing, Zaltbommel, The Netherlands (2011, 2nd edn)

Socially engineered change

Essence

Changes in organizations do not always succeed. This may be because management has no shared vision, there is no connection between the programme team and the organization, or between the project teams themselves, or because of fragmented communication. The model for socially engineered change provides guidelines on how a strategic change can be made a success, whether it involves the introduction of a new method, a reorganization or a (post-merger) integration of organizations.

FIGURE 17.3 Socially engineered change

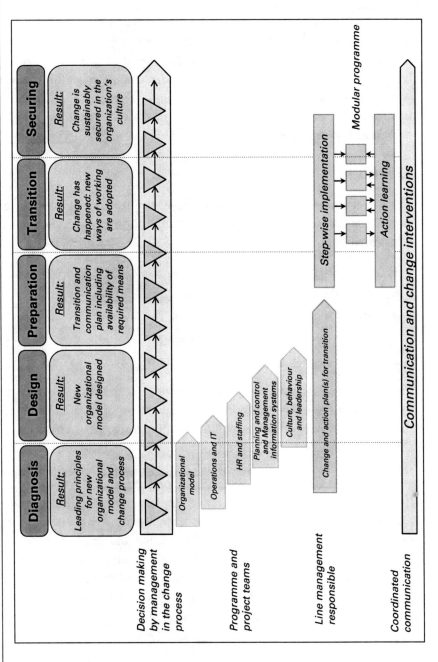

SOURCE: after Wobben, Kalshoven and De Groot (2009)

Usefulness

For strategy implementation, socially engineered change is a useful concept and model. It offers help in embedding a chosen strategy in the organization and getting a fast but structured pay-off. The socially engineered change model increases the likelihood of success in strategy implementation. The basic principle is that change must be planned well in advance, with clarity about the end situation. The likelihood of success increases when the strategy is translated into fairly detailed principles for implementation.

Execution

The socially engineered change model uses five main principles, which provide guidance on the approach for change and which can be used as a benchmark:

- Use an integral approach for change.
- Reflect the final result in the approach.
- Position management and key people.
- See communication as a two-way street.
- Change through learning.

The change process itself involves a number of core activities. Once the new strategy has been determined, it needs to be operationalized into the design of a new organization and the preparation of a change plan. Direction from the top management team during all the steps is at the core of the change process. In addition, managers and possibly employees are responsible for various improvement projects, possibly coordinated by a programme manager. The actual implementation is based on an experiential learning programme. The central pivot is at the heart of the organization: the executives effectively manage and implement change in the workplace. This is achieved in a modular manner. Finally, throughout the process, communication and cultural interventions are directed at employees to inform them about the change and/or boost willingness to change.

Verdict

Socially engineered change is a useful concept and model for many types of organizational change. Hence the name, socially engineered change, is based on the conviction that change in organizations can be engineered as long as there is a good plan that is executed correctly. In practice, however, change programmes often aren't as idealistic as had been hoped when they were instigated. Particularly in highly unpredictable situations and in situations where evolution seems more appropriate than revolutionary changes, socially engineered change fares worse. Where change is driven by strategy and can be planned and/or centrally directed, as in strategy processes using the strategic dialogue model, socially engineered change fits seamlessly.

Literature

For the socially engineered change model we refer to the following source:

- Wobben, J J, Kalshoven, A and Groot, R de (2009) *Socially Engineered Change: A targeted approach for successful change* [translated from Dutch: *De maakbare verandering: een doelgerichte aanpak voor succesvol veranderen*], Academic Service, The Hague

Change quadrants model

FIGURE 17.4   Change quadrants model

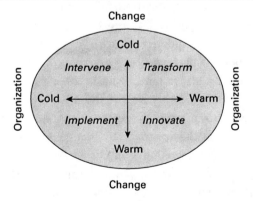

Essence

The change quadrants model states that the best-suited approach for organizational change and strategy implementation depends on both the type of organization and the motivation for the desired change. The basic premise is that an organization is either 'warm' or 'cold' and that a change can also be either 'warm' or 'cold'. In a warm organization, people are very involved with each other, whereas a cold organization is more bureaucratic. A warm change arises from an ambition to improve and cold change arises from necessity. When both these elements are plotted on a graph, four quadrants can be identified: the change quadrants (see also Figure 17.4). In each quadrant a different approach to managing change is suggested: intervention, transformation, innovation or implementation.

Usefulness

The change quadrants model is useful for determining change agents, identifying active participants in the change process and establishing the scope and timing of the change in order to maximize its success. The change quadrants model is used to choose the right approach for change, given the type of change and the type of organization in which the change is to take place.

Execution

Through interviews with key employees in the organization, you can assess the type of organization. This qualitative analysis is key to the use of the change quadrants model. A distinction must be made between cold and warm types of organization. Within an organization, there are cold storage rules, regulations, systems, structures, management procedures, control and coordination to achieve results. There is little or no intrinsic willingness to perform (better than expected). A warm organization has a common understanding and shared values that ensure that the organization runs smoothly. Warm and cold organizations can both be effective; this is not a value judgement. It is, however, an important distinction to make, as the approach to change will be different in each type. In a cold organization, change should be based around systems and bureaucracy: for example, first make a change plan, then execute that plan and ensure you stick to it. In a warm organization, change should be based more around intrinsic motivation: for example, inspire people to achieve objectives jointly and facilitate their attempts.

Next, the type of change is determined. This largely depends on necessity and momentum: fuelled either by urgency (external; cold) or by drive (from within; warm). Cold motivation for change is an objective response to a situation or emergency, such as an imminent bankruptcy, a drastic decline in market share or profits, or an inevitable (new) competitive threat. Warm motivation for change, however, is primarily dictated by personal and professional ambitions and entrepreneurship.

After assessing the type of organization and type of change, the appropriate change quadrant can be used to derive the best-suited approach to change for the organization:

- *Intervention.* This is cold change in a cold organization. For instance, the organizational restructuring of a business unit.
- *Implementation.* This is warm change in a cold organization. For instance, executing a change plan with enthusiastic project teams and employees, although they are free to choose their approach and timelines.
- *Transformation.* This is cold change in a warm organization. For instance, giving fixed objectives to project teams and employees, which they have to pursue according to a prescribed approach and strict timelines.
- *Innovation/renewal.* This is warm change in a warm organization. For instance, setting up teams to come up with new ideas and experiment with them.

Verdict

The change quadrants model gives a good idea of the approach to change that an organization should take. The distinction between type of organization and type of change is considered helpful and practical. In reality, however, the cold approach to change in a warm organization and a warm approach to change in a cold organization are the most difficult. People may not be as committed to the organization and as willing to change as management thinks, as a result of which nothing really happens. Or, worse, the erosion of commitment can result in a strong negative response to change that may cause irreparable damage to the organization.

A shortcoming of the change quadrants model is that besides the type of organization and type of change, the style and preferences of management should also be considered when choosing the approach to change. Be aware that a cold change is easier to plan and communicate than a warm change, and that many organizations assess themselves as being warmer than they actually are. Thus the sentiments and style of management should be aligned with the chosen approach to change, if the change process is not to be hindered. Therefore, the change quadrants model is often used in combination with models such as Kotter's eight phases of change (p 229) and the change communication model below.

Literature

The change quadrants model is based on the following sources:

- Van Assen, M F, Van den Berg, G J J B and Pietersma, P (2008) *Key Management Models: The 60+ models every manager needs to know*, 2nd edn, Prentice Hall, Upper Saddle River, NJ
- Kotter, J P (1990) *Force for Change: How leadership differs from management*, Free Press, New York

Change communication model

FIGURE 17.5   Change communication model

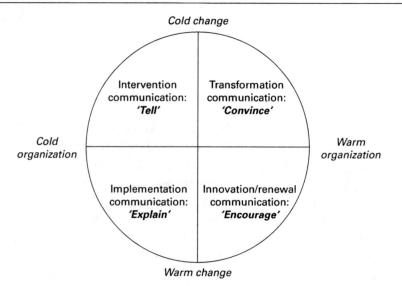

Essence

The change communication model builds on the same premise of 'warm' and 'cold' organizations and types of change as the change quadrants model (p 217) and suggests a matching approach to change communication as for the chosen approach to change. The model helps to select the style, method and instruments for communication to support the change process effectively.

Usefulness

In any change process, communication about the change (its purpose, its objectives, its progress etc) is of crucial importance. But the appropriate communication style, methods and instruments depend on the type of change intended and the type of organization in which the change is to take place. The basic premise is that an organization is either 'warm' or 'cold' and that a change can also be either 'warm' or 'cold'. In a warm organization, people are very involved with each other, whereas a cold organization is more bureaucratic. A warm change arises from an ambition to improve and cold change arises from necessity. When both these elements are plotted on a graph, four quadrants can be identified, each with a different approach to managing change: intervention, transformation, innovation and implementation (see Figure 17.4). For each approach to change, a matching communication style, methods and instruments must be chosen (see Figure 17.5).

Execution

After determining the most appropriate approach to change, the matching approach to change communication can be determined:

- *Intervention communication.* This is communication for a cold change in a cold organization. As change is imposed on the organization, a traditional top-down approach is also chosen for change communication: carried out by line management and characterized as informing and telling. It requires a balance between mass communication and personal attention: clear and direct in group communication, attentive and specific in individual (one-to-one) communication. The messenger (the manager) is the 'face' of the message and is regarded as the personification of the change. The manager's emotions, personal touch and communication style set the tone.

- *Implementation communication.* This is communication for a warm change in a cold organization. As change is driven more by ambition than necessity, the communication style and method reflect this. It is about convincing people of the benefits of the change and motivating them to help realize the change. Communication is thus about sharing information (results, figures) and about keeping everyone focused on, and motivated to achieve, the same end result. Often it is characterized as a public relations style of communication. Either project teams or management can be the communicator, although management is often more fitting. Be aware that the communicator is also expected to lead by example: not just tell, but show.

- *Transformation communication.* This is communication for a cold change in a warm organization. As management is forced to take the initiative for change, communication is aimed at facilitating the realization of the necessary changes. Often management will set the framework and then professionals in the organization will be invited to tell them what can best be done within that framework to realize the intended change. Communication is about closing the formal and informal information loops in the organization, making sure that information is not only shared with the rest of the organization by the people involved but that this is done from a central point in the organization. This requires balancing tight control with the orchestration and facilitation of professionals.

- *Innovation/renewal communication.* This is communication for warm change in a warm organization. As change is initiated by ambitions within the organization, communication should also be organized in a bottom-up fashion, with the joint goal of realizing the change being the objective of communication. This approach to change communication is characterized by a strictly monitored communication process but with broad and extensive guidance and facilitation for communication by those leading change projects. Communication is thus decentralized and is often organized as a two-way interaction: informing people about progress but also explicitly asking for suggestions and input through instruments such as E-Boardroom (see p 250).

Verdict

The change communication model complements the change quadrants model. For each quadrant in the change quadrants model, an appropriate approach to change communication can be determined. The change quadrants model indicates that a communication strategy is always situational. In practice, change communication is not obviously linked to the situation or to the approach to change. All too often, change communication runs on autopilot.

Literature

The change communication model is based on the following source:

- Gehrels, C, Van Venetië, E and Thevenet, J (2003) *Management Models for Communication [translated from Dutch: Managementmodellen voor communicatie]*, Nieuwezijds/ Academic Service, The Hague

18 Models for Step 7: Execution

 ## Step 7: Execution

In *Step 7: Execution*, the new strategy and the proposed changes are implemented. The various change and action plans that were developed in the operationalization step are carried out. The execution step is about action. It is about realizing the desired changes and incorporating them in the organization, and having them adopted by key stakeholders.

Many strategy and strategy implementation models can be used in the execution step, particularly models that facilitate change management.

MODELS THAT CAN BE USED IN STEP 7: EXECUTION ARE:

- stakeholder management;
- Kotter's eight phases of change;
- the seven forces for effective change model.

Stakeholder management model

FIGURE 18.1 Stakeholder management model

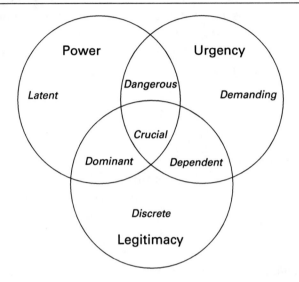

SOURCE: After Mitchell, Agle and Wood

Essence

Every company interacts with its environment and therefore has to deal with individuals, groups, companies and other organizations: the stakeholders. Some of these relationships are intentional and desirable, others are not. All have in common the fact that they are involved with the organization in a certain way and thus have an interest in the activities and objectives of the organization.

Usefulness

The stakeholder management model is an instrument that is useful for aligning the interests of the organization and the interests of its stakeholders. It provides a framework to map the interests of all stakeholders and to assess the areas of concern (issues) these stakeholders have with respect to the organization's – newly stated – strategic objectives. Any resistance arising from these concerns can then be determined and an appropriate approach and communication plan drawn up for each stakeholder and each point of concern, to convince them of the organization's intentions.

The stakeholder management model is complementary to the stakeholder analysis model (p 156), which is about identifying and understanding stakeholders' interests. The stakeholder management model helps to act upon the interests of the stakeholders in relation to the organization's new strategy. It is useful in the execution step, as only now have the organization's interests become clear and the organization wants to act on its goals. So in this step it makes sense to try to align the organization's interests with those of the stakeholders.

Execution

Stakeholder management begins with an inventory of the organization's stakeholders. They are put into groups, for example 'the environmental movement', 'the staff' or 'the government'. Within any group, there are key people to identify who can be communicated to directly. Each key figure has a determining role in the stakeholder group, and is someone that people follow.

Not all stakeholders are equally important for an organization. By classifying them, the organization can prioritize relations with certain stakeholders. The classification is based on three characteristics of the relationship:

- the power of the parties to influence the organization;
- the legitimacy of the relationship and actions of the stakeholders with the organization in terms of desirability, accuracy or appropriateness;
- the urgency of the demands on the organization made by the interested party and the extent to which that party requires sensitive handling.

Stakeholders who score highly on only one of the three characteristics are called latent stakeholders. Those who score highly on all three are crucial partners for the organization (see also Figure 18.1). Their interests and concerns should always be considered by the organization.

After drawing up the inventory and any prioritization, the organization should determine, for each stakeholder or interested group, what their interests are and what concerns they might have about the new strategy. Based on these concerns an estimate can be made of which stakeholders will support the organization's objectives and which still have doubts. Supporters are called movers. They will probably contribute actively and look for others to do so, too. Opponents are called blockers and those who are not in favour or oppose are called floaters. Depending on the importance given to the relationship with an interested party, targeted action should be chosen as soon as that person's attitude seems to be moving in the same direction as the organization. Movers should be informed about objectives and (planned) activities, so that they can contribute. Floaters can usually be won over, as the organization can overcome their doubts by explaining how their interests are served by the new plans. Blockers should be asked to explain what they perceive to be a threat and what the organization could do to remove that perception. Usually too much attention is given to blockers and too little to floaters.

For all actions and communications with the different stakeholder groups, performance indicators are chosen to monitor whether the action actually contributes to the mobilization or creation of a win–win situation with that stakeholder. A stakeholder action card is a suitable tool to keep track of these (see Figure 18.2). It is a practical tool that gives a good overview of the interests, positions and roles of stakeholders and the approach taken towards them, and helps to keep track of progress and developments. It also allows actions and communication with the stakeholder to be further fine-tuned if necessary.

Verdict

The stakeholder management model is used to achieve specific changes in the actions, behaviour or attitude of one or more of the organization's stakeholders. It provides practical guidance on how to convince any (internal or external) opponents and thus create support for the (desired) change. The stakeholder management model can be applied to any decision that requires change in the actions, behaviour or attitude of stakeholders. It can be also used in any situation where there is resistance to (proposed) decisions and changes among stakeholders.

Literature

The stakeholder management model is based on the following resource:

- Mitchell, R K, Agle, B R and Wood, D J (1997) Toward a theory of stakeholder identification and salience: defining the principle of who and what really counts, *Academy of Management Review*, 22 (4), pp 853–86

FIGURE 18.2 Stakeholder action card

Stakeholder (name)	Classification (latent–crucial)	Interest	Issue(s)	Coalition with	Attitude ('Mover'–'Floater'–'Blocker')	Resistance /response	Approach	KPI for approach	Monitoring method	Communication means

Kotter's eight phases of change

Essence

Kotter's eight phases of change is a systematic approach to a successful, sustainable way to achieve change in 8 steps. It is based on a survey in the 1990s of over a hundred companies that had gone through a change. John Kotter found that the most common mistakes during change were: too much self-importance, lacking a supportive coalition, underestimating the need for a clear vision, failing to communicate the vision clearly, permitting obstacles, forgetting to realize 'quick wins', declaring victory too soon and not anchoring changes in the organizational culture. Kotter argues that these errors can be avoided by understanding why organizations change, what steps are required to bring about change and what phases an organization goes through when changing.

Usefulness

In today's dynamic business world, the ability to manage and realize change is an important requirement for success in any organization. In his books (1990, 1996, 2002), Kotter makes a clear distinction between management and leadership in change. To him, management is a set of activities that keeps a complex system of people and technology running smoothly. Leadership, on the other hand, is what defines the future (gives a vision) and gets people lined up for that vision and inspired to pursue it. The eight phases of change model provides a systematic instrument for taking leadership in change. It enables a company to instil lasting changes in the organization, avoid (possibly) fatal mistakes and get people inspired.

Execution

Kotter emphasizes the importance of not skipping any of the eight phases. For lasting change, an organization has to go through all eight. The phases are:

- *Create a sense of urgency.* To address complacency, it is important that false signs of security are removed. Management must ensure that people feel a sense of urgency because of an (impending) crisis and that they are convinced that continuing as usual is no longer acceptable.

FIGURE 18.3 Kotter's eight phases of change

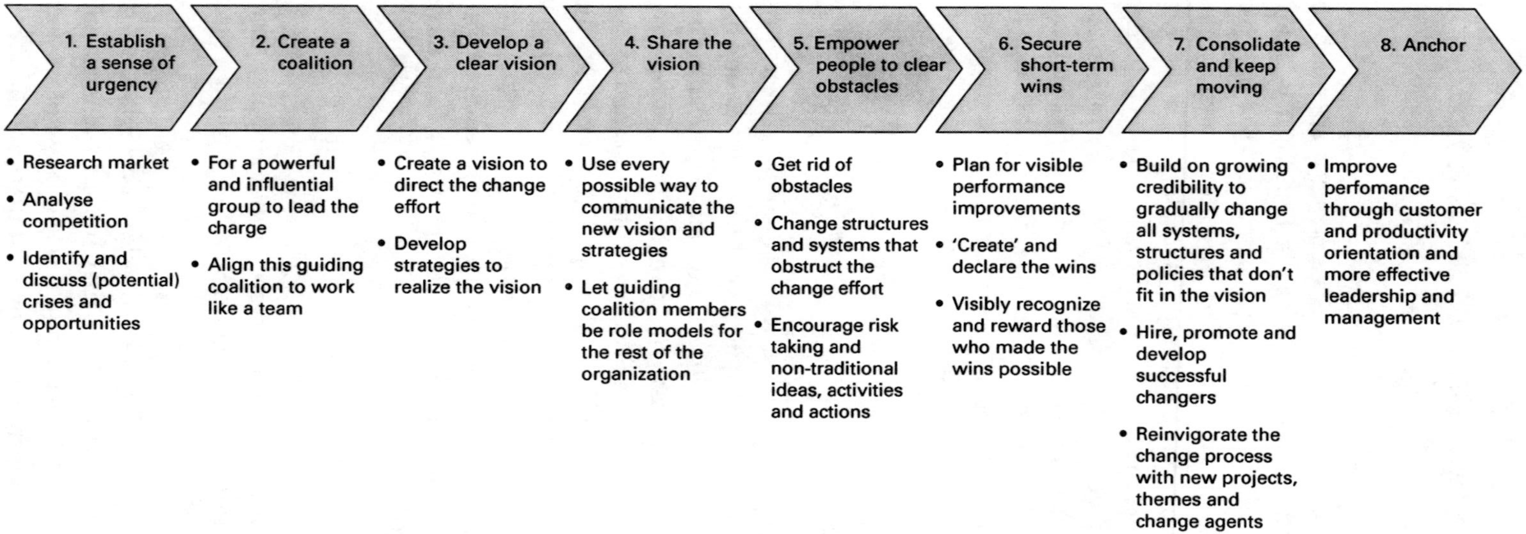

1. Establish a sense of urgency	2. Create a coalition	3. Develop a clear vision	4. Share the vision	5. Empower people to clear obstacles	6. Secure short-term wins	7. Consolidate and keep moving	8. Anchor
• Research market • Analyse competition • Identify and discuss (potential) crises and opportunities	• For a powerful and influential group to lead the charge • Align this guiding coalition to work like a team	• Create a vision to direct the change effort • Develop strategies to realize the vision	• Use every possible way to communicate the new vision and strategies • Let guiding coalition members be role models for the rest of the organization	• Get rid of obstacles • Change structures and systems that obstruct the change effort • Encourage risk taking and non-traditional ideas, activities and actions	• Plan for visible performance improvements • 'Create' and declare the wins • Visibly recognize and reward those who made the wins possible	• Build on growing credibility to gradually change all systems, structures and policies that don't fit in the vision • Hire, promote and develop successful changers • Reinvigorate the change process with new projects, themes and change agents	• Improve performance through customer and productivity orientation and more effective leadership and management

SOURCE: after Kotter (1990 and 1996)

- *Appoint a change team.* A strong coalition is needed to create change in an organization. The members of this group must appreciate the value of the proposed change and realize that they need to obtain trust and commitment from the people in the organization. Furthermore, they should be credible and have the skills, connections, reputation and formal authority to demonstrate leadership in change.

- *Have a clear vision.* Vision is a key element in successfully realizing change. Vision, according to Kotter, is the bridge between existing and future conditions. When implementing a new strategy, this vision should thus already be clear: it portrays the new strategy and why the organization wants to take on that strategic direction. A clear vision is then instrumental in giving a sense of direction for the desired change and in aligning activities. The best visions are formulated clearly, and they are simple, uplifting and situation-specific.

- *Communicate the change vision.* Communicating the vision is essential to ensuring that everyone understands and connects with the change. Inconsistent messages are major pitfalls that hinder successful change.

- *Make people self-reliant.* The change team should remove all barriers to action for anyone involved. These are embedded in the organizational processes and structures or exist in people's minds. Everyone should be in a position to assess the change and pursue it themselves.

- *Achieve success in the short term.* Change usually requires a great deal of time and effort. For this reason, people should be encouraged to realize 'quick wins'. These short-term successes support willingness to keep on pursuing the change. Successes must be clearly visible to all and closely linked to the effort for change.

- *Consolidate and enable more change.* Create momentum by celebrating successes. And then consolidate the achievements and results and use these as a stepping stone to more success. Ask people to come up with additional suggestions and new activities to realize the desired change.

● *Anchor new approaches in the culture.* As effective changes are achieved, prevent things from returning to what they were. Kotter argues that the real key to lasting change lies in the change of the organizational culture itself through consistent successful action over a sufficiently long period.

Verdict

Kotter warns about the complexity of organizational change. He recognizes that there are many ways to make mistakes during a change process. More importantly, even successful change can be full of surprises. But anyone who attempts to achieve change in an organization using Kotter's eight phases of change model must take into account the usual issues and be able to face up to the challenges that are specific to his or her situation.

Complexity increases even further when an organization is in the last phase of a previous change and already starting a new change process: it might find itself in more than one phase of the model simultaneously. This requires even more from the organization and its management and from the leadership in the respective change processes.

Literature

For Kotter's eight phases of change we refer to the following sources:

● Kotter, J P (1990) *Force for Change: How leadership differs from management*, Free Press, New York

● Kotter, J P (1996) *Leading Change*, Harvard Business School Press, Cambridge, MA

● Kotter, J P (2002) *The Heart of Change: Real-life stories of how people change their organizations*, Harvard Business School Press, Cambridge, MA

The seven forces for effective change model

FIGURE 18.4   The seven forces for effective change model

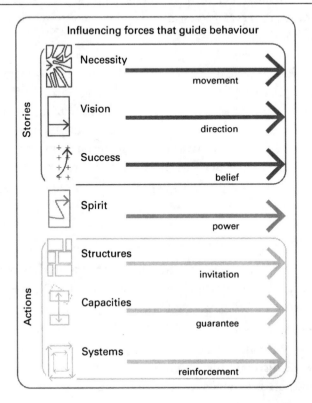

Essence

The seven forces for effective change model helps management to detect (expected) issues in the organization that can become bottlenecks in realizing desired changes. The model gives useful clues to overcome or solve those bottlenecks. It is a tool for managing and guiding effective change in an organization. The model is built on the premise that suitable behaviour within an organization (culture) is one of the key factors of success for an organization. Effective change is thus about getting suitable behaviour in place.

The seven forces are clusters of management activities that help to influence and change employee behaviour.

Usefulness

The seven forces for effective change model states that there are seven forces (or elements) that help to realize change. The model arranges these elements. All seven forces should be in equilibrium with each other to realize change effectively.

The model looks for causes that can stall a change process: it looks at what could go wrong. Usually a stalled change process is caused by non-equilibrium of the seven forces: one or more of them has insufficient attention. The seven forces for effective change model helps to identify which elements need more attention and focus on giving the appropriate attention to those elements. The model is therefore ideal for continuous diagnosis of the change process and to identify in a timely manner where and what interventions are required.

The seven forces in the model are:

- *Necessity*. Necessity feeds change, as without need there is no change. The manager must explain the need for change (awareness) to all concerned. Necessity promotes movement: people will feel the need or even want to change.

- *Vision*. Without vision, change is rudderless. A clear vision provides direction for organizational change. Managers and those responsible for change must communicate that vision. Vision gives direction.

- *Success*. An organization can only be changed effectively if people see that the changes lead to success and that the new behaviour makes them more successful. Success makes people believe in the change.

- *Structures*. The structural conditions accommodate the desired situation and new behaviour (culture). Old structures should be adjusted or abandoned. Clear new structures give an invitation to change: old habits no longer bring (enough) success.

- *Capacities*. Capacities make the change feasible. The capabilities of employees, the leadership style, the competences of management and the project management skills for the change project all deserve attention. Appropriate capacities give guarantees for change.

- *Systems*. Changes only become permanent if everyone involved can see and acknowledge their own contribution to the total change process. Everyone should thus be continuously informed and all activities should be monitored and evaluated with immediate feedback. Systems reinforce change.

- *Spirit*. Change requires some levels of attractiveness and appeal. Spirit represents the driving force behind the change, the source of energy from which the change will come. Spirit gives power to the change.

Execution

The seven forces for effective change model is used by first analysing all the forces for the change process at hand: has sufficient attention been paid to all forces? If not, take action. Next, keep the model at hand during the change process: continuously check whether all the forces are still in equilibrium and all getting the required attention.

For the seven forces, different actions can be taken. The first three forces, 'necessity', 'vision' and 'success', are so-called narrative forces. Their effects can be achieved by interaction and engagement with key stake-holders. Actions for these forces involve creating awareness, confrontation and/or inspiration. The 'structures', 'capacities' and 'systems' forces are the so-called 'hard' action forces. Their effects can be achieved by making tangible adjustments in the organization, for instance changes in team composition, in collective capacity-building workshops or skills training, or in installing new performance management procedures. Actions for these forces involve setting all preconditions for lasting change and preventing the organization from falling back into old habits. The seventh force, 'spirit', is the so-called 'soft' action force. Its effect can be achieved by strengthening the appeal of, and enthusiasm for, the desired change. Actions for this force include continually radiating enthusiasm and drive, and expressing enthusiasm in daily conduct and during events specifically organized around moments of success.

When using the seven forces for effective change model during a change process, the following points are important:

- Constantly focus on all forces. Management of behaviour is not a project but a process.

- Be able to work on all forces. Ensure management has sufficient instruments at their disposal to take action on each of the seven forces.
- Connect with the organization. Do the most urgent things first.
- Provide continuous communication. Have 'tell and repeat' running as a thread through the activities. Good communication is a prerequisite for success.
- Take small steps. Major change comes from many small steps. An increasing number of actions reduce resistance more than one giant leap forward.

Literature

For the seven forces for effective change model we refer to the following source:

- Kleinen, B *et al* (1998) Managing change of organizational culture [translated from Dutch: Management van cultuurverandering], *Elan*, 3 (12)

Models for Step 8: Monitoring

 ## Step 8: Monitoring

In *Step 8: Monitoring* the performance of the organization is followed, evaluated and checked to establish to what extent the organization actually realizes its strategic goals. The monitoring step is about continually reviewing progress on the organization's strategic goals and taking corrective action where and when needed. And it is about periodically validating the strategic direction itself, by monitoring the early-warning signals identified in the option and choice steps. Step 8 is the last step in the strategic dialogue model. It ensures that the organization acts according to the strategic choice. But it can also be the start of new steps if adjustment is needed.

Several strategy models are useful in the monitoring step, particularly those that help collect and interpret information on the organization's performance in a structured manner and those that help measure progress and identify steering measures.

MODELS THAT CAN BE USED IN STEP 8: MONITORING ARE:

- the PDCA (or Deming) cycle;
- the EFQM model;
- the balanced scorecard.

The PDCA (or Deming) cycle

FIGURE 19.1   The PDCA (or Deming) cycle

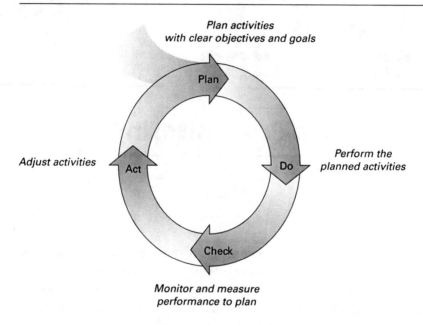

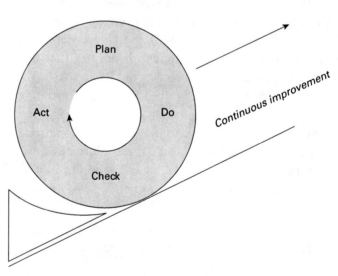

SOURCE: after Walton and Deming (1986)

Essence

The PDCA cycle, introduced by Walton and Deming in the 1980s, is a method to structure improvement and change projects. It refers to a logical sequence of four repetitive steps for continuous improvement and learning: plan, do, check and act. Planning (plan) the improvement of an activity should be followed by the execution of the activity (do) according to the plan. Next, enter the results and measure and study the improvement (check), and take possible actions (act) to adapt or improve the activities to better realize the desired goals.

Usefulness

The PDCA (or Deming) cycle enables an organization to lead improvement initiatives and change processes in a disciplined way and guarantees results. The model is used to structure the process of continuous improvement and learning. Any problem-solving cycle corresponds to a PDCA cycle. Metaphorically, the PDCA cycle can be seen as a wheel that is pushed up the hill during an improvement or change process (see also Figure 19.1). If results are consolidated in a timely manner, the wheel will not roll back. So, adequate planning, doing, checking and – in particular – acting will ensure that the organization can be 'rolled' to a higher level. By explicitly using the PDCA cycle, people will become aware of improvements and their benefits. This will encourage them to continue improving (or changing).

Execution

The PDCA (or Deming) cycle works by systematically following these four steps:

1 *Plan*. Plan changes ahead. Analyse the current situation and the possible consequences of the desired change before doing anything. Predict the expected results, with or without substantiation. Draft a plan that states goals, links to the organization's mission statement, sets preconditions and procedures, and allocates responsibilities, resources and activities – and includes measurement of results (or even the development of a measurement method for this purpose).

2 *Do*. During the execution of the plan, take small steps. This helps to keep control of progress and to attribute success to activities. It also prevents large relapses.

3 *Check*. Periodically check progress and results. Analyse why success is realized or why desired results were not achieved.

4 *Act*. Take action when results are not as desired. Try to standardize procedures by including those actions that have already been proved to contribute to success and eliminating those that do not contribute.

Verdict

Many organizations are not capable of specifying the desired results and successes, let alone be able to systematically plan and consistently follow up on their own plans, with or without the PDCA cycle. Following the entire PDCA cycle requires a lot of discipline.

Literature

For the PDCA (or Deming) cycle we refer to the following source:

- Walton, M and Deming, W E (1986) *The Deming Management Method*, Dodd, Mead, New York

The EFQM model

FIGURE 19.2   The EFQM model

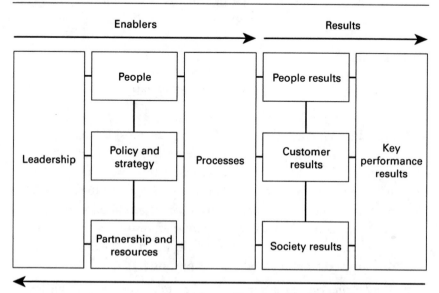

Innovation and learning

SOURCE: after EFQM (1992)

Essence

The EFQM model, developed by the European Foundation for Quality Management, is a model that helps translate strategy into five organizational areas ('leadership', 'policy and strategy', 'people', 'partnerships and resources' and 'processes') and four different result areas. The underlying philosophy is that, if the strategy is properly translated and implemented, the five organizational areas are aligned and contribute to all four result areas, the outcome of which will be satisfied customers and suppliers, satisfied employees, a satisfied society and satisfactory organizational performance and goal realization. The model helps to identify whether the translation of the strategy into these five areas is adequate, whether each of these areas contributes enough to the result areas and whether any gaps in performance can be identified.

Usefulness

Originally the EFQM model was introduced as a tool to evaluate and improve the overall quality of the company, based on total quality management principles, by improving the alignment between the organizational areas and/or increasing their contribution to the results of the organization.

In a strategy process, the EFQM model is also very useful for maintaining a clear overview of the interrelationships between the organizational areas of a company and how they contribute to the results of the organization. In other words, to monitor the performance of the organization and to identify, from this overview, possible gaps in performance and determine what underlying factors (in what operational area) for that gap need to be addressed to improve performance again.

Execution

The EFQM model is a strategy model that consists of five organizational areas and four result areas. The organizational areas describe the way in which the company is organized and are key elements for managing an organization effectively. For an excellent organization and excellence in achieving results, the five organizational areas require:

- *Leadership*. This requires managers with a mission statement, vision and values who are role models of a culture of excellence, who are personally involved in the development and improvement of the organization, who care about customers, suppliers, partners and representatives of society, and who can motivate and support people in the organization.

- *Policy and strategy.* This requires incorporation of current and future needs of all stakeholders, of information for performance measurement, of research and learning, of continuous development and improvement, and of communication.

- *People.* Employees play a key role: they should be carefully planned, managed and developed, their knowledge and competences should be identified, developed and sustained, they must be involved and empowered, they should interact at all levels in the organization, and they should be rewarded and cared for.

- *Partnerships and resources.* This requires excellent management of external relationships, of finances, of buildings, equipment and materials, of technology, and of information and knowledge.

- *Processes.* This requires systematic design and management of processes which meet customer demands innovatively and increase value, which produce and deliver well-designed and well-developed products that meet customer needs and expectations, and which are well organized in order to contribute to and enhance customer relations.

Using the model starts with (checking) the translation of the strategy in these five organizational areas. Next, the desired results are mapped to the result areas. In the EFQM model the organizational areas all contribute to the four result areas. These four result areas represent the different types of results an organization can aspire to with its strategy. The result areas, 'employees', 'customers and suppliers', 'society' and 'financial return', show what the activities of the company deliver.

Then an assessment is made between the desired results and the results actually achieved. In the EFQM model, the actual results are measured per result area using key performance indicators (KPIs). For the result areas customer, employee and society, perception indicators are also used to measure results.

Any gaps in performance (ie lower performance levels than desired) are then identified. Suggestions for improvement in the organizational areas affected can subsequently be determined. Ideally, these improvements are realized structurally. In the EFQM model there is a feedback loop between the result areas and the organizational areas that represents a coordinated learning effect: it is the essential link between 'what we do' and 'what's in it'. Performance improvement efforts preferably utilize this learning loop.

Verdict

The EFQM model provides companies with a structured approach to translating their strategy into functional areas in their organization and to improving the organization's overall quality. It is a recognized tool to improve the efficacy and professionalism of a company's planning and control cycle. The model provides core elements for the effective analysis, assessment, structuring, improvement and management of an organization. The model also works well in conjunction with the balanced scorecard (p 244). A useful source of additional information on the EFQM model and its use is the EFQM website, where benchmarks and tools for self-evaluation are also offered.

Literature

For the EFQM model we refer to the following sources:

- Hakes, C (2007) *The EFQM Excellence Model For Assessing Organizational Performance – A management guide*, Van Haren Publishing, Zaltbommel, The Netherlands
- EFQM (1992) *Total Quality Management: The European model for self-appraisal*, European Foundation for Quality Management, Brussels
- Oakland, J (1994) *Total Quality Management: The route to improving performance*, Butterworth-Heinemann, Oxford

The balanced scorecard

FIGURE 19.3   The balanced scorecard

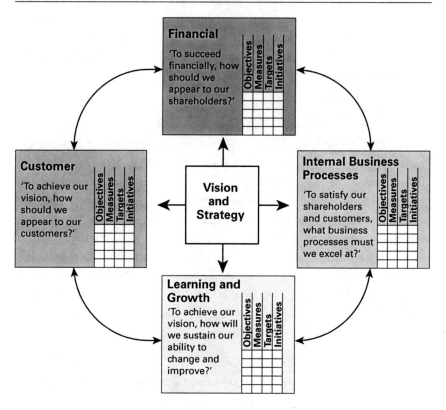

SOURCE: after Kaplan and Norton (1992 and 1996)

Essence

The balanced scorecard (BSC) was developed by Kaplan and Norton in 1992 as an alternative to traditional approaches to performance measurement, which focus exclusively on financial indicators and mostly on the historical performance of a company. The balanced scorecard is a method used to measure the progress of an organization towards its objectives. It holds four different perspectives in which progress is monitored. For each perspective, relevant key performance indicators (KPIs) are identified. Using all four perspectives and monitoring performance structurally enables organizations to make any necessary corrective adjustments promptly.

Usefulness

The balanced scorecard measures the company's performance on four aspects: 'financial', 'internal business processes', 'learning and growth' and 'customers'. Financial measures are complemented with non-financial measures that drive the long-term success of the organization. The balanced scorecard monitors not only past performance but also present performance, and tries to capture information about how well the organization is positioned for the future. It is used to monitor organizational performance transparently through multiple measures in its various perspectives. It enables management to take appropriate action where required, which will eventually lead to significant and lasting performance improvements.

Execution

To create a balanced scorecard, a company must first define its mission statement and vision, because this determines the desired performance. Then KPIs are determined in each of the four perspectives:

- *Financial perspective.* Timely and accurate financial information is needed to manage a business successfully. Important indicators in this perspective are return on investment (ROI) and economic value added (EVA), but other criteria may be included, depending on the characteristics of the company and the industry in which it operates.

- *Customer perspective.* Customer service and satisfaction are considered important issues for all organizations. You should know how your client perceives your company. Important indicators in this perspective are customer satisfaction, customer profitability, customer retention, customer contacts handling, market share in target segments and number of complaints.

- *Internal business processes.* Information on the performance of the company's operational activities helps to monitor and steer the effectiveness of the organization's activities. Important indicators in this perspective are quality, response times, cycle times, costs, time to market, realized break-even times and new sales as a percentage of total sales.

- *Learning and growth.* Insights into the degree of success of personnel management, knowledge management and innovation help to monitor and steer the organization's positioning for future performance. Important indicators in this perspective are employee satisfaction, staff retention rate, turnover or added value per employee ratios, information availability in relation to need, and number of new ideas per employee ratio.

Verdict

The balanced scorecard helps an organization to direct itself towards future performance and success. The balanced set of performance indicators in the four perspectives helps organizations to articulate and communicate their strategic objectives and desired results. It helps to align individual, organizational and cross-departmental initiatives to a common goal and lasting performance.

However, it is not easy to find a well-balanced set of KPIs. An appropriate number of indicators for a balanced scorecard is up to 12 to 16 when there is full consensus concerning these indicators. In addition, these KPIs have to be broken down further in underlying sets of performance indicators. This increases the difficulty in finding the correct set of KPIs. Otherwise, there is the risk that employees focus only on the few overall goals and on delivering only to the KPIs on the balanced scorecard.

A last note is that the balanced scorecard needs to be updated quite regularly to prevent the right performance being overlooked.

Literature

For the balanced scorecard we refer to the following sources:

- Kaplan, R and Norton, D (1992) The balanced scorecard: measures that drive performance, *Harvard Business Review*, January–February, pp 71–80
- Kaplan, R and Norton, D (1996) *The Balanced Scorecard: Translating strategy into action*, Harvard Business School Press, Cambridge, MA
- Kaplan, R and Norton, D (2004) *Strategy Maps: Converting intangible assets into tangible outcomes*, Harvard Business School Press, Cambridge, MA

PART 4
Key engagement methods

Each strategy process has a number of characteristics. And in every step of a strategy process, explicit attention must be given to each of these characteristics. But where in one step the emphasis will be more on increasing creativity, a different step requires more analysis. In the strategy process with the strategic dialogue five characteristics can be distinguished (see Part 1):

- participatory;
- creative;
- analytic;
- decisive;
- committing.

In Part 2 of this book, for each of the 8 steps of the strategic dialogue the characteristics that usually require the most attention in that step are described. In each step of the strategy process, specific attention to a characteristic or characteristics can be associated with explicit methods of engagement. These methods can be used to engage the right people to be involved in that step (see Part 2) and to engage them in the intended way in that step to give more (or less) emphasis to a specific characteristic of that step. For instance, to increase creativity, methods for the characteristic creative should be applied to the people that you want to participate and contribute creatively.

This part provides methods of engagement that correspond to each of the five characteristics, which in turn relate to each of the 8 steps of the strategic dialogue model.

Methods for the 'participatory' characteristic

 ## The 'participatory' characteristic

A strategy process with the strategic dialogue model is characterized by a high degree of engagement and participation. This participative characteristic means on the one hand 'involving the right people', that is, involving people with relevant knowledge and insights, and on the other 'involving more people', that is, involving more participants in the strategy process to increase the general acceptance of, and organizational support for, the new strategy.

In Step 1 (Searchlight) there is a reasonably high level of participation, both in the number of stakeholders – as well as the board of directors, also management, key employees, (external) experts, key customers and/or key suppliers – and in the level of participation of each of those involved.

Step 2 (Outside-in) also usually has a strongly participative character, involving both key (commercial) employees and network partners (including experts, customers and suppliers) to map out future developments together.

Step 3 (Inside-out) has a more limited participative character, involving some key employees in addition to the board and management.

Steps 4 (Options) and 5 (Choice) have a limited participative character. In these steps it is mainly (and sometimes only) the board and management who are involved. Although one of the principles underlying the strategic dialogue model is to use high levels of participation, it is not necessarily implied in the model that decision making in these steps should be democratic (see Part 1).

Steps 6 (Operationalization), 7 (Execution) and 8 (Monitoring) can be characterized as being very participative. In these steps, management takes the initiative and is responsible for implementing the new strategy and managing all strategic projects in, and changes throughout, the organization.

In this chapter, several methods of engagement which correspond to the participatory characteristic are introduced, which in turn relate to each of the 8 steps of the strategic dialogue model.

The methods for the 'participatory' characteristic are presented in random order:

- the e-Boardroom;
- crowdsourcing;
- buzzing;
- forming subgroups;
- brown paper session.

The e-Boardroom

The big picture

The e-Boardroom is a system for computer-supported meetings, brainstorming sessions and decision making. Participants can give their opinions anonymously. The e-Boardroom enables faster data collection than through individual interviews. It is also a useful tool to focus discussions as results are immediately available through digital reporting. Using the e-Boardroom changes the way meetings with large groups of people are organized. Often its efficiency inspires participants to contribute even more ideas and suggestions. Using this method for engagement encourages openness, which furthers exhaustiveness.

When to use it

The e-Boardroom is ideal for situations where a large number of people, both from within and from outside the organization, must simultaneously be involved in the strategy process. This method facilitates an open process for groups that normally would be too big for such an open approach: first the exchange of ideas, than later selecting, judging and deciding. For these processes with large groups the e-Boardroom is a quick, efficient and useful method.

Additionally, the e-Boardroom promotes equality between participants: each voice or opinion has an equal weight. This makes the method even more relevant in situations where equivalence is not obvious, for example when one participant is very dominant.

How to use it

The e-Boardroom exists on a network of laptops (or tablet computers) which participants operate in parallel. Each participant operates his or her own laptop. Data entries from participants are centrally collected, anonymously if desired. Results can be centrally projected or printed as a report. The e-Boardroom is often a real-time meeting in which participants sit in the same room, each with an individual laptop connected. It can also be a virtual meeting, with participants working from different locations of choice, connected via their laptop. The only constraint of the e-Boardroom is that participants are not able to participate at their individually chosen moment of time. The e-Boardroom always is about same-time participation.

In theory, the number of participants has no maximum, although the dynamics in an e-Boardroom meeting with 10 participants obviously differs from a meeting with 100 participants.

Crowdsourcing

The big picture

Crowdsourcing is a method that captures the knowledge, ideas and creativity of a large group of people or even a group as large as society as a whole. Through interaction with the group by purposefully posing questions, the organization can get useful, collective feedback.

This method can be used both externally (with key stakeholders) and internally (with key employees). A good medium for crowdsourcing is the internet or the intranet environment.

When to use it

Submitting a question to a relevant, interested audience or just to people in another field can generate new insights that help solve a problem or situation. Typically, crowdsourcing should be used in stages where (still) no decisions have to be taken, furthering the use of input of relevant stakeholders who are not involved in the decision-making stage itself.

In B2C environments, crowdsourcing methods are increasingly used for collecting information for strategic decisions, for example in marketing strategies. An example is a large chip manufacturer that organized a competition: not only did it invite consumers (the general public) to give suggestions for new flavours, it also invited the general public to vote for the best suggestion before putting the winner into production.

How to use it

For crowdsourcing you will need access to a large, relevant network or community of the target group, that is, the stakeholders with whom you wish to interact. A good approach is to ask a question via social media and thus launch a discussion, or to let people vote on ideas or products. On a smaller scale, crowdsourcing can be done using industry-related discussion platforms or intranets.

Buzzing

The big picture

Buzzing is a method of engagement in which a facilitator gives an assignment to a group to briefly exchange ideas with another member of the group on a topic provided by the facilitator. The outcome of the exchange is shared in a discussion with the whole group. The topic given can be a small issue, a problem situation, a theorem or a question. The method gets its name from the hubbub that occurs when participants pair up together in conversation (a buzzing sound).

When to use it

The buzzing method is useful in the following situations:

- To get responses when a group is silent after prompting them with a question, for example when evaluating outcomes of analysis. Using buzzing first typically produces more comments that are of better quality than posing the questions directly.

- To put topics on the agenda that normally are not easily discussed in a (large) group, for example regarding the way organizational changes are experienced.

- To activate participants in (very) large groups, for example as part of a presentation.

How to use it

The preparation of buzzing involves collecting a set of relevant questions, cases or theorems. Using real-life cases adds a sense of relevance and encourages participants to apply the outcomes.

When desired, buzzing can be organized as two rounds: in the first round participants exchange ideas with one neighbour and in the second round with the neighbour on the other side, with no central discussion in between. Buzzing in two rounds gives more nuances to the discussion, which can be an advantage in sensitive situations or discussions that are likely to be too personal. The facilitator rounds off the pair-wise exchange when the buzzing sounds get softer, as that typically indicates that the main issues have been discussed enough. In the group discussion, a good facilitator (explicitly) invites all participants to describe their ideas. The facilitator closes the buzzing session after the central exchange and discussion.

Forming subgroups

The big picture

Forming sub-groups is a method that increases involvement within a group. Based on the content or the process component on which the group is working, participants are divided into subgroups or pairs. Each subgroup should then prepare (part of) an assignment. This assignment could be carried out on site, or as homework. The subgroups then present the outcomes to each other in a plenary session. The outcomes can also be shared in other ways, for example through a common knowledge platform or intranet.

When to use it

In situations under high time pressure, forming employee subgroups can stimulate an outcome. When a topic evokes discussion, the debate can be accelerated by first forming subgroups to discuss the topic. Subgroups can simultaneously discuss more aspects of the topic and/or more topics and they allow more profound discussions on every aspect of the topic.

Furthermore, forming subgroups allows every participant to make a substantive contribution. In this way, the facilitator can also follow up on the personal commitment of each participant, making it easier to decide whom to involve again in later steps of the strategy process.

How to use it

Forming subgroups requires a specific topic or question that needs to be answered. Each subgroup should be given a clear framework to work within. This framework should include, for example, timelines and planning, availability of resources that the group can use and/or templates for the outcomes of each subgroup.

Brown paper session

The big picture

A brown paper session is a method to jointly visualize something, such as a process or model. On a large piece of (brown) paper, participants can post or write relevant issues and organize or cluster them. This clarifies issues and processes and makes it evident where bottlenecks are, who is involved and what resources are needed. A brown paper session literally brings participants into action by gathering them around the paper. Participants themselves post or write answers to the question on the paper, and prioritize and organize their answers together.

As participants themselves are actively working, their awareness about the topic will grow, as will their willingness to solve the problem.

When to use it

Usually, brown paper sessions are used to outline and visualize (work) processes, either within a department or across departments. The goal is often to quickly find bottlenecks in processes and to clarify them. Also, brown paper sessions are used to jointly construct future processes and show the gap between those future processes and the current situation.

In strategy processes the brown paper session method can be extended to topics other than (work) processes. It can be used to further the comprehensiveness of the analysis and/or to involve large(r) groups in the analysis. Participants can then contribute, associate and analyse developments together. This often leads to a discussion about what is and what is not relevant for the future strategy. The method can also be used for the creation of an implementation plan for the strategy, with milestones that often span several years.

Regardless of the substantive goal of the brown paper session, this method of engagement allows participants to participate actively and often intensifies the debate. This makes it an excellent method when the energy of a group decreases significantly, for example after lunch, or when more discussion and equality are needed in the process, or when a wider scope or better prioritization is needed.

How to use it

A brown paper session requires the following attributes:

- large pieces of (brown) paper, preferably big enough to cover entire walls;
- markers in different colours;
- sticky notes in different colours.

Important considerations for a brown paper session are:

- Start with a clear goal in mind.
- Make this goal explicit for all participants.
- Give participants a clear procedure to follow, by structuring the various activities.
- Stimulate participants to express themselves and to contribute.

Methods for the 'creative' characteristic

 ## The 'creative' characteristic

Formulating a new strategy is a process of discovering future opportunities and impossibilities. It therefore demands some creativity. In some situations it is better to think 'outside the box' or even not to think in terms of boxes at all. Looking at an issue from different perspectives can provide new insights which may also be relevant.

By its very nature, Step 1 (Searchlight) can be strongly characterized as creative. The known precedents are for a brief moment irrelevant, as the organization looks for its future playing field and games to play on it.

Step 2 (Outside-in) requires some creativity. The emphasis is not only on correct analysis of external developments, but participants are also invited to think of (and imagine) possible futures to which the organization must respond.

In Step 3 (Inside-out) participants are also invited to think of (and imagine) future possibilities for the current organization. This requires a little creativity.

Participants in Step 4 (Options) should again be highly creative. The outcomes of Steps 2 and 3 will be combined in this step, but the best combination is not always obvious. By putting together different combinations, for instance successively taking the outcomes of Steps 2 and 3 as variable input, more original options will be generated and more interesting ideas can be discussed. This process also helps in creating support for the options, as all points of view are taken into account, even though this sometimes means that people are forced out of their comfort zone during discussions. This chapter introduces methods of engagement that promote creativity.

The following methods are introduced in random order:

- moving values: depicting emotions and visions;
- energizers: constructing a tower together;
- futuring;
- reverse thinking;
- De Bono's 'six thinking hats'.

Moving values: depicting emotions and visions

The big picture

The moving values method actually consists of a big pile of images of very different things: individuals, groups, animals, objects, buildings, landscapes and situations. Images can move people, motivate them and touch them. The idea behind the moving values method is that words and concepts only gain meaning when people can relate to them through their own perception, when they personally associate images with themselves. People are naturally inclined to think and reason verbally. Associating images instead of discussing verbally anticipates sentiment and perception, allowing participants to think of their own, less obvious answer to a posed question and to better remember the outcomes of the discussion.

When to use it

Moving values stimulates people to think about themselves in relation to the organizational issue or strategy. It demands from participants that they think in images and thoughts that only secondarily need to be expressed in words. This method is therefore very suitable at the beginning of a meeting to let participants get acquainted with each other or to express their personal expectations or presumptions on the future of the organization.

The latter can be done by asking participants to select an image from the pile which symbolizes for them the biggest challenge the organization is facing or which symbolizes the organization when the new strategy brings the desired successes. Similarly, it is also possible to ask participants to select an image that symbolizes the implications of the new strategy for their personal situation (position or role). Participants then verbally explain their selected image and/or the meaning of the symbols depicted. As this will help them experience what the strategy actually means to individuals, it will accelerate support for the strategy.

How to use it

For this method, about a hundred different images (photographic originals/ cards) of individuals, groups, animals, things, buildings and landscapes are needed. The duration of this method is about half an hour. Spread the pictures on the floor or on a large table and let participants quietly have a look at them. Then let each participant choose an image that symbolizes their opinion, statement or answer to the central question posed by the facilitator. Round off the session by letting each participant briefly explain why he or she has chosen a particular image.

Energizers: constructing a tower together

The big picture

Snacks, jokes, incitements, interactions or whatever you call them, energizers are useful to loosen up discussions and to 'recharge' participants. They provide energy, stimulate involvement and bring participants together.

Constructing a tower together from a pack of paper is a group assignment to build the highest possible tower. It is an energizer under the theme 'cooperation'.

The method gives insights into the preferential roles and management styles of the participants, as they are free to choose the way they work together to construct the tower. In the debriefing the facilitator will point out the chosen roles and method of collaborating. The facilitator also relates these observations to the daily practice of the participants or to the roles of the participants in the strategy process.

When to use it

Energizers can be used as the focus weakens or after a break in the programme, for example to counter the 'post-lunch energy dip'. The method can be used with an existing team or with a new team that faces a joint challenge. It can also be used in a meeting in which cooperation is central or important, for instance in the first meetings of the teams that perform (part of) the analysis in the strategy process. Letting the team construct a tower together gives insights into the preferred styles of the participants. In a playful manner it can be observed who, by nature, are doers, thinkers, decision makers and/or dreamers. In a team, all kinds of individuals with complementary styles are needed. By being aware of your naturally preferred style, you are better able to take on a complementary role in the team.

How to use it

For constructing a tower together, a minimum of five and a maximum of eight participants per group is required. When there are more than eight, split the participants into subgroups that build in parallel in the same space. This also adds other elements, such as competition and cooperation among themselves.

Next, a pack of A4 paper of approximately 250 sheets per group (the raw material for building the tower) is needed. And each group needs a description of the assignment, which in essence should say: 'Construct from this pack of paper, without glue, staples, walls, chairs or other tools, a tower as high as possible in the next 15 minutes.'

Futuring

The big picture

Futuring is a method of engagement that is often described as a way of strategic thinking. The method aims for participants to anticipate future events and opportunities, especially those that are not expected from extrapolating from known developments. Through techniques and models such as scenario planning and vision development, futures that are deemed unrealistic are brought closer for participants and they will become more inspired and motivated. Futuring consists of several steps, starting from a specific question: distinguish relevant trends, translate those trends to day-to-day practice, link them to your own organization, and translate them into specific actions, decisions, products or services.

When to use it

Futuring is a method that enhances creativity, which is particularly useful when groups or individuals are too fixed on familiar outcomes. In futuring, participants are positively invited to think beyond the comfortable and obvious: seemingly impossible future possibilities can be brought to life in an inspiring way. Futuring always involves both external developments (macroeconomic, market and customer level) and internal developments (activities and products). Because this method helps to translate the abstract to specific, day-to-day practice, it helps break a potentially cynical atmosphere in a group (typically recognized by statements such as 'it won't work' or 'we have tried it 10 times already'). Hence, futuring is frequently used not only in strategy processes but also in innovation processes.

How to use it

Not much preparation is needed for futuring. The main ingredients are a clear framework (a step-by-step approach), availability of relevant information on the most important future developments, and the time to process this information. A flip chart or other appropriate means to capture the insights from the group is the only other requirement.

Reverse thinking

The big picture

Reverse thinking is, like futuring, a method that brings a new and often seemingly impossible situation closer, only in this case it is not so much a situation further away in time as one further removed from the organization itself. Reverse thinking is derived from lateral thinking. An organization has, for example, a question: 'How can we attract new customers?' The reverse thinking method reverses the question: 'What must we do to have maximal appeal to our existing customers?' The answers to the reversed question can then be translated to the original question and will provide inspiring new ideas to attract new customers, in this example.

When to use it

Reverse thinking offers a solution if no innovative ideas emerge when answering the original question. It is also an appropriate method to check whether all creative solutions have already been given. By exploring the opposite direction of the desired solution, much will become clear about what it takes to reach it.

How to use it

The reverse thinking method requires little preparation. All that is needed is a problem statement or question that can be reversed, and some tools such as a flip chart or laptop to capture the participants' ideas.

De Bono's six thinking hats

The big picture

In his 1985 book of the same name, Edward de Bono introduced six thinking hats, each with its own colour, that correspond to the input and the way of thinking of participants. Each participant is given a hat of a certain colour and told to think and talk from a specific perspective. By thinking from a certain angle, represented by the coloured hat, the participants' initial responses will be changed. Someone who, for example, always talks about facts (white hat) is invited also to look at the possibilities (green hat). Thinking hats can also be used in a team to get a picture of how and what is communicated and where possible gaps in team cooperation might occur.

When to use it

The thinking hats provide insight into the way people communicate with each other. They help people to use a different mindset. This method thereby makes it possible for participants to contribute in a way they would never have imagined and to express opinions they wouldn't normally hold. It also forces the participants to nuance their own perspective. Finally, it is a convenient method when a team has to be reminded what it means to act as a team and to contribute in a manner that is complementary to each other. De Bono's six thinking hats is a method that looks at options from all angles, improving the quality of the final decision.

How to use it

For this method all that is required is some coloured paper for making paper hats or badges in six different colours:

- white (facts and figures);
- red (feeling and intuition);
- black (negative);
- yellow (positive);
- green(fertile);
- blue (control and distance).

22 Methods for the 'analytic' characteristic

The 'analytic' characteristic

A dialogue on strategic choices requires considerations based on facts and on the outcomes of thorough analyses. These analyses should also guarantee the rationality and objectivity of the decision-making process. Therefore, the strategic dialogue model maps out both the current and future playing fields with both qualitative and quantitative analysis of the implication(s) of the different strategic choices.

The analytical content is not constantly required and differs per phase. In two steps as introduced in Part 2 of this book, the analytic characteristic is evident: the name of Step 3 (Inside-out: analysis) implies that this phase is for a large part about analyses. Step 2 (Outside-in: scenarios) also has a strong analytical component. As much information on the outside world as possible is collected, interpreted and looked at from multiple angles, including the less obvious ones. Lastly, in Step 8 (Monitoring), analyses of performance to strategy are made to keep the organization on course. Constant analyses of developments in the context of the organization will identify if the chosen course is still the right one.

In this chapter, methods of engagement that can enhance the analytical characteristic are introduced: either to bring the right facts to the table, to increase and safeguard objectivity, or both.

The following methods are introduced in random order:

- document research (desk research);
- interviews (with stakeholders);
- House of Commons debate;
- benchmarking.

Document research (desk research)

The big picture

Document research (or desk research) is a collective term for gathering information and analysing it directly. Research is based on as many relevant sources as possible, and the analysis often results not only in new insights but also in additional sources for more and/or other relevant information. For proper document research, it is important to proceed in a structured manner. Otherwise there is a risk that the researcher doesn't see the wood for the trees or, even worse, has only subjective sources. A good approach is to determine references and a framework for research in advance, and to consider which (type of) insights the analysis should yield. Those who work in this structured way can never collect too much information.

When to use it

Document research provides the possibility of processing large amounts of information in a structured way and distilling the most important information. Thus it can be used for obtaining information about the company itself (annual reports or financial statements, profitability analysis, employee performance etc), market information, supply chain information, competitor data, customer information and even trends and developments at the macroeconomic level. Document research is essential in the strategic dialogue model, particularly in Step 2 (Outside-in) and Step 3 (Inside-out). But at other times it is equally good to put some distance between the researchers and the issue and/or stakeholders at hand and look at the topic through structured analysis of (objective) information. This distance can be furthered by letting people who have not been involved before do the document research, which also increases the objectivity of the analysis.

How to use it

The information to be analysed through document research will mostly be already available in the organization, for example in business management software solutions systems or in archives, but often not all of it. Contemporary management information systems will have business intelligence modules, connecting and disclosing many of the organization's data. Also, software that works with so-called Big Data can be used to obtain the right data or to process them.

Other ways to get information include from the internet, from interviews (see the next method in this chapter) or by collecting or buying market information or competitor benchmark information (see later in this chapter).

Interviews (with stakeholders)

The big picture

Interviewing is all about gathering information from and about the most important stakeholders. These stakeholders are of interest to the organization either in general or for the specific issue at hand. This requires a good notion of who these most important stakeholders are: they can be found both within and outside the organization. Interviewees' opinions are almost by definition subjective: even when asked about observable events or objective facts, interviewees will always put their own spin on them. That is also one of the key added values of interviews: the facts that come to light are a reflection of the opinion of the stakeholders and the importance they attach to them.

Obtaining information through interviews can be done in either a quantitative or qualitative way. Quantitative research is useful for consulting a large number of stakeholders, resulting in the possibility of displaying, for example, percentage ratios. Quantitative research can take place through personal contact (face-to-face interview), by phone, in writing, and of course also via the internet.

Qualitative research can give more in-depth and background information. It provides an image of the opinions, wishes, requirements, experiences and needs of the interviewees (the target group). Qualitative research can be carried out by means of in-depth interviews and group discussions.

When to use it

Qualitative interviews are particularly suitable for getting to know the story behind the story. By thoroughly discussing a topic with a number of stakeholders, it is easier to identify what is really important to them or what exactly the issue is about. Quantitative interviews are like surveys: they are generally more suitable when the nature of the problem is known but not its scale and magnitude.

By gathering information very broadly and from a large group of stakeholders, it will become clear for whom the topic is most relevant and what the opinions on the topic are, revealing both majority and minority views.

How to use it

For quantitative research:

- a standardized questionnaire with a clear introduction;
- a tight schedule for release of the questionnaire;
- an invitation to participants;
- a reminder to participate;
- closure of the questionnaire as planned;
- analysis of the results;
- presentation of the results (online or in writing).

For qualitative research:

- a (semi-)structured questionnaire or list of topics;
- a good recording method, preferably with a voice recorder so that the interviewer is not occupied with taking notes but is free to do the interview. Otherwise, pen and paper will do equally well.

House of Commons debate

The big picture

Named after the British House of Commons, this method is about debating a topic using arguments, not emotion. In this method, all relevant – and also some less relevant – arguments come to the table, and it becomes clear who takes which standpoint in the debate. In every debate, emotion will be displayed, but owing to the visibility of the arguments and the overall motivation of the participants, emotion will strengthen the overall experience without eclipsing the arguments.

To start the method, a facilitator formulates, with the participants, a strong statement around a topic, for which there are about as many supporters as opponents. Next, the participants have the opportunity to engage in debate with each other. During the debate, everyone gets the chance to put forward their arguments; the debating environment challenges them to put forward clear and well-considered arguments. The debate stops when all supporters and opponents have expressed their arguments and are convinced that they have expressed their opinions properly. The goal is not to reach consensus, but to reach mutual insight into the arguments (and motivation and emotion) of others.

When to use it

A manager can use this method when a team seems to be in disagreement on a particular topic. The method is particularly useful when discussions become polarized. By organizing a structured debate, motivations and emotions can be explicitly expressed, so that everyone becomes aware of the perceptions of others and it becomes clear that there are more sides to the question than perhaps they had realized. The effect is that emotions are less dominant and participants gain more insight into the positions and corresponding justifications of the others. Often, differences in opinions turn out to be much smaller than expected upfront. At that point in time it is good to go back to the content, for example by proposing a procedure for reporting jointly on this topic.

A House of Commons debate improves relationships as everyone gets clear visibility of the motives and rationale of others.

How to use it

A House of Commons debate is useful when there is a group or team of participants, preferably between 8 and 20, which has a topic on which the group members do not agree and where discussion tends to polarize quickly, letting spontaneous discussion get out of control. The debate is led by a facilitator who is not allowed to interfere with the content in any way (he or she should not express any personal opinion on the matter). For topics where the group's superior or manager is strongly involved, a neutral facilitator should be appointed. Also, the facilitator must be able to maintain discipline and order and pay particular attention to time management. The debate should take place in a closed room with a central row of tables, so that supporters and opponents can sit opposite each other and about five feet apart (at 'sword length').

Benchmarking

The big picture

Benchmarking provides answers to two questions: is the grass really greener on the other side of the fence, and if so, how did they achieve that? Benchmarking is often regarded as a model, not a method. In its purest form, it is nothing more than comparing information: how do we stand relative to others? Often this comparison is made on the basis of information that is structured: in other words, a model. For example, if you are benchmarking a company's overheads, the composition of staff departments and the methods used to measure the performance of these departments are compared to those of other organizations, following a fixed procedure.

There are several ways to benchmark. An internal benchmark compares teams or business units within an organization. An industry benchmark compares organizations within a particular industry. A competitor benchmark does the same, but more specifically for the most similar organizations that target the same (potential) customers. It is also possible to buy expert databases containing information on competitors or other organizations and use them for your benchmarking exercise, but often the information they hold is not clearly defined or it is ambiguous.

Usually, benchmarking is about comparing the organization to the average of the benchmark population. This gives companies insight into their own situation and how the organization performs compared to the average. Often, however, it is more insightful for the organization to compare itself not to the average but to the best, for example the top 25 per cent. By coupling this comparison with certain good or best practices, the areas in which improvement is needed often become very clear. However, benchmarking doesn't tell you how to improve (it usually can't specify the differences in performance), but rather gives insights into what to improve. Benchmarks don't make judgements, and only when there is no explanation for a deviation from expected performance does it makes sense to look for improvement (eg relatively high training costs can be the result of a strategic choice concerned with investing in employee skills).

When to use it

Traditionally, benchmarking has mainly been used for financial or competitor analyses. Today, it is increasingly used to improve efficiency and processes. Historical benchmarking can sometimes lead to new and surprising insights: by comparing current performance to that of an earlier point in time, progress can be made visible. There is a downside to this, though: comparing the organization to itself carries the danger of too much introspection. It also ignores external changes, such as technological or macroeconomic developments.

Another warning regarding benchmarking is that the outcome of the benchmark (ie the relative performance of the organization) should never be a goal in itself: no organization will beat the competition by being equally as good as them!

How to use it

Good benchmarking is often trickier than it appears at first sight. First, you must have very clear and unambiguous definitions. Then, you must define measurement methods that objectively and properly measure what the organization wants to compare. While measuring within the organization itself is difficult, measuring other organizations will probably be even more difficult, if not impossible. Besides, organizations in general are often reluctant to disclose information to a competitor, even when the outcomes of the benchmark are made available to all participants. Therefore, many organizations make use of (independent) benchmark databases. After carrying out the benchmark, a report on the comparative performance of each participant is written and directions for improvement defined.

23 Methods for the 'decisive' characteristic

 ## The 'decisive' characteristic

A common critique of decision making through dialogue is that the method is all about talking and does not result in any actual decisions. In the strategy process with the strategic dialogue model, dialogue is a means, not an end. Making strategic choices is its central activity. Using a dialogue to come to a decision has value in winning support for the choice made in the process. A dialogue also helps the substantiation of the choice, by safeguarding the consideration of both external and internal input.

In the strategic dialogue model, decision making is most prominent in Step 5 (Choice): here the strategic options identified are weighed and choices made. Most of the other steps are less characterized by decision making. In Steps 2 (Outside-in), 3 (Inside-out), 5 (Choice) and 7 (Execution), decisions are mostly made regarding the process (in particular on the approach and/or methods), not so much regarding the content. In Step 1 (Searchlight) there are some important decisions to be made: regarding both the scope of the strategy (what game does the organization want to play) and the strategy process (whom to involve, what analyses to do, when to be ready etc). In Step 6 (Operationalization), decisions related to the content are made: after choosing the strategic direction, decisions on how the organization wants to execute the strategy (the tactics of the game) are made. And in Step 8 (Monitoring), choices regarding performance which is in line with the strategic direction or deviating from it are made. Decisions in this step are mostly on whether or not action should be taken.

It is generally not so difficult to come up with ways to make decisions. Just raise your hand when in favour is universally the easiest way, but it is hardly ever done in today's management teams. Therefore, other methods are introduced in this chapter. Many are suited for decision making by larger groups and have been redesigned for decision making in strategy processes with the strategic dialogue model.

In this chapter the following methods are presented in random order:

- metaplan;
- tokamak ('nuclear pressure-cooker');
- voting with your feet;
- pyramid discussion.

Metaplan

The big picture

A metaplan is intended to combine the contributions of large numbers of participants. It starts with the formulation of a central question in a group session. All participants then contribute to the metaplan by writing their ideas on a shared piece of paper (sticky notes are often used). Together with the participants, a moderator then categorizes the notes and decisions can be made for each category. Participants can thus commit themselves to a number of agreements. In each subsequent group session the metaplan is brought out again in order to keep these agreements in mind.

When to use it

A metaplan can be used in assessments, brainstorming sessions, vision development sessions or when trying to make knowledge or information from employees specific. It provides a common outcome, based on the diverse contributions of the participants. The metaplan brings a discussion (more) alive and enhances a sense of shared decision making. It so increases support – essential within a strategy process with the strategic dialogue model – for the choices and agreements that are made. This method is effective both for large groups with up to 200 participants and for small groups, for example a management team.

How to use it

For a metaplan you will need the following:

- sticky notes, preferably large and in different colours;
- markers (one per person);
- a blank wall on which the sticky notes can remain and some large pieces of paper;
- some tape.

Tokamak ('nuclear pressure-cooker')

The big picture

Named after a nuclear fusion process, tokamak is the bringing together of the energy of experts to come to new insights. In the world of nuclear physics, tokamak is the name for a process in which a series of explosions are created through extreme heat. This exploding mass of fire moves like a whirlpool and at a given point in time goes into perpetual motion. It becomes a kind of generator. The reactor in which this process takes place is called the 'tokamak'. Similarly, the tokamak method aims to provide the same process of energy propagation: at first consuming but then generating energy and insights. In a session of half a day, 8–15 people come together. They have all prepared their own insight or good idea in advance. These ideas are then further developed in the tokamak and enriched with the ideas and suggestions of the other participants. The entire process takes place in one room. Owing to working under the pressure of time constraints, it is possible to come up with a lot of results in a short time, not only through enforced creativity, but also in converging towards specific and ultimately practical actions. For each action, an 'owner' is named before the end of the tokamak session and key performance indicators are defined.

When to use it

A tokamak enables quick selection from a large number of alternatives and the production of a clear action plan. This may be useful, for example, when an organization wants to enter new markets quickly, or to identify and solve organizational bottlenecks efficiently. The tokamak provides direction and acceleration in situations where there are many different ideas.

How to use it

A tokamak should take place in a room which allows participants to be sealed off from any outside disturbances and which is not too large for the group. The participants' discussion follows a structured procedure, but one which leaves room for creativity. A strict timetable and an itera-tive procedure speed up the process. Every participant provides input in every step. There are two to three people to guide the process, keep track of the time and ensure that the procedures are followed and that appointments and outcomes are guaranteed.

Voting with your feet

The big picture

In the voting with your feet method, participants discuss the topic and then vote by moving to a position in the room that matches their choice. They vote with their feet, so to say. This method is useful when there are more than two options, but it is also an interesting method for binary questions. Although it is not meant for making choices, the method makes the positions of the participants on the topic at hand clearly visible. When used for decision making, it forces people to take a posi-tion openly and doesn't allow them to hide.

When to use it

Voting with your feet is a good method for involving everyone in the discussion and making the various opinions in the group explicit. Often it is also a way to get some energy into groups: using this method liter-ally means that participants must stand up and take a position. In such situations, this method is used as a starting point for discussion by getting everyone involved. In other situations, when discussions tend to become an endless repetition of arguments, the voting with your feet method clarifies the opinions and relationships of the participants in a fun and energetic way. To this end, this method is especially useful when holding discussions and/or making decisions with large groups.

How to use it

Voting with your feet requires:

- a sharp thesis that can trigger discussion and division in the group;
- tape to create division lines on the floor.

Pyramid discussion

The big picture

The pyramid discussion is a method that enables a large group to discuss a topic and make a decision without taking too much time over it. The pyramid discussion begins with discussions among small groups (pairs) of participants. After the first round of discussions, two (or more) small groups merge and discussion resumes in this larger group. Groups merge after every subsequent discussion, until there is a plenary discussion about two alternatives. The debate goes as follows:

- Start off in pairs: decide jointly how to answer the question or statement after a short discussion and note the result on a map (for example: 'These are the four main developments in our market').

- Merge into foursomes: an equally brief discussion between the two pairs in which their initial results are exchanged and reinforced, which leads to as many answers as the first discussion. Write down these results on a map (for example: 'These are the four most important developments in our market').

- Merge into octets: the two foursomes present their results as before, and the octet jointly comes to a new, shared choice (for example: 'These are the four most critical developments in our market').

- Continue until four teams remain (more than 16 people per team is not recommended). Each team appoints a representative, chosen in a separate brief discussion in the team.

- The four representatives meet separately and again try to come to a joint decision. When this has been achieved, they write it down for all to see. Then, all participants are invited to rejoin the discussion. Using a method such as voting with your feet, participants can express their consent (or not) to the compromise achieved by the four representatives. This is repeated until a majority vote is achieved, with the compromise adjusted as and when requested by the participants.

When to use it

The pyramid discussion method is suitable when a large group of people need to think about a particular subject and take a position on it. Support for a proposal increases with each subsequent round, in which participants repeatedly defend their idea as they naturally want it to go forward to the next round. Owing to time constraints, the group will still need to make compromises. This method is less appropriate in situations where additional analyses are required before decision making can proceed.

How to use it

For the pyramid discussion method, all that is required are flip charts (or large pieces of paper), plenty of markers (one for each subgroup) and a large room.

24 Methods for the 'committing' characteristic

 ## The 'committing' characteristic

Participation, creativity, analysis and decision making are all very important, of course, but useless if they are not linked to a certain degree of involvement. Participants and responsible parties must stand behind the outcomes and choices: they must give their commitment to it. By linking a certain degree of involvement to the choices made, participants will be motivated to actually follow up on the outcomes and choices. This requires an understanding of the choices made and of the factors driving them, and an awareness of the consequences. Good communication about the choices and the selection process is crucial for this. In Steps 6 (Operationalization) and 7 (Execution), a high degree of commitment is required. In particular, line management and staff departments that will have an important role in the implementation of the strategic choices will have to commit to them, in order to take the lead correctly in implementation and realization. Step 5 (Choices) also requires a lot of commitment, albeit from a different group, namely policymakers, management and the board. Step 1 (Searchlight) also calls for commitment from people to get behind a shared ambition.

Many of the methods presented in the earlier chapters of this part of the book also have elements that encourage commitment from participants. But for anyone seeking methods which enable participants to be explicit about their support for the conclusions and outcomes and/or methods that drive participants to follow up on the outcomes, this last chapter will present some useful suggestions for methods that encourage commitment.

In this chapter the following methods are presented in random order:

- signing up for allocated tasks;
- simulations;
- elevator pitch.

Signing up for allocated tasks

The big picture

Letting participants in a discussion put their signature to the conclusions and outcomes guarantees that all members of the group will actually stand behind the conclusions: they signed up to them. Allocating tasks and making participants sign up to them will make sure that participants really relate to the(ir) task(s) in the implementation of the strategy. This gets realization of the strategic choices off to a good start: each person has signed up for a specific responsibility. Putting their signature to it – it is even better if this is done at an event created for that purpose, for example signing it as a historical document in a place with suitable decor, a photographer and invited dignitaries or actors – puts just that little bit of extra emphasis and playfulness on what for most people seems self-evident and logical but for others seems just a little bit scary.

When to use it

This method is designed to reinforce what has been agreed, or to ensure that everyone has the same purpose or direction. The method is best used at the end of a step to capture the outcomes. In addition, this method ensures that people cannot hide, but must take responsibility and stand behind a group decision. The signature later serves as a big stick, if anyone does not do what he or she is expected to do and signed up for.

How to use it

For this method, in principle only pen and paper are needed, or a modern-day equivalent such as a tablet computer or equivalent. But when a more theatrical approach is desired, a stately writing desk, a special pen or quill, flags, champagne and other attributes that make it into a solemn event serve the occasion and add to the fun.

Simulations

The big picture

A simulation is 'the mimicking of reality'. To really understand a strategic direction, it helps to experience it. This can be done by simulating the outcomes and consequences of the new strategic direction and by mimicking the future situation to which the strategic direction will lead. These simulations can be in the form of a play, a movie, a story, appropriate music, storytelling, role play etc.

A more advanced method of simulation is serious gaming. Serious gaming mimics the consequences of a strategic direction with a computerized game. This way, participants can experience virtually what working according to new processes will be like, or they can experiment with a new style of leadership. In this way, participants can learn about the new situation before it becomes reality. Through this first-hand experience, participants get acquainted with the new situation and, with the positive experience from the simulation, look forward to it: they are more committed to it than they were before their experience with the simulation.

When to use it

Simulation is an appropriate method to allow a group of participants to experience and really understand the strategic direction to which the organization aspires, and to get feedback about the consequences of the new strategic direction even before the new situation materializes.

How to use it

For each situation the requirements are different. A fully developed serious game is usually costly because of high development costs and therefore it is usually only of interest for large or disruptive change programmes. But a simulation using a few actors in a role-play situation based on a self-written script is usually quite easy to arrange.

Elevator pitch

The big picture

An elevator pitch is a catchy and unique storytelling method that management can use to convey where the organization stands now and in the future. The elevator pitch is similar to a chat in an elevator, which takes about 90 seconds: the time taken by the elevator to go from the ground floor to the 20th floor. What do you say in this short time to get someone interested in strategic choices about where the organization stands now and what will make it successful in the future?

When to use it

An elevator pitch is a kind of 'story-selling' – it is about selling your ideas through a very short but convincing story. The method can bring both the current and the future situation to the attention of participants and let them discuss it.

This method also enables participants to put the desired future situation and direction of the organization into their own words. Also, in situations where alleged obstacles stand in the way of real progress, it is an effective means of clarifying the future picture. This method can be used in practically all steps.

How to use it

Preferably an elevator (lift) is used, or a short film with a lift that runs in the background. But essentially only a timer is needed.

PART 5
Applying the strategic dialogue

We introduced the strategic dialogue model in Parts 1 and 2 of this book. The model consists of 8 steps, allowing us to make maximum use of the participative and inclusive approach to strategy it entails. The strategic dialogue model lets you unleash the power of engagement. But how can you apply it to your own strategy process? Are there any points of attention or pitfalls to avoid?

In Part 5, we present some points of attention on how to best get started with your own strategy process with the strategic dialogue model. We will show that some aspects and steps in the strategy process with the strategic dialogue will differ depending on the situation at hand. For different contexts we will present some hints and clues as to how to use the strategic dialogue model differently from in a 'normal' context.

This final part then concludes with some suggestions on how to avoid the most common pitfalls in a strategy process.

Points of attention when applying the strategic dialogue model

In Part 1 of this book we introduced the strategic dialogue model, consisting of 8 steps through which strategy can be formulated and implemented. There are two important points of attention when applying the strategic dialogue model. The first is the recommendation of proper preparation and strong facilitation of the strategy process. The second is about recognizing the actual starting point of the strategy process.

Any strategy process must always be prepared in advance. This also holds for going through the 8 steps of the strategic dialogue model. Before the start of the process, the sequence of activities and the different roles of participants (and when they will be required) must be clear to all those likely to be involved. Often a core strategy team is formed in this preparatory stage, a facilitator is appointed and, not least, time is reserved in the stakeholders' schedules. Proper preparation will smooth the process. And clear roles and facilitation (with an appointed facilitator) helps to keep the process on track.

To complete the strategy process successfully, we highly recommend that you appoint a facilitator. Ideally the facilitator should be independent, well informed, very capable and with the right level of seniority. All participants and all those involved and engaged in the strategy process should naturally accept this person in the role of facilitator, which is a very important role in a strategy process. Appointing a facilitator enables timely follow-through of all activities, appropriate involvement of stakeholders and good conduct during the process. The facilitator can also initiate all the preparations for the strategy process, including planning and sequencing of activities, sending invitations to participants and stakeholders, the formation of the strategy team and the division of roles and responsibilities between the strategy team and the board of directors and management. As mentioned in Part 1, proper preparation and clear roles will smooth the process, and appropriate facilitation helps to keep the process on track.

The facilitator should actively steer the process. Each step in a strategy process with the strategic dialogue model involves elements of participation, creativity, decision making, analysis and commitment. These five important characteristics can be actively influenced in each of the 8 steps by a facilitator, who can guide participants effectively towards the desired outcomes of the strategy process.

Often a facilitator is only appointed when it is decided that a strategy process should take place. However, in reality strategy processes do not always start at Step 1, but are often triggered by a finding in one of the other steps. The starting point can thus be almost any step (see Figure 25.1). For example, if you are sure that the mission statement and ambition are still relevant and that all the necessary information about the context and environment is at hand, you can start at Step 3 (Inside-out). As long as you are sure that there is sufficient information on the previous steps, you can start wherever seems to be most appropriate – but the information you have must be consistent and up to date, and you must take the direction of the arrows into account.

The strategy process with the strategic dialogue model is thus not necessarily a linear one, as already mentioned in Part 1. But even when you start at a point of your choosing, you must understand and have an overview of the coherence and interactions among all phases before you begin, if you are to complete the strategy process successfully. Very often in our consulting practice, we find that difficulties with implementation are the result of not having analysed all relevant data in previous steps and that choices have been made too easily. At any starting point, proper preparation of the strategy process and the timely appointment of a facilitator are key to ensuring that you obtain an overview of all steps and that you obtain and consult the information from previous steps.

FIGURE 25.1 Different starting points in the strategic dialogue model

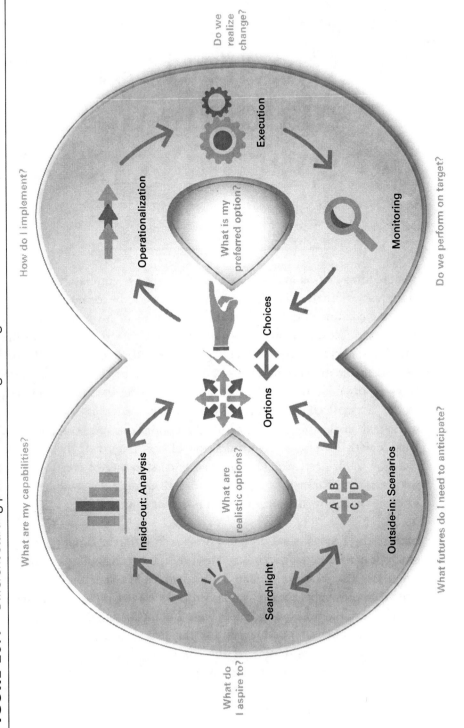

26 Applying the strategic dialogue in specific contexts

In the Introduction and in Part 1 of the book, we emphasized that the context or situation in which a new strategy is to be formulated affects both the content of the strategy and the process of how the strategy is formulated. This, of course, also holds for a strategy process with the strategic dialogue model, the scope and depth of which are also highly dependent on the specific context. This chapter presents the different ways to organize the strategic process in specific contexts compared to the 'normal' context. This includes contexts such as restructuring, mergers or acquisitions and external disruptions (new technologies etc). Part 2, with its extensive introduction of the 8 steps of the strategic dialogue model, has provided a basic understanding of each of the 8 steps and their characteristics in the 'normal' context. This will help you to understand how to adjust them in different contexts.

Each of the 8 steps has a different process in different situations. How much or how little factual information on the organization is available will affect the progress of Step 3 (Inside-out). Whether the market in which the company operates is relatively stable and simple, or extremely dynamic and complex, will affect Step 2 (Outside-in). Do you expect to carry out only a limited revision of the defined strategy or will there be a thorough repositioning of the company? Is there a high degree of freedom in formulating the company's strategy or only limited room for manoeuvre? Both will affect Steps 1 (Searchlight), 4 (Options) and 5 (Choice). Context matters!

Below we discuss/provide guidelines on how best to factor in the context in a strategy process with the strategic dialogue for some commonly found contexts.

This chapter discusses the following situations:

- restructuring;
- external shock or disruption;
- merger or acquisition.

In each of these situations, compromises must be made between different aspects of the strategy process as circumstances dictate. It may be that there is very little time available, and the lead-time will therefore be limited. It might be the case that confidentiality requirements limit the ability of the people involved to express themselves. The nature of a specific situation determines the strategy process, sometimes creating more constraints than would be the case in a 'regular' strategy process.

Restructuring

Where restructuring is needed, it is probable that results have been bad for a long period of time, there is now even more deterioration, and the company's banks will be pressing the entrepreneur to research new perspectives. There is great urgency to improve both the rate of return and cash flow, and drastic measures are required. This will affect how the strategy process with the strategic dialogue model can and must be carried out:

- A shorter lead-time means less opportunity to involve many people, both from inside and outside the company. The process will therefore be narrower than in a normal setting.
- More internal parties than external parties will be involved, since involving the latter takes more time. Confidentiality also plays an important role in this.
- The short-term solution will have to be found in the context of the current organization and competences. The focus is on

exploitation rather than exploration, although some attention should be paid to long-term prospects.

- Analysis will be focused on the main causes of the problems in order to obtain a complete picture of them, so that the right decision can be made within a short period of time.

- Decision making will be more directive, as there is no time for consensus and people in an emergency situation are more likely to take immediate action, having in mind the adage 'If there is a fire, you had better start fighting it instead of having meetings.'

External shock or disruption

Sometimes a drastic distortion of the market occurs, for whatever reason. Often the cause is unforeseen. In this situation, the existing rules in the market and value chain become invalid. An inventive solution must be found quickly. Examples of external changes include the entry of a new competitor in the market, the emergence of a new technology or the introduction of new products that perform far better than the old ones. These external shocks or disruptions have the following effects on the strategy process with the strategic dialogue model:

- A shorter lead-time means less opportunity to involve many people, both from inside and outside the company. The strategy process will therefore be more narrowly focused than in a normal setting.

- The strategy process will involve more external parties than employees, since the reason for the strategic reorientation lies within the market. It is important to get a clear view as soon as possible of customer, supplier and competitor responses to the market distortion.

- The short-term solution should be sought within the market. This means that the focus is on exploration, although some attention needs to be paid to exploitation, for example to anticipate the short-term drop in demand.

- Analysis will preferably be focused on the main causes of the problem and making a quick exploration of it in order to develop ideas in the short term.

- Decision making will, in spite of the desired speed, be focused on achieving consensus and involving as many people as possible in order to mobilize them to anticipate the shock and feel committed to the solution.

Merger or acquisition

The most important characteristic of a merger or acquisition is that there is negotiation about the proposed agreement, which involves a small group of people and, to a lesser extent, the owners and financers of the companies, accountants and other financial services providers. The desired confidentiality restricts the possibilities for broad dialogue and engagement within the company. This applies to both the buyer and the seller. Furthermore, it is almost impossible to have a dialogue and engagement with external parties. The pressure is higher than in a regular strategy process, and there is no desire for slow, detailed negotiations, though this is less so than in a crisis situation. Strategic exploration is of great importance, not only to determine the merger's benefits and synergies, but also because the growth prospects largely determine the valuation. The main consequences for the strategy process with the strategic dialogue model are:

- The lead-time will be limited, which decreases opportunities for dialogue and engagement. Also, planning is often driven by the course of the negotiations.

- Creativity is mainly explorative. You should also look at the advantages of economies of scale, thus also exploitation. But the real value creation of mergers and acquisitions comes from combining the joint core competences and markets and developing new initiatives.

- Analysis must therefore be broad. Since it focuses on the long term (an acquisition is not initiated for just a couple of years), it cannot be very deep because many uncertainties are involved.

- Decision making will be directive; no large groups will be involved. Dedication from the top management of both companies is required. In the later stages of implementation of the synergy, more parts of the company should be mobilized, but in the case of rationalization this will not involve the entire company.

Differences when compared to the 'normal' context

Figure 26.1 provides an overview of the main consequences of the strategy process with the strategic dialogue model for each of the specific, common situations described in this chapter. The effects are compared to a 'normal' context to emphasize the effect of a specific context.

FIGURE 26.1 Overview of differences in strategy processes in different contexts

	Restructuring In times of financial distress	External shock Disruptive technology, market entry or exit of dominant player	Merger/acquisition Taking over or being taken over	'Normal' context
Participatory Participation of external parties and/or internal staff	Internal high External low	Internal low External high	Internal low External low	Internal high External high
Creative Focused on exploring (respond to opportunities and threats etc) or on exploitation (dealing with strengths and weaknesses)	Exploitation	Exploration	Exploration and exploitation	Exploration
Analytical General and broad (whole market and company-wide), or narrow (focused issues) and deep analyses	Narrow and deep	Narrow and general	Broad and general	Broad and deep
Decisive Decision-making process focused on consensus or on a directive approach	Directive	Consensus	Directive	Consensus
Committing Seeking commitment of the entire organization or mainly of the board and management team.	Board and management team	Entire organization	Board and management team	Entire organization

27 Try to avoid the most common pitfalls in a strategy process

In any strategy process there are a number of pitfalls to be avoided. These pitfalls relate both to the content of the strategy and to the strategy process. The most common pitfalls are:

- *'Me too.'* Companies tend to blindly follow their most important (or annoying) competitor. Do not be tempted to look up to 'the wrong guy'. Stay true to yourself and build on your own DNA.

- *'The grass is always greener on the other side of the fence.'* Organizations (like people) tend to be attracted to new initiatives or possibilities. Do not be tempted to set foot in new markets or take on new activities blindly. Make rational considerations and stick to your mission statement and core objectives.

- *'It's all about the money.'* Strategy tends to be dominated by the bottom line. Don't make strategy into an investment prospectus! Keep a broad perspective on your organization's raison d'être: it has more to offer than ROI.

- *'Chase after hockey stick effects.'* Organizations' directors often have very high ambitions regardless of actual developments. Planned performance then often looks like a hockey stick: year 1 +5%, year 2 +5% and suddenly in year 3 +50%. Don't be fooled when trends appear not to be developing at such speeds. Focus on rational analyses and make feasible projections for future performance.

- *'What are we really doing here?'* Sometimes organizations are so caught up in their own dynamics and almost routine activities that they are aware neither of the added value which customers attribute to the company's products and services nor of customers' overall perception of the company. Don't base decisions on assumptions about customers. Thoroughly analyse what your customers want and how you fulfil their needs now and could do so in the future.

- *'It's an exclusive matter.'* Strategy is often considered the domain of top management and directors. Don't consider yourself capable enough to do strategy all by yourself. Include input from employees, customers, suppliers and other key stakeholders to enrich your own insights and come to better-informed, and better, decisions.

- *'Paralysis by analysis.'* Management and directors often have a 'risk-oriented mindset'. Don't be tempted to pursue analysis to the nth degree. Strategy isn't solely about mathematics. It is also about decision making based on only a few facts and a lot of gut feel.

- *'Pulling a dead (hobby) horse.'* In every strategy process, individual preferences and pet projects come to light. Don't be tempted to endlessly promote or impose your own preferred idea. Build on objective analysis and choose what is best for the organization as a whole.

- *'Strategy as compromise.'* Sometimes management and directors have the best intentions to make everybody happy. Don't be tempted to keep everyone satisfied. Strategy is first and foremost about making choices, so don't hesitate to do so, even if it means that someone doesn't get his or her own way.

- *'Talk about people, not with people.'* Directors and management often find it difficult, inappropriate or inconvenient to engage with employees or other stakeholders. Don't stay locked up in an 'ivory tower' during the strategy process. Engage! Engage! Engage!

REFERENCES

Aaker, D A and McLoughlin, D (2010) *Strategic Market Management: Global perspectives*, John Wiley & Sons, Chichester

Abell, D F (1980) *Defining the Business: The starting point of strategic planning*, Prentice Hall, Englewood Cliffs, NJ

Abell, D F and Hammond, J S (1979) *Strategic Marketing Planning: Problems and analytical approaches*, Prentice Hall, Englewood Cliffs, NJ

Alsem, K J (2006) *Strategic Marketing: A practical approach*, McGraw-Hill, Maidenhead

Barnes, C, Blake, H and Pinder, D (2009) *Creating and Delivering Your Value Proposition: Managing customer experience for profit*, Kogan Page, London

Bodie, Z, Kane, A and Marcus, A J (2004) *Essentials of Investments*, Irwin/McGraw-Hill, New York

Burt, R S (2009) *Social Capital: Reaching out, reaching in*, Elgar Publishing, Northhampton, MA

Collins, J and Porras, J (1994) *Built to Last: Successful habits of visionary companies*, Harper Business, New York

Collins, J and Porras, J (1996) Building your company's vision, *Harvard Business Review*, 74 (5), pp 65–77

Curry, J (1992) *Know Your Customers: How customer marketing can increase profits*, Kogan Page, London

Curry, J and Curry, A (2000) *The Customer Marketing Method: How to implement and profit from customer relationship management*, Free Press, New York

EFQM (1992) *Total Quality Management: The European model for self-appraisal*, European Foundation for Quality Management, Brussels

Freeman, R E (1984 and 2010) *Strategic Management: A stakeholder approach*, Cambridge University Press, Cambridge

Freeman, R E and Harrison, J S (2010) *Stakeholder Theory: The state of the art*, Cambridge University Press, Cambridge

Gehrels, C, Van Venetië, E and Thevenet, J (2003) *Management Models for Communication* [translated from Dutch: *Managementmodellen voor communicatie*], Nieuwezijds/Academic Service, The Hague

Groppelli, A A and Nikbakht, E (2000) *Finance*, Barron's Educational Series, Hauppauge, NY

Hakes, C (2007) *The EFQM Excellence Model for Assessing Organizational Performance – A Management Guide*, Van Haren Publishing, Zaltbommel, The Netherlands

Hamel, G and Prahalad, C K (1994) *Competing for the Future: Breakthrough strategies for seizing control of your industry and creating the markets of tomorrow*, Harvard Business School Press, Cambridge, MA

Hill, T and Westbrook, R (1997) SWOT analysis: it's time for a product recall, *Long Range Planning*, 30 (1), pp 46–52

Johnson, G and Scholes, K (1998 and 2011) *Exploring Strategy*, Prentice Hall, Upper Saddle River, NJ (2011, 9th edn)

Kaplan, R and Norton, D (1992) The balanced scorecard: measures that drive performance, *Harvard Business Review*, January–February, pp 71–80

Kaplan, R and Norton, D (1996) *The Balanced Scorecard: Translating strategy into action*, Harvard Business School Press, Cambridge, MA

Kaplan, R and Norton, D (2004) *Strategy Maps: Converting intangible assets into tangible outcomes*, Harvard Business School Press, Cambridge, MA

Kelly, K (1997) New rules for the new economy: twelve dependable principles for thriving in a turbulent world, *Wired*, Issue 5.09, September

Keown, A J *et al* (1994) *Foundations of Finance: The logic and practice of financial management*, Prentice Hall, Englewood Cliffs, NJ

Kleinen, B *et al* (1998) Managing change of organizational culture [translated from Dutch: Management van cultuurverandering], *Elan*, 3 (12)

Kotler, P and Armstrong, G (1967 and 2011) *Marketing Management*, Prentice Hall, Upper Saddle River, NJ (2011, 14th edn)

Kotler, P, Kartajaya, H and Setiawan, I (2010) *Marketing 3.0: From products to customers to human spirit*, John Wiley & Sons Inc, Hoboken, NJ

Kotter, J P (1990) *Force for Change: How leadership differs from management*, Free Press, New York

Kotter, J P (1996) *Leading Change*, Harvard Business School Press, Cambridge, MA

Kotter, J P (2002) *The Heart of Change: Real-life stories of how people change their organizations*, Harvard Business School Press, Cambridge, MA

Maylor, H (2002) *Project Management*, 3rd edn, Financial Times/Pitman, London

Mitchell, R K, Agle, B R and Wood, D J (1997) Toward a theory of stakeholder identification and salience: defining the principle of who and what really counts, *Academy of Management Review*, 22 (4), pp 853–86

Moussault, A, Baardman, E and Brave, F (2006 and 2011) *International Project Management Association Anthology of Methods in Project Management* [translated from Dutch: *IPMA Wegwijzer voor methoden bij Projectmanagement*], Van Haren Publishing, Zaltbommel, The Netherlands (2011, 2nd edn)

Oakland, J (1994) *Total Quality Management: The route to improving performance*, Butterworth-Heinemann, Oxford

Osterwalder, A (2004) *The Business Model Ontology. A proposition in a design science approach*, University of Lausanne, Switzerland

Osterwalder, A and Pigneur, Y (2010) *Business Model Generation: A handbook for visionaries, game changers and challengers*, John Wiley & Sons, Chichester

Pietersma, P *et al* (2012) *The Grand Book on Strategy: In dialogue to strategic advantage* [translated from Dutch: *Het Groot Strategieboek: In dialoog naar een strategische voorsprong*], Academic Service, The Hague

Porter, M and Kramer, M (2011) Creating shared value: how to reinvent capitalism – and unleash a wave of innovation and growth, *Harvard Business Review*, 89 (1/2), pp 62–77

Porter, M E (1980 and 1998) *Competitive Strategy: Techniques for analyzing industries and competitors*, Free Press, New York

Porter, ME (1985) *Competitive Advantage*, Free Press, New York

Ragiel, E M and Friga, P N (2001) *The McKinsey Mind: Understanding and implementing the problem solving tools and management techniques*, McGraw-Hill, New York

Ross, S A, Westerfield, R and Jaffe, J (1999) *Corporate Finance*, McGraw-Hill, New York

Schwartz, P (1991) *The Art of the Long View: Planning for the future in an uncertain world*, Currency Doubleday, New York

Sisodia, R, Wolfe, D B and Seth, J (2007) *Firms of Endearment: How world class companies profit from passion and purpose*, Wharton School Publishing, Upper Saddle River, NJ

Sperandeo, V (1998) *Trader Vic II: Principles or professional speculation*, John Wiley & Sons, New York

Surowiecki, J (2004) *The Wisdom of Crowds: Why the many are smarter than the few and how collective wisdom shapes business, economies, societies and nations*, Double Day, New York

Treacy, M and Wiersema, F (1995) *The Discipline of Market Leaders: Choose your customers, narrow your focus, dominate your market*, Perseus Books, New York

Van Assen, M F, Van den Berg, G J J B and Pietersma, P (2008) *Key Management Models: The 60+ models every manager needs to know*, 2nd edn, Prentice Hall, Upper Saddle River, NJ

Van der Heijden, K (1998) *Scenarios: The art of strategic conversation*, John Wiley & Sons, Chichester

Walton, M and Deming, W E (1986) *The Deming Management Method*, Dodd, Mead, New York

Wobben, J J, Kalshoven, A and Groot, R de (2009) *Socially Engineered Change: A targeted approach for successful change* [translated from Dutch: *De maakbare verandering: een doelgerichte aanpak voor succesvol veranderen*], Academic Service, The Hague

INDEX

figures in *italics* indicate a figure or table in text

CPSIA information can be obtained at www.ICGtesting.com
Printed in the USA
BVOW02s1429030114

340846BV00004B/11/P